PRAISE FOR *THE READING MIND*

"Daniel Willingham pulls back the curtain on the fascinating process of reading, explaining the discoveries of cognitive science in clear, accessible prose. For the many fans of *Why Don't Students Like School,* Willingham's new book offers more of the rigorous yet enjoyable science writing we love."

—**Annie Murphy Paul**, author of *The Brilliant Blog*

"This is a superb book. Willingham's ability to make cognitive research on reading coherent and comprehensible is exceptional. I wish that it had been available when I taught courses about research on reading to education doctoral students. This book should be standard fare in every doctoral education course on reading."

—**Isabel L. Beck**, professor emerita, School of Education, University of Pittsburgh

"What goes on in the mind as we read? How do people learn to read? What motivates some to read more than others? Does reading online differ from reading books? For those curious about these questions, and for those who care about children learning to read and growing as readers, this delightful, easy-to-read book explains this highly complex topic through fascinating studies and lively examples. With probing questions after each chapter, *The Reading Mind* will make a terrific book club read or textbook."

—**Ellen McIntyre**, dean and professor, College of Education, University of North Carolina, Charlotte

"This is the book we've been waiting for. Willingham captures the magic of reading while simultaneously demystifying how we read. He brings key experimental findings to light as he takes us on the journey from recognizing individual words to constructing meaning from text. Beautifully written, clear and accessible, yet still embracing complexities rather than shying away from them—this book is essential reading for anyone interested in how we read."

—**Kate Nation**, professor of Experimental Psychology, University of Oxford; fellow and tutor in Psychology, St. John's College

"Yet again, Daniel Willingham proves himself genius extraordinaire at translating research to practice! At once a brilliant tutorial on how the bitwise investigations of the research lab have evolved into the ever more powerful and comprehensive models that now dominate cognitive science, and a blueprint for educational excellence, this book is a must for educational practitioners, policymakers, and students. No more top-down versus bottom-up reading wars: language, literacy, and knowledge are all of one piece and so, too, must be their development."

—**Marilyn Jager Adams**, visiting scholar at Brown University

"Dan Willingham has done it again! This is another of his essential books for educational professionals, and anyone else interested in the reading process—sharing the cognitive science and practical implications of research in the domain of reading. No one does this kind of book better than Willingham!"

—**Keith Stanovich**, author of *Progress in Understanding Reading* and *The Rationality Quotient*

"This book is like a Malcolm Gladwell for anyone who is fascinated with how the mind works in literacy development. Willingham mixes his wonderful sense of humor with examples that are simply fun to read while conveying very important concepts about reading. Students will love it; parents will understand it; and scholars will wish that they wrote it!"

—**Susan B. Neuman**, professor of childhood education and literacy development, New York University

"*The Reading Mind* is an indispensable exploration of not only how we read, but why we read. An easy and entertaining read that draws on the science of the brain, books, and behavior, Willingham's work will deepen your understanding of the many facets of reading and literacy, as well as how the brain processes what amounts to an astoundingly complex and historically unlikely process. *The Reading Mind* should be required reading for anyone with a vested interest in the written word."

—**Kristofor Lauricella**, history teacher, High School for Youth & Community Development, Brooklyn, New York

THE READING MIND

THE READING MIND

A Cognitive Approach to Understanding How the Mind Reads

DANIEL T. WILLINGHAM

JB JOSSEY-BASS™

A Wiley Brand

Published by Jossey-Bass
A Wiley Brand
One Montgomery Street, Suite 1000, San Francisco, CA 94104-4594—www.josseybass.com

Jossey-Bass books and products are available through most bookstores. To contact Jossey-Bass directly call our Customer Care Department within the U.S. at 800-956-7739, outside the U.S. at 317-572-3986, or fax 317-572-4002.

Wiley publishes in a variety of print and electronic formats and by print-on-demand. Some material included with standard print versions of this book may not be included in e-books or in print-on-demand. If this book refers to media such as a CD or DVD that is not included in the version you purchased, you may download this material at http://booksupport.wiley.com. For more information about Wiley products, visit www.wiley.com.

Library of Congress Cataloging-in-Publication Data

Names: Willingham, Daniel T., author.
Title: The reading mind : a cognitive approach to understanding how the mind reads / Daniel T. Willingham.
Description: San Francisco, CA : Jossey-Bass, 2017. | Includes index.
Identifiers: LCCN 2017004432 (print) | LCCN 2016059823 (ebook) | ISBN 9781119301370 (cloth) | ISBN 9781119301387 (Adobe PDF) | ISBN 9781119301363 (ePub)
Subjects: LCSH: Reading. | Reading comprehension. | Cognitive psychology.
Classification: LCC LB1050.2 .W55 2017 (ebook) | LCC LB1050.2 (print) | DDC 418/.4019—dc23
LC record available at https://lccn.loc.gov/2017004432

Cover design: Wiley
Cover image: © seamartini/Getty Images, Inc., © flytosky11/Getty Images, Inc.

Printed in the United States of America
FIRST EDITION

HB Printing   10 9 8 7 6 5 4

*This book is dedicated to five of my teachers
who taught me to love reading:
Gene Doherty, Joan Goodman, Joyce Gustafson,
Richard Liewer, and Janet Stellenwerf.*

We are absurdly accustomed to the miracle of a few written signs being able to contain immortal imagery, involutions of thought, new worlds with live people, speaking, weeping, laughing. We take it for granted so simply that in a sense, by the very act of brutish routine acceptance, we undo the work of the ages, the history of the gradual elaboration of poetical description and construction, from the treeman to Browning, from the caveman to Keats. . . . I wish you to gasp not only at what you read but at the miracle of its being readable.

Vladimir Nabokov, *Pale Fire*

CONTENTS

LIST OF TABLES AND FIGURES

Tables

Figures

ABOUT THE AUTHOR

Daniel Willingham earned his B.A. from Duke University in 1983 and his Ph.D. in Cognitive Psychology from Harvard University in 1990. He is currently Professor of Psychology at the University of Virginia, where he has taught since 1992. Until about 2000, his research focused solely on the brain basis of learning and memory. Today, all of his research concerns the application of cognitive psychology to K–16 education. He writes the "Ask the Cognitive Scientist" column for *American Educator* magazine, and is the author of *Why Don't Students Like School?* (Jossey-Bass, 2009), *When Can You Trust the Experts?* (Jossey-Bass, 2012), and *Raising Kids Who Read* (Jossey-Bass, 2015). His writing on education has appeared in 14 languages. His website is www.danielwillingham.com.

ACKNOWLEDGMENT

My thanks to Marcia Invernizzi, Gail Lovette, and Mark Seidenberg for generously sharing their expertise in reading, and to Karin Chenoweth, Lisa Jakub, and Robert Pondiscio for providing feedback on parts of the manuscript. Steph Tatel and five anonymous reviewers were kind enough to read the whole thing, and offered useful, detailed reactions. I especially thank Chuck Clifton for taking on this chore—his comments greatly improved the manuscript. As always, my literary agent, Esmond Harmsworth, was generous with his wisdom and guidance. My colleagues at Jossey-Bass, particularly my editor, Kate Gagnon, were superb. Finally, I thank Trisha Willingham, who provided astute feedback at all stages of the book, from conception to execution.

THE READING MIND

Introduction

The Chicken Milanese Problem

Agenda for the Introduction

To consider the question "how does the mind read?" More specifically, to understand why it is a terrible scientific question, and why we pose it anyway.

Picture this commonplace scene. I was on an airplane, reading E. L. Doctorow's *Billy Bathgate* on my Kindle. The following passage is found near the end of the book, and when I read it, I softly gasped.

Before he got through it I was hearing the distant sound of police sirens, and it was so arduous for him to speak it that he died of the effort: "Right," he said. "Three three. Left twice. Two seven. Right twice. Three three."[1]

My goal in this book is to account for what happened in the few moments it took me to read those 43 words.

The environment held nothing more remarkable than black marks on a white screen, yet somehow I was mentally transported to another world, indeed, to a world quite alien to me: New York City some 30 years before my birth, populated by gangsters. How does the mind create a mental world from black marks? And why would I care enough about Otto "Abbadabba" Berman—a real-life gangster portrayed sympathetically in this novel—to gasp when he's murdered?

The approach I'll take to answering these questions is cognitive. I'll describe what the mind is doing as we read, but I'll seldom consider what the brain is doing. That may sound shortsighted (the mind is, after all, what the brain does), but it's a common scientific approach taken over the last fifty years. Computer science offers an analogy. You can describe the steps of a calculation—say, figuring out the date of the next lunar eclipse viewable in Toronto—without describing what's happening in the electronic guts of the computer during this calculation. In the same way, I'm going to describe the steps by which your mind reads without specifying how the brain carries out those steps.

Cognitive psychologists commonly tackle large, daunting questions by breaking them down into smaller, more manageable questions. We do that by thinking through what *had* to happen in order for some bit of mental work to get done.

What had to happen between my seeing the letters on the screen and my emotional reaction to the events in an imagined world? I had to see the letters and identify them. I had to assemble the letters into words, and then the words into sentences, which I comprehended by applying grammatical rules. My emotional reaction entails not just comprehension, but memory. "He died of the effort" prompts pity only if you feel like you know Berman. So over the course of the novel I must have built and updated a sort of personality picture of this character. And of course memory is needed to organize the sequence of events into a coherent sense of the plot.

So, will this skeletal outline of what happened as I read *Billy Bathgate* serve as a starting point for a theory of reading?

How Do You Make Chicken Milanese?

Even my crude analysis shows that "what happens when we read?" is a bad scientific question, the type of question psychologists usually don't pose. Why? Think of all the millions of activities your mind can direct: you can guess the cost of a paperweight you see in an antique store, ride a child's tricycle for comic effect, make Chicken Milanese, invent a plausible excuse for missing your neighbor's son's middle school play, and so on. For each of these we might pose the question "What's happening in the mind when you do that?" But scientists don't. The reasons that scientists don't ask how you cook Chicken Milanese inform what I've included and excluded in this book, so it's worth describing these reasons in some detail.

The first reason is that task descriptions are not quite as simple as I've made out. I said "let's consider what had to happen" as I read that passage from *Billy Bathgate,* and then I said something like "you have to perceive the letters, and understand the words," and so on. The history of psychology shows that it's easy to be fooled when you try to describe a task.

Here's a simple example. When we read it feels as if we move our eyes smoothly—we sweep from the start of a line to the end, and then snap back to the far left of the page for the next line. That impression is easily disconfirmed by watching the eyes of another person as she reads. Her eyes don't move smoothly, but instead jump from one spot to the next, usually a distance of seven to nine letters.[2] That's so easily observed it's probably been known for centuries. But even that observation—jumping movements, not smooth tracking—is an incomplete description. In fact, your eyes are not always pointing at the same letter when you read.[3] About half the time each eye looks at a different letter. They may even be slightly crossed.

The implications of this fact for an understanding of reading are not obvious. I raise the issue to point out that researchers have been working at an account of reading for over a century, and they are still finding ways of improving their description of *what's actually happening* when someone reads—not how they do it, but what they are doing. That's one reason psychologists usually don't try to explain really complicated behaviors. They figure that they probably shouldn't be confident they can adequately describe what they are explaining.

Suppose we give up on the idea that we'll have a perfect description of what people actually do during a complicated task, and we decide to settle for a provisional description. That's not a bad strategy—as we learn more, our description of the task will improve. One thing we're pretty confident about is that a complex task will require many different cognitive processes. My off-the-top-of-the-head analysis of reading called for vision, memory, grammatical analysis, language comprehension, and emotion. Any one of these mental processes is known to be terribly complicated.

Consider seeing letters. One challenge is that letters can take on quite different appearances, varying in size, typeface, and typographical emphasis (bold, italic, etc.) (Figure I.1). How does my visual system treat these very different-looking objects as equivalent?

A a **a** *A* *A* a

Figure I.1. One letter, different fonts. These letters must all be interpreted as equivalent, even though they look different.
© Daniel Willingham

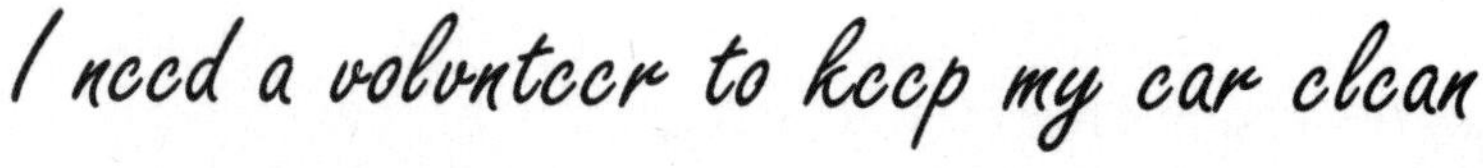

I need a volvnteer to keep my car clean

Figure I.2. Ambiguous letters. Although I'm sure you read this sentence easily, if you look closely you'll notice the "e"s in the word "need" are the same shape as the "c" in "clean." And the same shape is interpreted as a "v" and as a "u" in the word "volunteer."
© Daniel Willingham

Worse yet, the very same shape might be interpreted as representing different letters, depending on the surrounding context (Figure I.2). So we need to do more than define what makes an "A" an "A"; we need to specify the context in which it will be seen as an "A."

Finally, note that we've taken for granted that we're looking at black characters on a white background. How could it be otherwise? But what dictates that "the black bits define the objects, whereas the white is background"? Differentiating objects from their background is so embedded in our visual system that we seldom notice that it's an issue, unless we're looking at one of those clever images where the object and background are ambiguous (Figure I.3).

Now suppose the complicated work of identifying letters is complete, and I've assembled the letters into words. My mind is trying to sort out the meaning of what I've read. One problem is that some words have multiple meanings. In the *Billy Bathgate* passage, Berman starts his brief speech with the word "Right." What did I think he meant when I read that word? Morally correct, as in "the right thing to do"? Or perhaps agreeing with the facts of the matter, as in "You got that right." Or appropriate, as in "the right tool for the job." A few words later Berman uses the word "left" and so it becomes clearer that when he said "right" he was probably signifying a direction. But before I read "left," what did I

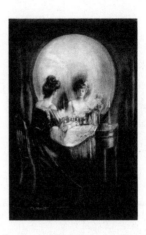

Figure I.3. Reversible figures. At left, the black area can be seen as an object (vase) and the white area as background, or the white area seen as the object (dog profiles) and the black as background. At right, the mirror is seen as background when we focus on the woman and her reflection, but it may also been seen as the foreground object—a skull.
Vase © Tasha Volkova via Shutterstock; "All is Vanity" by C. Allan Gilbert. Public Domain
http://bit.ly/2a2Nddd

suppose "right" meant? Did I suspend judgment, hoping for clarifying information later? It doesn't *feel* like we do that. For example, if you read, "Later that afternoon, he went to the bank," you probably don't think to yourself, "he might have gone to a financial institution or he might have gone to the edge of a river bed, but I don't know which." You pick one meaning and go with it. But how do you pick? And what about sentences that require you to keep more than one sense of the word in mind simultaneously? For example, in Chapter 1 of *The Adventures of Tom Sawyer,* Twain says that two fighting boys "covered themselves in dust and glory." So a single instance of the word "covered" is simultaneously literal (for dust) and figurative (for glory). How does that work?

I could go on and describe how reading depends on memory, on your powers of inference and problem solving, even on your ability to time movements with great precision—eye movements must be perfectly synchronized with ongoing reading—but you get the idea. Reading—or cooking Chicken Milanese, or any moderately complex task—calls on so many mental processes that an agenda to provide a cognitive explanation comes perilously close to the goal "I'm gonna explain the mind." There's too much.

Let's Do It Anyway

I've discussed two reasons psychologists don't pose questions like "how do people cook Chicken Milanese?" or "how do people read?" First, because the task is complex we suspect we'd botch our description of what people are doing as they attempt it, so our theory of the mental events underlying the task would be wrong from the start. Second, the complexity of the task suggests it calls on many mental processes, and a theory of how the mind achieves the task may be too ambitious.

But reading differs from cooking Chicken Milanese in an important way: it matters. Reading matters in our day-to-day affairs, in our culture, in our economy, in our civic lives, in the arts, and so on. There are stakes attached to people reading well or poorly (Figure I.4). It's true that psychologists seldom try to account for really complex tasks, but they make an exception for reading, as well as a handful of other consequential tasks, like driving a car.

Still, the Chicken Milanese problems are real, so we need to deal with them as best we can. What can we do about the task description problem? What if we're trying to account for how people read but we're getting wrong what *reading* really means, just as people used to get wrong the bit about eye movements during reading? The brute truth is that there's no solution. That's the nature of science, and the best we can do is keep the possibility in mind, and try to be clear-eyed when we describe the process of reading. Thus, in this book I'll devote a lot of energy to analyzing the task of reading.

How about the complexity problem, the fact that there are so many processes required to read? Here, we must accept that our account of reading will be incomplete. We can't fully describe how people identify letters, how they separate objects from background, and all the rest. So the question is, what will we try to explain, and what will we disregard?

We might say to ourselves "well, we don't need to explain how people separate letters from background because that's not really a reading process. It's a process for all of vision, and you happen to use it when you read. So let's set the goal of accounting for the reading stuff, and we'll leave the more general-purpose thinking processes for someone else to figure out." That won't work, because all of the mental machinery that

Figure I.4. Medicine packaging. Literate people likely do not notice how frequently they rely on the ability to read. Here I've blurred the print on medicine packaging to help you imagine being unable to read, and trying to select a medicine for your child's sore throat, perhaps by attempting to match packaging with your memory of television commercials.

supports reading is borrowed. Reading is less than 6,000 years old; that's precious little time for any reading-specific thinking processes to have evolved, and there's not much evidence that any have. The mental processes that contribute to reading evolved for another purpose, and we co-opt them for the act of reading.

A better principle will be for us to ignore the mental processes that don't vary much from person to person. Separating objects from background is a good example. Yes, it's a complicated, mysterious process, but somehow anyone with typical vision does it. Crucial to our purposes, when people struggle to read it's not due to a failure of this process. And strong readers are no better than average readers in separating objects from background. So although this process is indispensable for reading it's not the first thing we want to explain.

Researchers do know something about the mental differences between strong and weak readers. A strong reader has a broad vocabulary, and would know the meaning of the word "arduous" in the *Billy Bathgate* passage. A strong reader would comprehend that Berman is telling Billy the combination to a safe, even though the safe goes unmentioned in the passage. Come to that, we'd guess that a strong reader would be reading in the first place, on a plane, when he could be playing a game on his phone, watching a movie, or sleeping. These factors—broad vocabulary, good comprehension skills, motivation—are quite commonsensical. Accounting for them will get more interesting when we start to engage in task analysis, as I promised we would. What are the differences in personality or attitudes between the people on an airplane who choose to read and those who don't? Is reading from a Kindle different than reading from paper? How can you make sense of a passage that depends on your knowledge of combination safes, but doesn't mention a combination safe?

The Plan of the Book

I've emphasized the complexity of reading. We will therefore take it one step at a time, starting from the ground floor, so to speak: how readers see letters, then moving on to how they see words, then sentences, and so on, with one chapter devoted to each topic. In keeping with the emphasis on close analysis of the task, each chapter frames an aspect of reading as a problem: how is *this* bit of mental work accomplished?

That emphasis on task analysis will also prompt us to begin not with reading, but with writing (Chapter 1). Considering its purpose will help us better appreciate what readers actually do when they read letters and words (Chapters 2 and 3). From there we can consider word meaning (Chapter 4), and the comprehension of sentences and paragraphs (Chapter 5). Having this understanding of the process of reading will prepare us to consider why people might be motivated to read—or not (Chapter 6). Finally, we'll consider the possibility that digital technologies should prompt us to rethink everything we know about reading, as they have so radically changed other aspects of our lives (Chapter 7).

Before we plunge into this content, let me draw your attention to two limitations of the topics covered. First, this book is offered as a summary of one scientific approach to the study of reading—namely, the cognitive approach. That's not the only scientific perspective on reading. Another scientific literature employs the sociocultural view, which emphasizes the role of the social environment in reading; what you read, how often you read, your interpretation of what you read, and your thoughts and beliefs about reading are all influenced by the people around you and your relationship to them. The cognitive approach is not in opposition to this view; it's just different. As you'll see over the course of the book, it is more concerned with picking apart the mind of the reading individual. It's no accident that I titled the book *The Reading Mind*, and not *The Science of Reading*.

The second limitation of this book is that it's not about how people learn to read. I aim to describe how an experienced reader reads, not how a novice learns. That said, a great deal of reading research has been conducted with novice readers, and some it will be relevant to our purpose. I'll flag these studies when I refer to them, to help keep clear in your mind the difference between the mind of the expert reader and the mind of the learner.

Although this book is not offered as a summary of the learning-to-read research, some of the conclusions drawn may be applicable to education. However, these implications must be drawn with caution. This book is based on basic science, and basic science seeks to describe the world as it is; in this case, to describe the mind of a reader. Education is not a basic science, but an applied science. Applied sciences do not seek to describe the world as it is, but rather to change the world, to make it more like some ideal vision of what the world ought to be like. In the case of reading education the "change" is the transformation of people who cannot read into readers.

Applying findings from basic science to that effort is not straightforward.[4] For example, many of the studies I'll cite were conducted with experienced readers, and their reading may be different than that of those learning to read. In addition, many studies deal with one, isolated aspect of reading—how we know the meaning of a word, for example, or how we read a misspelled word in the middle of a text. But when we consider reading education, we can't think about aspects of reading in isolation. Doing so entails the risk that we'll change instruction to improve one aspect of reading and unwittingly worsen another aspect. To provide an obvious example, long practice sessions studying letter-sound relationships may help improve decoding, but it may also prompt a decline in reading motivation. With these cautions in mind, I will offer some thoughts at the end of each chapter as to conclusions that scientists can offer that might be useful to practitioners.

But I'm getting ahead of myself. Before we contemplate how the science of reading can be useful to educators, let's review some of the science of reading. True to our commitment to examine carefully what a task really entails, we will begin our analysis not with the reading mind, but with the alphabet.

Summary

- Cognitive psychologists describe the workings of the mind, not the brain.
- Psychologists typically do not seek to explain the workings of very complex mental acts like reading because (1) they are not confident they could describe the task adequately and (2) most of the mind is recruited to address even moderately complex tasks, so the explanation would be dauntingly complex.
- Psychologists *do* try to explain complex tasks that are of great importance in human affairs. Reading is one such task.
- We will try to avoid the traps of accounting for complex tasks by (1) engaging in careful task analysis and (2) seeking to describe only those processes of reading that separate successful readers from struggling readers.

References

1. Doctorow, E. L. (1989). *Billy Bathgate*. New York: Harper & Row.
2. Rayner, K, Pollatsek, A., Ashby, J., & Clifton, C. (2012). *The Psychology of Reading*. New York: Psychology Press.
3. Liversedge, S. P., White, S. J., Findlay, J. M., & Rayner, K. (2006). Binocular coordination of eye movements during reading. *Vision Research*, *46*(15), 2363–2374.
4. For more on the relationship of basic science and education, see Willingham, D. T. (2012). *When can you trust the experts?* San Francisco: Jossey-Bass.

1

ON YOUR MARKS

Agenda for Chapter 1

To understand the purpose of reading. Before trying to understand how it works, it's useful to be clear on what the product of reading is—that is, what the act of reading accomplishes.

In the Introduction we began our analysis of some of the mental processes that are used to read. For example, we said, "well, somehow you've got to recognize the letters on the page, and then figure out what word those letters signify." That seems clear enough, but it will help if we back up a step and consider what reading is *for*. Cognitive psychologists often begin their study of a mental process by trying to understand the "why" before they tackle the "how."

Visual scientist David Marr is often credited with this idea because he emphasized its importance in such a clear way, via this example.[1] Suppose you want to know the mechanism inside a cash register, but you aren't allowed to tear it open. That's akin to being a psychologist trying to understand how the mind reads; you want to describe how something works, but you can't look inside. If we watched a cash register in operation, we might say things like "when a button is pushed, there's a beeping sound," and "sometimes a drawer opens and the operator puts in cash or takes some out, or both," and so on. Fine, but what's the purpose of the beeps and the drawer? What's the goal here?

If we watched the cash register in operation and paid attention to function (not just what we're seeing), we might make observations like *the order of purchases doesn't affect the total*, and *if you buy something and then*

13

Table 1.1. **Watching a cash register.** Observations of a cash register might lead to basic principles of arithmetic.

Observation	Arithmetic expression	Principle
The order of purchases doesn't affect the total	$A + B + C = A + C + B = B + A + C$, etc.	Commutativity
If you buy something, and then return it, you end up the same amount of money you started with	$X - Y + Y = X$	Negative numbers
If you pay for items individually or all at once, the cost is the same	$(A) + (B) + (C) = (A + B + C)$	Associativity

return it, you end up with the same amount of money, and *if you pay for items individually or all at once, the cost is the same.* A sharp observer might derive some basic principles of arithmetic, as shown in Table 1.1.

Knowing that the purpose of a cash register is to implement principles of arithmetic puts our earlier observations—keys to be pushed, numerals displayed—in a different perspective. We know what these components of cash register operation contribute to.

Let's try that idea with reading. What is reading for? We read in order to understand thoughts: either someone else's thoughts, or our own thoughts from the past. That characterization of the function of reading highlights that another mental act had to precede it: the mental act of writing. So perhaps we should begin by thinking about the function of writing. I think *I need milk,* I write that thought on a note to myself, and later I read what I've written and I recover the thought again: *I need milk.* Writing is an extension of memory.

Researchers believe that this memory function was likely the impetus for the invention of writing. Writing was invented on at least three separate occasions: about 5,300 years ago in Mesopotamia, 3,400 years ago in China, and 2,700 years ago in Mesoamerica.[2] In each case, it is probable that writing began as an accounting system. It was needed to keep records about grain storage, property boundaries, taxation, and other legal matters. Writing is more objective than memory—if you and I disagree about how much money I owe you, it's helpful to have a written record. Writing not only extends memory, it expands it. Creating new memories takes effort. It's much easier to create new written records.

Writing also serves a second, perhaps more consequential function: writing is an extension of speech. Speech allows the transmission of thought. The ability to communicate confers an enormous advantage because it allows me to benefit from your experience rather than having to learn something myself. Much better if you were to tell me to stay out of the river because the current is dangerous than for me to learn that through direct experience. Writing represents a qualitative leap over and above speech in terms of the opportunity it creates for sharing knowledge. Speech requires that speaker and listener be in the same place at the same time. Writing does not. Speech is ephemeral but writing is (in principle) permanent. Speech occurs in just one place, but writing is portable.

Frances Bacon wrote "Knowledge is power" in 1597, presumably after entertaining this thought. When I read his words, I think what Bacon thought, separated in time and space by more than 400 years and 3,500 miles. As poet James Russell Lowell put it, "books are the bees which carry the quickening pollen from one to another mind."[3]

Let me remind you of the point of this discussion. We're trying to describe the function of writing as an entrée into our discussion of the mental process of reading. I'm suggesting that writing is meant to preserve one's own thoughts, and to transmit thoughts to others. So now we must ask, "how is writing designed, such that it enables the transmission of thoughts?"

How Writing Might Work

Suppose that we live in a culture without writing, and we encounter a need to transmit thoughts to others who are not present. What method of written communication would seem the most natural? Probably the drawing of pictures. For example, suppose I know that an especially aggressive ram frequents a particular place. I want to warn others, so I incise the image of a ram in a rock wall near where I've seen it before (Figure 1.1).

Figure 1.1. A pictograph of a ram.
Photo by David-O, Flickr, used under CC BY

The drawing I've made is called a pictograph, a picture that carries meaning. Pictographs have real functional advantages. Writing them requires no training, and they are readily interpretable; no one is illiterate when it comes to pictographs. But pictographs do have serious drawbacks. First, their very advantage—they are readily interpreted without study—also brings a disadvantage—they are open to misinterpretation (Figure 1.2). My intended warning may be taken to mean *Hey, there are lots of rams around here—good place to hunt!*

Another problem is that some thoughts I want to communicate do not lend themselves to pictographs. The ram image would have been less ambiguous if I had put a picture representing ***danger*** next to it . . . but what image would represent ***danger***? Or ***genius***? Or possessives like ***mine*** or ***his***? (When I want to signify a mental concept, that is, an idea someone is having, I'll use ***bold italics***).

The problem brings to mind the story Herodotus tells in *The Histories* concerning the fifth-century BC conflict between the Persians and Scythians.[4] The king of the Scythians sent the king of the Persians a mouse, a frog, a bird, and some arrows. What could such a message mean? The Persian King thought it was a message of capitulation: ***we surrender our land*** (mouse), ***water*** (frog), ***horses*** (which are swift like birds), and ***military***

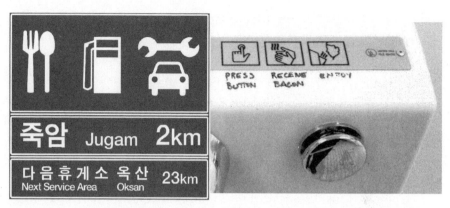

Figure 1.2. The ambiguity of pictographs. The Korean highway sign offers fairly unambiguous pictographs: food, gas, auto repair. Some jokester has added text to the pictographs on the bathroom hand drier showing that they are ambiguous, even if the alternative interpretation is improbable.

© P.Cps1120a, via Wikimedia Commons: http://bit.ly/2a2QSYy; Press button receive bacon © Sebastian Kuntz, Flickr

power (arrows). One of his advisors disagreed, saying the message meant *unless you can fly into the air* (like a bird), *hide in the ground* (like a mouse), *or hide in the water* (like a frog), *you will die from our arrows.* The image of an object might represent the object itself, but when we use it to represent anything else, it is subject to misinterpretation. Pictographs won't do. (By the way, the Persian King was wrong; the Scythians attacked.)

I might turn instead to *logographs*—images that need not look like what they are intended to represent. For example, I could represent the idea *mine* by, say, a circle with a square inscribed within. I've sacrificed the immediate legibility of pictographs—you need some training to read the writing now. But I've gained specificity and I've gained flexibility. I can represent abstract ideas like *danger* and *mine* and *surrender*.

But this solution carries a substantial disadvantage. I have introduced the requirement that the writer (and the reader) have some training. They have to memorize the abstract symbols. Educated adults know at least 50,000 words, and memorizing 50,000 symbols is no small job. We could find ways to reduce the burden, for example, by creating logographs so that words with similar meanings could be matched to similar-looking symbols, but we're still looking at a heavy burden of learning.

Furthermore, we are overlooking an enormous amount of vital grammatical machinery that conveys meaning. When we think about coding our thoughts into written symbols, it's natural to focus on nouns like *ram*, adjectives like ***aggressive***, and verbs like ***run***. But writing with only those symbols would be cramped Tarzan-talk: "Ram here. Aggressive. You run." We want to be able to convey other aspects of meaning like time (***The ram is here*** vs. ***The ram was here***), counterfactual states (***The ram is here*** vs. ***If the ram were here***), whether the aggression is habitual (***That ram acts aggressively*** vs. ***That ram is acting aggressively***), and whether or not I am to referring rams in general (***That ram is an aggressive animal*** vs. *A ram is an aggressive animal*).

Couldn't I just create symbols for all that stuff? For example, when I wanted to indicate that something happened in the past I could, I don't know, draw a horizontal line over the symbol that functions as a verb. Here's the problem. Grammar is complex. So complex that an entire field of study—linguistics—is devoted to describing how it works, and that description remains incomplete. That's a wild fact to contemplate, considering that children learn to use grammar effortlessly when they learn to talk. No one has to drill them in the rule that past tense is usually indicated by adding **ed** to a verb. (I will use boldface to indicate spoken language, whether a simple sound or a whole word.) But children (or adults) can describe very few of these rules; we use them without being fully aware of them, just as we know how to stay upright on a bicycle but can't tell anyone just how we do it. That we find it so hard to describe the rules of grammar is likely an important reason that there is not a fully logographic writing system that captures a spoken language. (Westerners often think that modern Chinese is a logographic language; actually, characters may also represent a syllable of spoken Chinese.)

SOUND AND MEANING

Some of the very earliest writing systems (e.g., Sumerian cuneiform and Egyptian hieroglyphics) included a partial solution to the problem of conveying grammar. Some of the logographs would be used as symbols for sound. For example, the symbol for duck might also, in some contexts, be used to signify the sound **d**. That allowed writers to denote grammatical features like conjugation. It also allowed the spelling of proper names.[5]

This strategy might have been a stepping stone to *phonetic writing systems*—systems in which symbols stand for sound, not meaning, such as how we use the Roman alphabet to correspond to the sounds of spoken English. More accurately, we should say *mostly* phonetic writing systems—all contain some logographs. For example, in English we use "$," "&," and emoticons such as ":-)." (I'll use quotation marks to indicate writing as it would appear on the page.) Sound-based systems have the enormous advantage of letting the writer use grammar unconsciously, just as we do when we speak. Writing is a code for what you say, not what you think (Figure 1.3). All known writing systems code the sound of spoken language.[6]

Here's another way to think about how reading works. Humans are born with the ability to learn spoken language with ease. Children don't need explicit instruction in vocabulary or syntax; exposure to a community of speakers is enough. So on the first day of school, before any reading instruction has begun, every child in the class has bicameral mental representations of words: they know the sound of a word (which scientists called *phonology*), and its meaning (which scientists call *semantics*) (Figure 1.4).

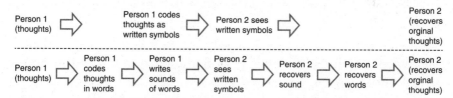

Figure 1.3. **Writing is a code for what you say.** The top row shows written communication that directly codes meaning. The bottom row shows written communication that codes thoughts into words, and then words into sound.
© Daniel Willingham

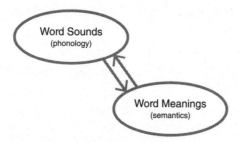

Figure 1.4. **The relationship of word sound and meaning.**
© Daniel Willingham

Notice that I've depicted the sound of words and the meaning of words as separate, but linked. How do we know they are separate? Maybe they are different aspects of a single entity in the mind, like a dictionary entry, which gives you the definition of the word and the pronunciation.

A lot of technical experiments indicate that sound and meaning are separate in the mind, but everyday examples will probably be enough to make this idea clear. We know meaning and sound are separate because you can know one without the other. For example, suppose you use the word **quotidian**. The word might sound familiar to me—I know I've heard it before—even if I don't know the meaning. The familiarity suggests I have some sound-based representation of the word; it's not like you said **pleeky**, about which I might think *that certainly could be a word, but it's not one I've ever heard*. The opposite situation is also possible; there's a concept with which you're familiar, but you have no word associated with it. For example, everyone knows that *people have a crease above their lips and below their nose*, but few people have a memory entry for the sound of the word naming this anatomic feature, the **philtrum**.

We also know that sound and meaning are located in separate parts of the brain. Brain damage can compromise one without much affecting the other. Damage to part of the brain toward the front and on the left side can result in terrible difficulty in finding words; the patient knows what she wants to say but cannot remember the words to express it.[7] It's the same feeling you have when you feel a word is on the tip of your tongue; you're trying to think of the name of the *Pennsylvania Dutch breakfast food made with ground pork and cornmeal*, and you *know* it's in your memory somewhere, you just can't quite find it.

But of course, most of the time, you *can* find it. If that word is in your memory, my providing the definition is very likely to make the sound of the word (**scrapple**) come to mind. And conversely, if someone says a word you know—**market**, for example—you automatically think of the word's meaning. So these mental representations—the sound and the meaning of a word—are separate, but linked; and the link is typically strong and works reliably.

Reading, then, will build on this existing relationship between sound and meaning. It will entail adding some translation process from letters to

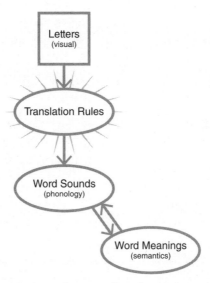

Figure 1.5. Letters, translation rules, sound, and meaning.
© Daniel Willingham

the sound representations, which already have a robust association with meaning (Figure 1.5).

It's all very nice to say, "we'll code sound instead of meaning," but it's not obvious how to do so. An architect of writing might first think of coding syllables because they are pretty easy for adults to distinguish. People can hear that **daddy** has two sounds: **da** and **dee**. So we create a symbol for **da**, another symbol for **dee**, one for **ka**, another for **ko**, and so on. There are some languages—Cherokee, for example, and Japanese kana—that use that strategy. But in English (and indeed, in most languages), there would still be a memorization problem. Spoken Japanese uses a relatively small number of syllables—fewer than 50. English has over 1,000! That's many fewer than the 50,000 symbols we were speculating that a logographic system might require, but it's still a lot of memorization.

Instead of syllables, English uses an alphabetic system. That means each symbol corresponds to a speech sound, also called a *phoneme*. There are about 44 phonemes in English (Figure 1.6).

Now the memorization problem seems manageable—just 44 sounds and 26 letters! That's nothing!

I hope it is now clear to you why we took this side trip through an analysis of writing. Our initial question was "how does the mind read

VOWELS			CONSONANTS	
IPA	**Examples**		**IPA**	**Examples**
ʌ	p<u>u</u>p, l<u>u</u>ck		b	<u>b</u>all, la<u>b</u>
a:	<u>a</u>rm, f<u>a</u>ther		d	<u>d</u>oor, la<u>d</u>y
æ	b<u>a</u>t, bl<u>a</u>ck		f	<u>f</u>ix, i<u>f</u>
ə	<u>a</u>way, cin<u>e</u>ma		g	<u>g</u>as, fla<u>g</u>
e	s<u>e</u>t, b<u>e</u>d		h	<u>h</u>ot, <u>h</u>ello
3:	b<u>ur</u>n, l<u>ear</u>n		j	<u>y</u>et, <u>y</u>ellow
I	sh<u>i</u>p, s<u>i</u>tting		k	<u>c</u>ap, ba<u>ck</u>
i:	thr<u>ee</u>, h<u>ea</u>t		l	<u>l</u>ight, litt<u>le</u>
ɒ	p<u>o</u>t, r<u>o</u>ck		m	<u>m</u>y, le<u>m</u>on
ɔ:	m<u>a</u>ll, f<u>ou</u>r		n	<u>n</u>o, te<u>n</u>
ʊ	b<u>oo</u>k, c<u>ou</u>ld		ŋ	bri<u>ng</u>, fi<u>ng</u>er
u:	tr<u>ue</u>, f<u>oo</u>d		p	<u>p</u>at, ma<u>p</u>
aI	h<u>i</u>ve, <u>eye</u>		r	<u>r</u>ing, t<u>r</u>y
aʊ	c<u>ow</u>, <u>out</u>		s	<u>s</u>ay, mi<u>ss</u>
əʊ	s<u>o</u>, h<u>o</u>me		ʃ	<u>sh</u>ut, cra<u>sh</u>
eə	th<u>e</u>re, <u>air</u>		t	<u>t</u>ee, ge<u>tt</u>ing
eI	pl<u>ay</u>, <u>eigh</u>t		tʃ	<u>ch</u>ime, <u>ch</u>ur<u>ch</u>
Iə	f<u>ear</u>, h<u>ere</u>		θ	<u>th</u>ing, bo<u>th</u>
I	t<u>oy</u>, j<u>oi</u>n		ð	<u>th</u>at, mo<u>th</u>er
ʊə	c<u>ure</u>, t<u>ou</u>rist		v	<u>v</u>oice, fi<u>v</u>e
			w	<u>w</u>ig, <u>w</u>indow
			z	<u>z</u>oo, la<u>z</u>y
			3	mea<u>s</u>ure, vi<u>s</u>ion
			dʒ	<u>j</u>et, lar<u>ge</u>

Figure 1.6. The phonemes used in American English. IPA stands for International Phonetic Alphabet.
© Anne Carlyle Lindsay

words?" Our analysis of writing gives us a much better idea of what "reading words" will actually involve. First, we must be able to visually distinguish one letter from another, to differentiate "b" from "p," for example. Second, because writing codes sound, we must be able to hear the difference between **bump** and **pump**. Actually, it's not enough to be able to hear that they are different words. We must be able to describe that difference, to say that one word begins with the sound corresponding to the letter "b" and the other begins with the sound corresponding to the letter "p." Third, we must know the mapping between the visual and auditory components, that is, how they match up. Reading brings challenges in all three processes, and we'll consider them in the next chapter.

Summary and Implications

Summary

- We consider the purpose of cognitive activities (like reading) because it's easier to think about the smaller-scale pieces of this activity if you know the larger goal to which they contribute.
- The purpose of reading is the communication of thought across time and space.
- Communicating thought directly into symbols would be impractical because it would require a lot of memorization, but a bigger obstacle is that we'd have to figure out how to represent grammar.
- Instead of writing down thoughts, we write down oral language. Writing codes sound.

Implications

- The fact that writing codes spoken language should lead us to expect that reading ability in adults will be closely related to their ability to understand spoken language. It is.[8] There is a strong relationship between oral comprehension and reading comprehension among people who can decode fluently. If you can't follow a complicated written argument, for example, you wouldn't be able to follow the argument if someone read it to you.
- The fact that writing codes spoken language should also lead us to expect that explicit teaching of that code will be an important part of learning to read. It is.[9] The amount of explicit instruction children need in the code varies, depending on other aspects of their oral language, but for some children this explicit instruction is vital.
- The fact that our writing system does not use many logographs indicates it would be a bad plan to treat words as though they are logographs—in other words, to teach children to focus on what words look like, rather than the sound they code. (The exception would be irregularly pronounced words that are very common, e.g., "be," and "have.")

Discussion Questions

1. Sometimes a tool can be developed for one purpose but then used for another purpose. Are there purposes other than "transmit thoughts" to which writing is put?

2. I said that one of the disadvantages of a logographic writing system is that reading and writing would require the memorization of a lot of symbols. Suppose we did use a logographic writing system. What would this change mean for schooling, and more broadly for society? Would different people be literate?

3. Consider the popularity of one type of logograph, the emoji. Their ubiquity, along with the fact that *all* writing systems use at least some logographs, suggests that there may be something that logographs communicate well that an alphabetic system does not capture well. What might that be?

4. Language is meant to transmit thoughts and it usually seems to serve that purpose well. Email messages, however, seem especially prone to misinterpretation. What tends to go wrong with email messages and why might that be?

5. I claimed that writing captures thoughts through oral language—you write what you say. But some types of communication seem to be closer to "what we say" than others. The writing in text messages, for example, is closer to the way I would speak to the person who will read it than, say, a letter I would write out. Should this matter to our characterization of what writing is?

REFERENCES

1. Marr, D. (1982). *Vision*. New York: Freeman.

2. Robinson, A. (2007). *The story of writing* (2nd ed.). London: Thames & Hudson.

3. "Review of Kavanagh, a Tale by Henry Wadsworth Longfellow." (1849, July). *The North American Review, 69*(144), 207.

4. Available at: http://perseus.uchicago.edu/perseus-cgi/citequery3. pl?dbname=GreekFeb2011&query=Hdt.%204.131.2&getid=1/.

5. Schmandt-Besserat, D., & Erard, M. (2008). Origins and forms of writing. In C. Bazerman (Ed.), *Handbook of research on writing* (pp. 7–22). New York: Erlbaum.

6. Perfetti, C. A. (2003). The universal grammar of reading. *Scientific Studies of Reading, 7*(1), 3–24. http://doi.org/10.1207/S1532799XSSR0701_02.

7. Dick, F., Bates, E., Wulfeck, B., Utman, J. A., Dronkers, N., & Gernsbacher, M. A. (2001). Language deficits, localization, and grammar: Evidence for a distributive model of language breakdown in aphasic patients and neurologically intact individuals. *Psychological Review, 108*(4), 759–788.

8. Bell, L. C., & Perfetti, C. A. (1994). Reading skill: Some adult comparisons. *Journal of Educational Psychology, 86*(2), 244–255; Gernsbacher, M. A., Varner, K. R., & Faust, M. E. (1990). Investigating differences in general comprehension skill. *Journal of Experimental Psychology: Learning, Memory, and Cognition, 16*(3), 430–445.

9. National Institute of Child Health and Human. (2000). National Reading Panel. Teaching children to read: An evidence-based assessment of the scientific research literature on reading and its implications for reading instruction. Report of the subgroups. Washington, DC. Retrieved from www.nichd.nih.gov/research/supported/Pages/nrp.aspx/.

2

Sound It Out

Agenda for Chapter 2

We've concluded that our alphabet codes spoken language. Being able to read means being able to decode writing to recover speech. The particulars of that task depend on the language represented (English) and the alphabet used to code it (the Roman alphabet). This chapter describes the particulars of the code used by English readers.

In Chapter 1 we concluded that writing is meant to preserve and communicate thoughts, but does so indirectly. It's a workaround, a cheat, because it doesn't communicate thought, it communicates the sound of spoken language. That means reading what someone has written requires three things. You need to be able to differentiate one symbol (i.e., letter) from another. You must be able to differentiate one sound from another, to hear the difference between **b** and **p**. And you must know what sound a letter or group of letters is associated with. Those challenges exist for experienced readers, but they are easiest to appreciate when they are fresh. So in this chapter I will use many examples of studies that have examined children learning to read.

Challenge 1: The Letters

If you were inventing an alphabet from scratch, how would you design the letters? I've just prompted you to think that it might be wise to create letters that would be easy to distinguish, so readers would not confuse them. Then again, it might be helpful to create letters that are easy to draw, for the sake of writers. That's logical enough, but alphabets respect neither principle.

Letters from the Environment

Mark Changizi and his colleagues analyzed 96 writing systems to determine which shapes they commonly used.[1] Then they examined a large set of photographs of natural scenes, to determine whether the shapes found in the alphabets also tended to appear in natural scenes. For example, "L" shapes and "T" shapes are very commonly observed in the environment because the former is created when two edges of an object meet, and the latter is formed when an object overlaps another object (Figure 2.1).

The researchers then looked for a relationship between the frequency that a shape was used by a writing system and the frequency that that shape was observed in the photographs of natural scenes. The researchers found that the most common letter shapes match the shapes that people most frequently encounter in their daily visual worlds.

A reasonable hypothesis is that the visual system has been tuned over time (either evolutionary time, or the lifetime of an individual, or both) to best perceive shapes that appear most frequently in the environment. People who invented alphabets unconsciously capitalized on that property of the visual system. The shapes that people see most easily were judged to make nice letters. It's a good example of what we mean when

Figure 2.1. Natural scene with T's and L's. T shapes and L shapes are commonly observed in the outlines of objects.
Original version © Dragan Milovanovic, Shutterstock

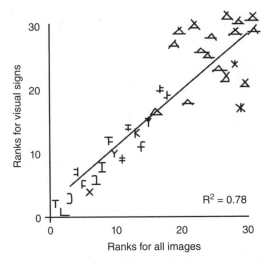

Figure 2.2. Alphabetic shapes. This graph shows that alphabets use shapes commonly seen in the natural environment. The vertical axis shows the frequency that a particular shape is observed in alphabets. The horizontal axis shows the frequency that the shape is observed in a large set of photographs of natural scenes.
Redrawn from Changizi, Zhang, Ye, & Shimojo (2006)

we say that the brain is not designed for reading and writing—rather, we co-opt existing mental mechanisms to make literacy work.

There are other design properties that alphabets *lack*. Letters are not designed to be easily written. Letters vary in how many hand movements they require. An "L" requires two hand movements. An "X" requires three, even though the letter is composed of just two strokes. If the Roman alphabet were designed to minimize work for writers, most letters would take just one or two strokes: for example, l, /, \,—, and J. But we have "E" and "H," each of which require five strokes.

Letter Confusability

Even though letters tend to be shapes that our visual system purportedly sees well, those shapes are often confusable. Many of our letters use a vertical line with a semicircle to the right: "B," "D," "P," "R." The letters "E," "F," and "H" differ by just one stroke, as do "I," "J," and "L." Some pairs are mirror images, like "M" and "W" or "b" and "d." If the goal were to make letters look really different from one another, why not use some

	a	b	c	d	e	f	g	h	i	j	k	l	m	n	o	p	q	r	s	t	u	v	w	x	y	z
a	123	3	3	5	0	0	0	0	0	0	0	0	0	0	0	5	1	2	0	0	0	0	0	0	0	0
b	0	99	0	88	0	0	4	0	0	0	0	1	0	0	0	32	21	0	0	0	0	0	0	2	0	0
c	1	0	133	0	3	0	0	0	0	0	0	0	0	0	0	2	0	0	0	0	0	0	0	0	0	0
d	0	96	0	121	0	0	0	0	0	0	0	0	0	0	0	24	22	0	0	0	0	0	0	0	0	0
e	0	1	5	0	132	0	1	0	0	0	0	0	0	0	0	0	0	0	0	0	0	0	0	0	0	0
f	0	0	0	0	0	129	0	0	0	0	3	0	0	0	0	0	0	0	0	47	0	0	0	0	0	0
g	0	2	0	3	0	0	128	0	0	2	0	0	0	0	0	2	2	0	0	0	0	0	0	0	0	0
h	0	0	0	1	0	0	0	117	0	0	0	0	0	0	0	8	0	0	0	0	0	0	4	0	0	0
i	0	0	0	0	0	0	0	0	135	6	0	6	0	0	0	0	0	0	0	0	0	0	0	0	0	0
j	0	0	0	0	0	0	0	0	6	131	0	0	0	0	0	0	0	0	0	0	0	0	0	0	0	0
k	0	0	0	0	0	0	0	0	0	0	120	0	0	0	0	0	0	0	0	0	2	0	0	8	0	0
l	0	0	0	0	0	0	0	1	7	4	0	128	0	0	0	0	0	1	0	0	0	0	0	0	0	0
m	0	0	0	0	0	0	0	0	0	0	0	0	138	0	0	0	0	0	0	0	0	0	0	7	0	0
n	1	0	0	0	0	0	0	7	0	0	0	0	0	112	0	0	0	0	0	0	22	0	0	0	0	0
o	4	0	13	0	0	0	0	0	0	0	0	0	0	0	126	0	0	0	0	0	0	0	0	0	0	0
p	0	22	0	19	0	0	0	0	0	0	0	0	0	0	0	102	71	0	0	0	0	0	0	0	0	0
q	1	20	0	21	0	0	0	1	0	0	0	0	0	0	0	88	99	0	0	0	0	0	0	0	0	0
r	0	0	0	0	0	3	0	0	0	1	0	0	0	0	0	0	0	120	0	3	0	0	0	0	0	0
s	0	0	0	0	0	0	0	0	0	0	0	0	0	0	0	0	0	0	118	0	0	0	0	0	0	5
t	0	0	0	0	0	40	0	0	0	0	2	0	0	0	0	0	0	0	0	122	0	0	0	0	0	0
u	1	0	0	0	0	0	0	3	0	0	0	0	0	2	24	0	0	0	2	0	11	0	0	0	0	0
v	0	0	0	0	0	0	0	0	0	0	0	0	0	0	2	0	0	0	0	0	2	125	0	0	0	0
w	0	0	0	0	0	0	0	0	0	0	0	0	0	4	0	0	0	0	0	0	2	0	133	0	0	0
x	0	0	0	0	0	0	0	0	0	0	5	0	0	0	0	0	0	0	0	0	0	0	0	141	0	0
y	0	0	0	0	0	0	0	0	0	0	0	0	0	0	0	0	0	0	0	0	0	0	0	0	143	0
z	0	0	0	0	0	0	0	0	0	0	0	0	0	0	0	1	1	0	5	0	0	0	0	3	0	129

Figure 2.3. Letter confusion matrix. Preschool children were shown a letter and were asked to name it. The rows show the letter presented, and the columns show what the child said, with the numbers showing how often each response was offered. Thus, the diagonal (the large numbers) represents correct responses. As you can see, "b" and "d" were highly confusable for these children.

© Daniel Willingham, data from Courrieu & De Falco (1989)

characters that have unconnected line segments, e.g., "ת" or "Ξ"? Why not have some closed figures that are not rounded, e.g., "Δ" or "☐"? Letters of our Roman alphabet are at least modestly confusable, and when children learn to read, they do indeed mix up letters that look similar, a phenomenon also observed with alphabets other than the Roman (Figure 2.3).[2–4]

That said, we shouldn't think this problem is worse than it is. There simply aren't that many letters to be learned. So even children who have received no reading instruction often learn a bit about letters simply through observation. Parents may notice that their child seems to read familiar signs like "McDonalds" or "Taco Bell." In truth, they are probably just recognizing the logo, but when a logo is not available they still may show letter learning, as when they recognize friends' names on their cubbies at preschool.[5]

And although similar letters may be confusing when they are first learned, with practice, telling them apart is not a problem. Children learn the critical features that differentiate letters. In one experiment, researchers presented two nonword letter strings and asked children to say whether the two were identical (e.g., "BMWQ BMWQ") or different (e.g., "BMWQ BWMQ"). The letters were quite large, so kids had to move their eyes around to see them. Where a kindergartener looked was some-what unpredictable, but third-graders looked at the parts of letters that tend to differ—those are the parts that carry the most information.[6]

But what about dyslexia? Isn't letter reversal at the heart of that read-ing problem? The hypothesis that dyslexia is rooted in visual problems goes back to at least the 1920s and was current until the 1970s. At that time some surprisingly simple experiments were conducted, showing that vision is usually not the problem. One experiment simply counted the number of errors dyslexic readers made that could be due to reversals and found they are relatively infrequent.[7] In another clever experiment, researchers flashed words on a screen one at a time and asked dyslexic readers to copy what they had seen, without trying to read the words aloud. They made very few errors, so the reading problem was not visual.[8]

Dealing with Letter Differences

What about the problem raised in the Introduction? How do readers deal with differences in fonts, type size, and typographical emphasis? I noted that this is a type of problem that your visual system has to solve all the time—all dogs must be identified as dogs, even if they look different— but how does that happen?

An influential approach is to think of letters as composed of con-stituents like horizontal lines, vertical lines, semicircles, and so on (Figure 2.4).

Figure 2.4. **Letter features.** These features are basic constituents of letters. "L" contains a horizontal line, vertical line, and a corner. "P" contains a vertical line and a semi-circle, and so on. More features would be needed to capture all the letters in the Roman alphabet.
© Daniel Willingham

Now imagine a network (Figure 2.5, Time 1). You can see there are two rows of circles, which we'll call *nodes*. Imagine that a node can have energy associated with it, as though it's vibrating, or has a voltage. When a letter appears out in the world, the visual system evaluates it for its constituent features: does it contain a horizontal line, a vertical line, a semicircle? If the letter contains the letter constituent, then the corresponding node becomes energized. In the example, the person sees the letter "L,"

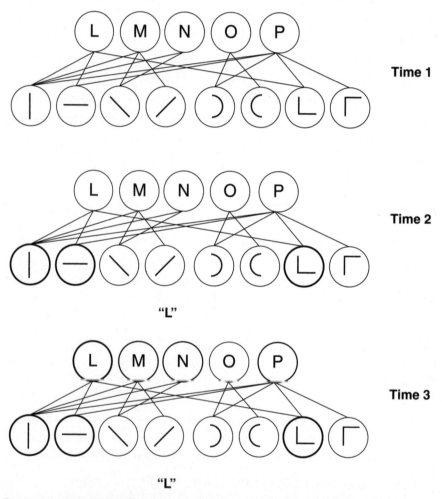

Figure 2.5. Letter identification network. Letters are composed of constituents shown as activated nodes in this model of visual letter recognition.
© Daniel Willingham

and so three of the letter constituents are active, which is symbolized by the thicker border of those nodes (Figure 2.5, Time 2). If the three constituents of the letter "L" are all active, they pass the energy to the "L" node, and it becomes active. The "M" node becomes somewhat active, because a vertical line is one of its constituents too. The system decides which letter is present simply by selecting the letter node with the greatest activity (Figure 2.5, Time 3).[9]

This model of how people identify letters is very successful. For one thing, it greatly reduces the too-many-fonts problem because most letters in different fonts or sizes still share the same features. In addition, we see why letters that share lots of features (e.g., "b" and "d") would be much more likely to be confused than letters that share no features (e.g., "b" and "w"). Furthermore, there is evidence that there are groups of cells in the visual system that do exactly this sort of constituent feature detection.[10]

In sum, even though alphabets were not created to ensure minimum confusability of letters, that doesn't seem to pose a problem. Good readers and struggling readers are more similar than different when it comes to differentiating "P" from "D." That's not the case, however, when it comes to hearing the sounds associated with each letter.

Challenge 2: The Sounds

Being able to hear the sounds associated with letters doesn't seem like it ought to be that hard. Isn't it obvious that a child can do that if she can hear the difference between **big** and **dig** in everyday speech? But that's not quite the same task because in order to learn to read and write, the child must be aware of what differentiates **big** and **dig**, so she can think *Aha, there's the letter 'd,' I know what sound that makes!* Many mental processes lie outside of awareness, and some seem destined to remain so. For example, you obviously know how to shift your weight to stay upright on a bicycle, but that knowledge is accessible only to the parts of the brain that control movement. You can't examine that knowledge or describe it. Other types of knowledge are unconscious, but can become conscious. For example, most people speak grammatically—even if they violate some rules taught in school, they speak in accordance with others in their linguistic community. People are unaware of these rules, but *can* consciously learn them. Hearing individual speech sounds is analogous. Any speaker can hear that **big** and **dig** differ and although people aren't born with the ability to describe the difference, most can learn to do so.

Why Speech Sounds Are Hard to Describe

We are not born with the ability to hear individual speech sounds, but the challenge is even greater than that. Young children have difficulty understanding where one spoken word ends and another begins. That's important for reading—you need to know which sounds are supposed to clump together to form a word. But kids don't hear individual words as well as adults do. In a standard test of this ability, an experimenter gives a child a short sentence to keep in mind—say, "I like yellow bananas." The child is given a small basket of blocks and asked to make a line of blocks, one for each word in the sentence. There's no guarantee that the child will pick four blocks for the sentence. It might be three, it might be five, it might be seven. They are just not sure where words begin and end.[11]

That's hard to believe, but this confusion actually reflects the physical stimulus of speech—it's more or less continuous. Our mind may *perceive* breaks between words, and we might assume that perception is due to very brief periods of silence; but those periods are actually infrequent, and are as likely to occur in the middle of a word as between words! (Figure 2.6)

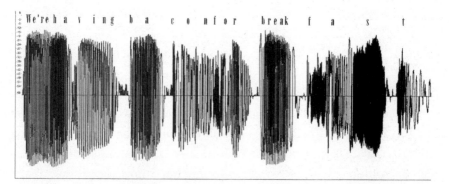

Figure 2.6. Visual representation of the sound of a spoken sentence. The author is saying "We're having bacon for breakfast." Time moves left to right, and the vertical axis shows sound intensity. You can see the words "We're" and "having" blend together, and there is a break in the middle of the word "bacon."
© Daniel Willingham

Brief pauses between words don't really exist in the speech stimulus, but rather are created by our minds as part of speech perception. To further persuade yourself that's so, think of what it sounds like when someone speaks a foreign language you don't understand. You don't hear any breaks.

There is a fairly standard progression by which children develop the ability to hear speech sounds: they learn to hear separate words, then words within compound words (**scarecrow** includes the words **scare** and **crow**), then individual syllables (**table** includes the syllables **tey** and **buhl**), and finally, individual speech sounds (**sat** includes three sounds: **s**, **æ**, and **t**). Hearing words, syllables, and speech sounds can be harder or easier depending on the particular task, and children needn't gain full expertise in one before starting to learn the other, but this rough order is typically observed.[12] Obviously, it's learning to hear speech sounds that is of greatest concern for reading, especially because that ability is less likely to develop spontaneously, and more likely to require some special activities on the part of parents and teachers.

Why is hearing individual speech sounds so hard? One problem is that people pronounce differently what we tell children ought to be same speech sound. That is, people have regional accents, and two people ostensibly saying the same thing can produce quite different speech sounds. So I'm supposed to understand that "b" goes with the final sound in the name **Bob**, but people with certain accents actually pronounce it **Bop** (Figure 2.7).

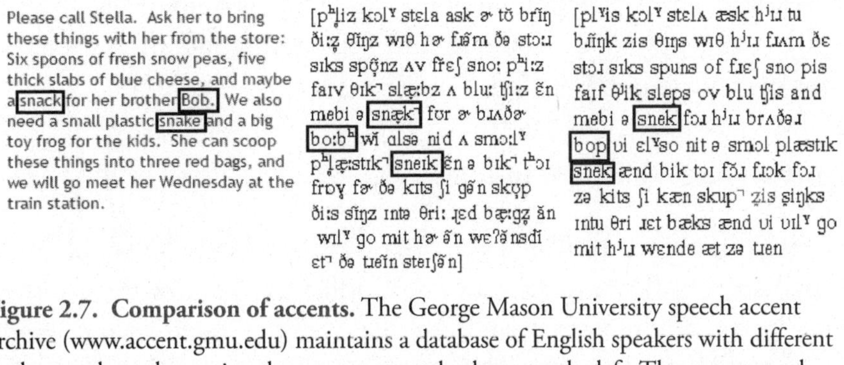

Please call Stella. Ask her to bring these things with her from the store: Six spoons of fresh snow peas, five thick slabs of blue cheese, and maybe a snack for her brother Bob. We also need a small plastic snake and a big toy frog for the kids. She can scoop these things into three red bags, and we will go meet her Wednesday at the train station.

[pʰɫiz kolˠ stɛla ask ɚ tö bɾĩŋ ðiːʒ θĩŋz wɪθ hɚ fɹ̃m ðə stoːɹ sɪks spõ̃nz ʌv fɹɛʃ snoː pʰiːz faɪv θɪkⁿ slæːbz ʌ bluː tʃiːz ɛ̃n mɛbi ə snæk̚ for ɚ bɹʌðɚ boːbʰ wĩ ɑlsə nid ʌ smoːlˠ pʰɫæːstɪk̚ sneɪk ɛ̃n ə bɪk̚ˀ tʰoɪ fɾoɣ fɚ ðə kɪts ʃi ɡə̃n skʊp ðiːs sĩŋz ɪntə θriː ɹɛd bæːɡʒ ã̃n wɪlˠ ɡo mɪt hɚ ð̃n wɛʔð̃nsdĩ ɛtⁿ ðə tɪẽɪ̃n steɪʃə̃n]

[plˠis kolˠ stɛlʌ æsk hʲɪɹ tu bɹ̃ɪ̃ŋk zis θɪŋs wɪθ hʲɪɹ fɪʌm ðɛ stoɹ sɪks spuns ov fɪɛʃ sno pis faɪf θʲik sleps ov blu tʃis and mɛbi ə snɛk fɔɹ hʲɪɹ bɹʌðəɹ bop ʋi ɛlˠso nit ə smol plæstɪk snɛk ænd bik toɪ fɔɹ fɪɔk foɹ zə kits ʃi kæn skʊpⁿ ʒis sɪŋks ɪntu θri ɹɛt bæks ænd ʋi ʋɪlˠ ɡo mit hʲɪɹ wɛnde æt zə tɪen]

Figure 2.7. Comparison of accents. The George Mason University speech accent archive (www.accent.gmu.edu) maintains a database of English speakers with different backgrounds, each uttering the same paragraph, shown at the left. The center panel shows the phonetic transcription of a 37-year-old Glasgow native, and at right, a Russian of the same age who has been learning English for one year. I've highlighted a few of the differences.

Composite of screenshots from www.accent.gmu.edu

But the problems in identifying individual speech sounds don't end with the fact that different people say them differently. An individual speaker also says them differently, depending on the context. People produce about 10 speech sounds per second, so it's no great surprise that the positions your lips, tongue, and vocal cords were in when you produced the last speech sound will influence the way the next one sounds. In fact, you also produce a speech sound differently because you anticipate the next sound you're going to say. For example, try this. Put your hand in front of your mouth and say **pot**. You feel the puff of air when you say the **p**. Now do the same thing, saying **spot**. The puff is stronger for **pot** than **spot**. So there's not a single sound associated with the letter "p." The same person says it a little differently, depending on the context.

For some speech sounds, the problem is still worse. Consider the letter "p" again. You actually can't say it aloud. You might think of it as **puh**—that's what parents often tell children—but that's *two* sounds: the sound associated with the letter "p" and then a vowel sound after it, **uh**. The sound associated with the letter "p" is simply a plosion of air. In fact, that's the same plosion of air you make for the letter "b." The only difference is that when you say **bee** your vocal chords vibrate to make the vowel sound *at the same time* you make the plosion of air, whereas when you say **pee** the vocal chords only start to vibrate about 0.04 seconds *after* the plosion. Yup. The difference between **pee** and **bee** hinges on this 0.04 second difference in timing. So asking "What sound does the letter 'p' make?" is nonsensical. The very definition of the sound that is supposed to go with the letter depends on its relationship to neighboring sounds. It's actually impossible to say **p** in isolation.

Context-Free Sounds and Reading

I've described three difficulties in hearing speech sounds: people pronounce them differently, the same individual pronounces them differently depending on context, and in some cases the sound itself depends on the neighboring sounds. The critical thing to notice is that each of these three challenges describes ways that context is important for understanding individual speech sounds. When someone is speaking you have that context available. But when you are learning which sounds go with

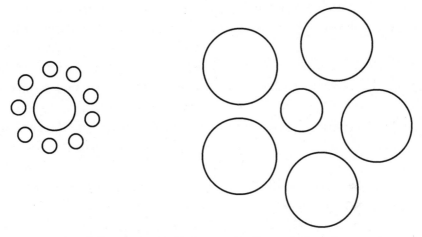

Figure 2.8. Visual illusion. You've likely seen this illusion before, the point being that the central circles appear to be different sizes because of the surrounding circles. In a similar fashion, context influences how we evaluate speech sounds, so thinking about them in isolation is very difficult.
© Daniel Willingham

which letters of the alphabet, that's context-free. The problem lies in isolating all the different ways you hear a sound in spoken speech, and then abstracting some ideal version of that sound so you can associate it with a letter (Figure 2.8).

The ability to hear individual speech sounds is called *phonemic awareness.* (Phonological awareness is the term for hearing any sort of speech sound, e.g., separate words, or separate syllables.) It is tested with several different tasks. Children might be asked to name the sound at the beginning of a word. They might be asked if two words begin with the same sound, or end with the same sound. In more challenging tasks, they might be asked to change a word by adding, removing, or manipulating sounds, e.g., if I took the word **top** and added a **ssss** at the beginning, what word would it make?

We would guess that phonological awareness would be important to learning to read. If reading is a code between symbols and speech sounds, it's going to be hard to learn the code if you can't hear the speech sounds. Lots of research indicates that this reasonable supposition is right. Children who have trouble learning to read often have difficulty with phonological awareness tasks.[13] At the other end of the spectrum, children who more or less teach themselves to read turn out to perform quite well on these tasks.[14] More generally, measures of phonological awareness and of letter knowledge show strong relationships with reading measures, not just in elementary school but continuing through high school.[15,16] This relationship between phonological awareness and reading is not unique to learning to read English—you see it across languages.[17,18]

But of course these studies just show a correlation. They can't support the stronger conclusion that phonological awareness is *required* for learning to read. Training studies are more persuasive. Children can be given practice in phonological awareness by, for example, playing games with rhyme (Who knows a bird's name that rhymes with **luck**?) or alliteration (Five fantastic falcons fanned four flipping foxes!). Training tasks tend to be quite similar to those used to measure phonological awareness, but include practice and feedback. We'd expect that children who get phonological awareness training would show improvements in learning to read compared to kids who don't get the training. They do.[19–21]

Some children get incidental training at home. That is, their parents play rhyming and alliteration games with them as a matter of course, for example, through read-alouds; Mother Goose, Dr. Seuss, and other children's favorites are packed with such wordplay. And research shows that children who encounter this sort of wordplay at home develop phonemic awareness and later find it easier to learn to read.[22]

Still, we might question whether sound is *necessary* for learning to read. Perhaps teachers make sound necessary by virtue of the way they teach reading. They emphasize the sound-based nature of the code and so it's no surprise that training students to hear sounds helps. What if a child had to bypass sound when learning to read because she cannot hear? The letters may signify sound, but the pattern of letters for each word is still unique (or nearly so). Would she learn to read by matching word spellings—their visual appearances—directly to their meaning?

It turns out that sound is difficult to bypass. Some deaf children try to match words to their American Sign Language counterparts, but that's tough to do—you're trying to match an alphabetic word to a symbol that corresponds to a meaning unit.[23,24] If you bypass sound, you're forced to focus on the visual aspect of the letters to differentiate words, and you're back to one of the problems with a logographic code—there is a huge number of symbols to memorize. Little wonder that many or most deaf readers code phonologically, and that's true even for beginning readers.[25] That's hard, obviously, and it results in poor reading performance; deaf high school graduates read, on average, at a fourth grade level.[26]

I've made it sound as though there's a strict order to these two mental processes: gain phonemic awareness, then learn to read. The processes are better characterized as reciprocal. It's hard to learn to read without some degree of phonemic awareness, but that awareness may be pretty crude—it improves with reading experience. One of the more dramatic demonstrations of this phenomenon came in an experiment of Portuguese adults who could not read. They had a terrible time with phonemic awareness tests. But once they learned how to read, their phonemic awareness improved dramatically.[27]

CHALLENGE 3: THE MAPPING

The third challenge inherent in reading English is that you must learn the *alphabetic principle*; the idea that letters correspond to sounds. Perceiving that idea is not intuitive, and children don't effortlessly learn it via exposure, the way they learn grammar by listening. They may learn that letters correspond to names or words (as in the cubby example above), but that's different than understanding that individual letters signify speech sounds.

For example, in one experiment children who could not yet read were taught to recognize the printed words "mat" and "sat." Once they could do so the experimenters showed them the words "mow" and "sow" to see whether the children could differentiate them. If so, that would indicate that they understood that individual letters signify individual sounds. The only children who could extend "mat/sat" knowledge to "mow/sow" were those who had good phonological awareness *and* who had learned the graphic symbols "m" and "s." The alphabetic principle—the idea of an association between letters and sounds—doesn't come naturally. The auditory *and* the visual pieces must be in place.

How Confusing is the Mapping in English?

The principle may not come naturally, but surely we could make the particulars easier. If you were creating an alphabet for English from scratch, you would probably create 44 letters and match each speech sound with one letter. We'd call that a one-to-one matching. Written English, alas, was not created from scratch. Our language is a mongrel: Germanic origins, heavily influenced by the Norman invasion and later by the adoption of Latinate and Greek words. That's a problem because when we borrowed words, we frequently retained the spelling conventions of the original language. The result is that English uses a many-to-many matching. One letter (or letter combination) can signify many sounds, as the letter "e" does: **red**, **flower**, **bee**. Then too, the same sound might be spelled via different letters or letter combinations, as in "boat," "doe," and "row." This complexity has caused misery among generations of school children, although it has provided fodder for light rimers.[28]

When the English
  tongue we speak.
Why is break not rhymed
  with freak?
Will you tell me why it's true
We say sew but likewise few?
And the maker of the verse,
Cannot rhyme his horse
  with worse?
Beard is not the same
  as heard
Cord is different from word.

Cow is cow but low is low
Shoe is never rhymed
  with foe.
Think of hose, dose, and lose

And think of goose and yet
  with choose
Think of comb, tomb and bomb,

Doll and roll or home and some.
Since pay is rhymed with say
Why not paid with said I pray?
Think of blood, food and good.

Mould is not pronounced
  like could.
Wherefore done, but gone
  and lone
Is there any reason known?
To sum up all, it seems to me

Sound and letters don't agree.

And yet things are not as bad as you might first think. English pronunciation looks more consistent when we take context into account. A well-known example of the anything-goes sensibility of English spelling is the invented word "ghoti," to be pronounced **fish**—provided one pronounces "gh" as in the word **enough**, "o" as in the word **women**, and "ti" as in the word **motion**. Cute, but there's a reason most would pronounce "ghoti" as **goatee**. The context of each letter matters. When "gh" appears at the start of a word, it's pronounced as a hard **g** (e.g., **ghastly**, **ghost**). In the middle of a word it's silent (e.g., **daughter**, **taught**). It's only pronounced as **f** at the end of a word (**laugh**, **tough**).

How much does context help constrain pronunciation? Researchers Brett Kessler and Becky Treiman analyzed the spelling and pronunciation of 3,117 single-syllable words. They found that consonants at the start of a word were pronounced consistently about 90% of the time. And the 10% of the time that the beginning consonants were not consistent, looking at the vowel that followed sometimes helped the reader figure out how to pronounce that initial consonant. For example, "c" is pronounced as **s** when it precedes "e," "i," or "y" (e.g., **cent**, **cinch**, or **cycle**), and "c" is pronounced as **k** when followed by other vowels (e.g., **cat**, **collar**, or **culprit**.) Final consonants were pronounced consistently about 94% of time. But context was of little help for those few inconsistencies.

Context helps even more when we consider vowels. But then again, vowels need more help because they are more often inconsistent; in Kessler and Treiman's analysis fully 40% of vowel sounds were exceptions. The initial consonant was *never* any help in predicting the pronunciation, but the final consonant was about 80% of the time. So for example, the vowel string "oo" is usually pronounced as in the word **boot**, but sometimes it's pronounced as in the word **book**. Well, it turns out that "oo" only has the latter pronunciation when it's followed by "k" or "r" (**book**, **brook**, **crook**, **shook**, **poor**, **door**, **floor**).

Of course, there are out-and-out rule violations in English spelling—enough that some educators suggest it makes more sense to use the term spelling patterns, rather than rules. Even for exceptions to the patterns, we can take heart. These are often high-frequency words—that is, they appear very often in the language.[29] "Gone," "give," "are," "were," and "done" all violate the pattern *when a word ends with 'e', the vowel sound is long.* (Hence, "give" should rhyme with "hive.") Although these violate the pattern, they appear so commonly they are good candidates simply to be memorized as exceptions.

So in the end just how many letter-sound pairings must children learn? It depends on whether you include only the words that seven-year-olds are likely to encounter, or *all* English words. The lowest estimate would be at least 200 pairings.

Learning the Mapping

A couple hundred letter-sound pairings does seem like a lot to learn. It's also not the type of learning that humans find easiest, but we're not terrible at it, either. Psychologists call it arbitrary paired-associate learning; we're supposed to know that "A" and "B" go together. If I see "A", I think of "B", and vice versa, but there's no special rhyme or reason as to why "A" goes with "B" instead of going with "C". It's arbitrary. In the same way, there's no reason that the shape "c" goes with the sounds it does.

We do this sort of learning all the time, for example, associating people's names and faces, or associating the names of sports teams with the cities they play in. If you follow football in the fall and baseball in the summer, that's 62 city-team associations you know. So the idea of children learning a couple of hundred associations seems . . . well, frustrating, given that there are 44 speech sounds, but not insurmountable.

Naturally, some people are a little better at it than others, and there is evidence that children who are good at learning paired-associates learn to read faster.[30] Interestingly, you only see the advantage if children are good at the very specific type of association called for in reading, namely, learning a verbal response to a visual stimulus. For example, you show children an arbitrary shape, and ask them to learn that it's called a **maluma**. When the association goes in the other direction—I say **maluma** and you have to pick out the shape—learning is unrelated to reading. [31–33]

It's little wonder we use the word "decode" to refer to the process of translating print to sounds. Print is a code. And although the code may not be as haphazard as it first appears, it's definitely a problem for

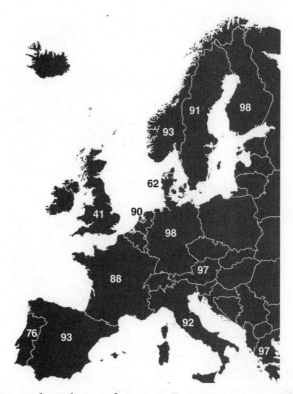

Figure 2.9. First-grade reading proficiency in European countries. The numbers are the average percentages of one-syllable words that children could read correctly at the end of first grade. Portuguese, French, and Danish, like English, have less consistent mappings between sounds and letters than other languages do.

Map of Europe: modified, original © hektoR, Shutterstock; data from Seymour, Aro, & Erskine (2003)

beginning readers, a problem that kids learning to read more consistent spelling systems don't face. Finnish, Spanish, and Italian, for example, are *very* consistent, with a near one-to-one mapping between letters and speech sounds and very few exception words. Kids learn to decode quite quickly in those countries. In a matter of months, almost all children can read aloud one or two syllable words with few errors. English-speaking children lag far behind (Figure 2.9).

First-graders do have a hard time in countries where the sound of the language maps inconsistently to writing. But most of the children learn the mapping, complex though it may be. By the time they reach fourth grade, the difficulty of the mapping is no longer the primary reason that children read well or poorly (Figure 2.10).

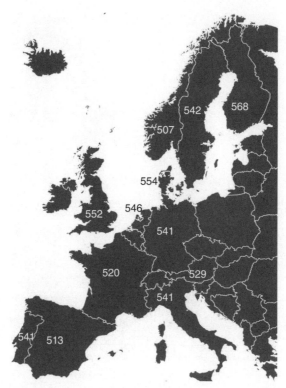

Figure 2.10. Average results from the Progress in International Reading Literacy Study (PIRLS) administered to 10-year-olds around the world. The scale goes from 0-1,000, with higher numbers reflecting better performance. The fourth-graders in England, Portugal, and Denmark score quite well, even though first-graders in those countries struggle with the difficult letter-sound mapping. These results show that most children are able to learn the mapping.
Map of Europe: modified, original © hektoR, Shutterstock; data from Mullis, Martin, Foy, & Drucker (2012)

All right, most children learn the letter-sound mappings in English, despite the difficulty. But must it be so difficult? Why not simplify English spelling?

This seemingly obvious idea has not been enacted because there are some non-obvious obstacles. First, such a movement could not be universal due to differences in pronunciation. If you really tried to respect pronunciation, you'd have different spellings of the same word in many of the countries that use English as an official language: Australia, Cameroon, Canada, England, Gambia, Malawi, Scotland, and so on. Second, simplified spelling would carry some costs. English has a lot of homophones: "I" and "eye," "bear" and "bare," and so on. The different spellings are troublesome to learn, but once you know them, they make reading easier. If these were spelled the same way, readers would have to use context to know which sense was meant. Third, it has proven harder than you might think to develop an accepted list of spelling patterns. The problem is that our current list of patterns is a mish-mash of those found in German, French, Latin, and Greek. Schemes to simplify spelling tend to privilege one of these four languages, so the number of words affected ends up being huge.

A goal more modest than the complete regularization of spelling might be achievable: reduce redundancies. The letter "x" could be replaced by "ks." Hard "c" could be replaced by "k," and soft "c" could be replaced by "s." Even this less ambitious goal has little chance of realization, as attempts at spelling simplification have historically encountered strong public opposition. English, unlike many other languages, does not have a central regulatory body with the authority to dictate changes, so public enthusiasm (or at least, acquiescence) would be essential.

Summing Up

In Chapter 1 we noted that English writing—and all other writing—codes sound, not meaning. In the case of our alphabetic system, that means that children must learn to discriminate only a small number of visual symbols, namely the letters of the Roman alphabet. That visual discrimination is relatively easy. More difficult is learning the mapping between letters and sounds. It's more complicated than it needs to be, but the mind is not ill equipped to learn this sort of association, so with time and practice, children catch on. The hardest aspect of learning to decode is the hearing of individual speech sounds. *That* your brain is not designed to do, and although some children pick up this skill with ease, many do not. It's the weak spot in learning to decode, the aspect of reading that is most likely to give kids trouble.

I've emphasized sound so much you may well have concluded the story of decoding ends there. Print allows us to talk to ourselves, and that's reading. But there's more to it. For example, have a look at this passage:

Wunce uhpawn uh thyme, thare wuz uh liddle gurl hoo lift wif hurr muhther inna liddle coddij, awn thuh ehj uhva larj fahrrust. Dis liddle gurl offun war a liddle kloke wif a priddy liddle rehd hood, anfer dis reesun peepl calder Liddle Rehd Rye Din Hood.

How'd that go? I expect you could work out the meaning, probably helped by the fact that the story is familiar. But note how much more quickly you can read the same passage with standard spelling:

Once upon a time, there was a little girl who lived with her mother in a little cottage on the edge of a large forest. This little girl often wore a little cloak with a pretty little red hood, and for this reason people called her Little Red Riding Hood.

If reading is a matter of translating print to sound and mentally "listening" to what we've decoded, shouldn't the passage be easier to read? Why should "coddij" be harder to read than "cottage"? In laboratory experiments we see that it takes a little longer to reject as a nonword a letter string that sounds like a word (e.g., "chare") compared to one that doesn't sound like a word (e.g., "pleck").[34]

An obvious explanation is that we have had some practice reading "cottage" and "chair," and none reading "coddij" or "pleck." That may mean that reading is more than the application of spelling-sound conversion rules—we know what words look like. But it may not mean that. It may be that some translation rules are used less often than others, we're slower to read when we use those unusual rules, and the "Liddle Rehd Rye Din Hood" paragraph used a lot of those unusual translation rules.

We consider these possibilities in the next chapter.

Summary and Implications

Summary

- To decode text, a reader must (1) distinguish one letter from another, (2) hear individual speech sounds, and (3) know the mapping between letters (and letter groups) and speech sounds.
- Letters are not designed for the sake of being easily distinguishable, and readers do confuse the ones that look similar. Still, there aren't that many to learn, so most children learn them without difficulty.
- Humans are not born with the ability to hear individual speech sounds. In fact, individual speech sounds are influenced by context: they vary in speakers with different regional accents for example, and the same person says the same speech sound differently depending on the other speech sounds in the word. So when we think of the sound associated with a letter, we're really thinking of an ideal, an abstraction.
- Being able to hear individual speech sounds is associated with reading success, and when children have trouble learning to read, this process is the most common stumbling block.
- In contrast to some other languages, English uses a complicated mapping of speech sounds to letters (and letter groups). Still, the mapping is more orderly than you might guess, because the context in which a letter appears may provide information about its sound.
- The mapping could be simpler. Still, most children learn it.

Implications

- If the hearing of individual speech sounds is usually the trouble spot for children learning to read, that might mean that it's the biggest contributor to diagnosed cases of dyslexia. That seems to be true,[35] but dyslexia is complicated and the extent to which other factors contribute remains actively debated.[36]

(*continued*)

- If the basic components of decoding are hearing sounds, appreciating the differences among letters, and learning the mapping between them, then anything that promotes those abilities ought to help once reading instruction starts. I've mentioned phonological awareness is improved by wordplay like rhyme and alliteration. Adults reading aloud with children can also draw their attention to letters by pointing out the very fact that it's the marks on the page that carry meaning, that some letters look the same, that we start at the left of a line and move to the right when we read, and so on. All these measures (and others that are similar in spirit) teach children about letters and print, and give them an edge when reading instruction begins.[37]

- We might think that, when teaching children letters, we should label them with the sound they make, rather than the commonly used name. For example, when pointing out a "t" we shouldn't say **that's a tee**, but instead say **that letter says t**, approximating as closely as possible the sound **t** in isolation, rather than saying **tuh**. This practice sounds logical because we're implicitly teaching the letter-sound correspondence. Logical, but there's no evidence that this practice helps, probably because almost all letter names at least contain the right sound.[38–40]

- The data shown in Figure 2.10 indicate that, even though the letter-sound mapping in English is difficult, children do learn it, and by fourth grade their reading comprehension is comparable to their peers in countries where the letter-sound mapping is easier to learn. We should bear this finding in mind when thinking about reading progress *within* the US too. I can't see an advantage to a school starting reading instruction especially early because of the difficulty of the English mapping, and indeed, research indicates that any advantage to the early start is transient. Kids who started later eventually become fluent decoders, and read as well as their early starting peers.[41]

Discussion Questions

1. If more children came to school with good phonological awareness, more would experience quick success in reading. Some children get incidental practice in phonological awareness (via read-alouds, for example), but many don't. If you were the head of programming for children's television for a major network, what might you do to address this issue?

2. The text provides an account of how we are able to read letters that look different. It assumes that letters share basic features, irrespective of typeface, size, and so on. That is, a capital "B" always has a vertical line and two semicircles on the right. But how, then, are you able to read print that is upside down?

3. Suppose a child grew up in a household with parents who were born in another country and who speak English with heavy accents. Do you think that child would have more difficulty learning the mapping between letters and sounds because the examples used in reading instruction—the word "cat," for example—are pronounced with different speech sounds at home and at school?

4. I noted that learning to distinguish letters usually does not present a big problem for children learning to read. Nevertheless, perhaps it would be worthwhile to change fonts in beginning readers to make confusable letters less confusable, for example, by printing "d" with a dot inside the circle and "b" as it usually appears. As children move on to more advanced reading material, they will of course lose this cue, but by that time they likely won't need it. Do you think such a measure would prove useful?

REFERENCES

1. Changizi, M. A., Zhang, Q., Ye, H., & Shimojo, S. (2006). The structures of letters and symbols throughout human history are selected to match those found in objects in natural scenes. *The American Naturalist, 167*(5), E117–E139. http://doi.org/10.1086/502806.

2. Treiman, R., & Kessler, B. (2003). The role of letter names in the acquisition of literacy. In *Advances in child development and behavior* (Vol. 31, pp. 105–135). San Diego, CA: Academic Press.

3. Treiman, R., Kessler, B., & Pollo, T. C. (2006). Learning about the letter name subset of the vocabulary: Evidence from US and Brazilian preschoolers. *Applied Psycholinguistics, 27*, 211–227.

4. Treiman, R., Levin, I., & Kessler, B. (2012). Linking the shapes of alphabet letters to their sounds: the case of Hebrew. *Reading and Writing, 25*(2), 569–585. http://doi.org/10.1007/s11145-010-9286-3.

5. Treiman, R., & Broderick, V. (1998). What's in a name: Children's knowledge about the letters in their own names. *Journal of Experimental Child Psychology, 70*(2), 97–116. http://doi.org/10.1006/jecp.1998.2448.

6. Nodine, C. F., & Lang, N. J. (1971). Development of visual scanning strategies for differentiating words. *Developmental Psychology, 5*(2), 221–232. http://doi.org/10.1037/h0031428.

7. Liberman, I. Y., Shankweiler, D., Orlando, C., Harris, K. S., & Berti, F. B. (1971). Letter confusions and reversals of sequence in the beginning reader: Implications for Orton's Theory of Developmental Dyslexia. *Cortex, 7*(2), 127–142. http://doi.org/10.1016/S0010-9452(71)80009-6.

8. Vellutino, F. R., Smith, H., Steger, J. A., & Kaman, M. (1975). Reading disability: Age differences and the perceptual-deficit hypothesis. *Child Development, 46*(2), 487–493. Retrieved from www.jstor.org/stable/1128146.

9. Grainger, J., Rey, A., & Dufau, S. (2008). Letter perception: From pixels to pandemonium. *Trends in Cognitive Sciences, 12*(10), 381–387. http://doi.org/10.1016/j.tics.2008.06.006.

10. Hubel, D., & Wiesel, T. (1962). Receptive fields, binocular interaction and functional architecture in the cat's visual cortex. *The Journal of Physiology, 160*(1), 106–154. Retrieved from http://onlinelibrary.wiley.com/doi/10.1113/jphysiol.1962.sp006837/full/.

11. Holden, M. H., & MacGinitie, W. H. (1972). Children's conceptions of word boundaries in speech and print. *Journal of Educational Psychology, 63*(6), 551–557. Retrieved from http://psycnet.apa.orgjournals/edu/63/6/551.

12. Cunningham, A. E., & Zibulsky, J. (2014). *Book smart.* New York: Oxford University Press.

13. Melby-Lervåg, M., Lyster, S. A. H., & Hulme, C. (2012). Phonological skills and their role in learning to read: A meta-analytic review. *Psychological Bulletin, 138*(2), 322–52. http://doi.org/10.1037/a0026744.

14. Backman, J. (1983). The role of psycholinguistic skills in reading acquisition: A look at early readers. *Reading Research Quarterly, 18*(4), 466–479.

15. Storch, S. A., & Whitehurst, G. J. (2002). Oral language and code-related precursors to reading: Evidence from a longitudinal structural model. *Developmental Psychology, 38*(6), 934–947. http://doi.org/10.1037//0012-1649.38.6.934.

16. Calfee, R. C., Lindamood, P., & Lindamood, C. (1973). Acoustic-phonetic skills and reading: Kindergarten through twelfth grade. *Journal of Educational Psychology, 64*(3), 293–298. Retrieved from www.ncbi.nlm.nih.gov/pubmed/4710951.

17. Anthony, J. L., & Francis, D. J. (2005). Development of phonological awareness. *Current Directions in Psychological Science, 14*(5), 255–259. http://doi.org/10.1111/j.0963-7214.2005.00376.x.

18. Hu, C.-F., & Catts, H. W. (1998). The role of phonological processing in early reading ability: What we can learn from Chinese. *Scientific Studies of Reading, 2*(1), 55–79.

19. Bradley, L., & Bryant, P. E. (1983). Categorizing sounds and learning to read: A causal connection. *Nature, 301,* 419–421.

20. Ehri, L. C., Nunes, S. R., Stahl, S. a., & Willows, D. M. (2001). Systematic phonics instruction helps students learn to read: evidence from the National Reading Panel's Meta-Analysis. *Review of Educational Research, 71*(3), 393–447. http://doi .org/10.3102/00346543071003393.

21. Bus, A. G., & van IJzendoorn, M. H. (1999). Phonological aware- ness and early reading: A meta-analysis of experimental training studies. *Journal of Educational Psychology, 91*(3), 403–414.

22. Rodriguez, E. T., & Tamis-Lemonda, C. S. (2011). Trajectories of the home learning environment across the first 5 years: Associations with children's vocabulary and literacy skills at prekindergarten. *Child Development, 82*(4), 1058–1075. http://doi.org/10.1111/ j.1467-8624.2011.01614.x.

23. Hanson, V. L., Liberman, I. Y., & Shankweiler, D. (1984). Linguistic coding by deaf children in relation to beginning reading success. *Journal of Experimental Child Psychology, 37*(2), 1984.

24. Morford, J. P., Wilkinson, E., Villwock, A., Piñar, P., & Kroll, J. F. (2011). When deaf signers read English: Do written words acti- vate their sign translations? *Cognition, 118*(2), 286–292. http://doi .org/10.1016/j.cognition.2010.11.006.

25. Hanson, V. L., Goodell, E. W., & Perfetti, C. A. (1991). Tongue- twister effects in the silent reading of hearing and deaf college stu- dents. *Journal of Memory and Language, 30*, 319–330.

26. Traxler, C. B. (2000). The Stanford Achievement Test, 9th edition: National norming and performance standards for deaf and Hard-of- Hearing Students. *Journal of Deaf Studies and deaf education, 5*(4), 337–348. http://doi.org/10.1093/deafed/5.4.337.

27. Morais, J., Luz, G., Alegria, J., & Bertels, P. (1979). Does awareness of speech as a sequence of phones arise spontaneously? *Cognition, 7*, 323–331.

28. Vaughn, J. S. (1902, August). Our strange language. *The Spectator*, 187.

29. Ziegler, J. C., Stone, G. O., & Jacobs, A. M. (1997). What is the pronunciation for -ough and the for computing spelling for /u /?

A database for computing feedforward and feedback consistency in English. *Behavior Research Methods, Instruments, & Computers*, *29*(4), 600–618.

30. Windfuhr, K. L., & Snowling, M. J. (2001). The relationship between paired associate learning and phonological skills in normally developing readers. *Journal of Experimental Child Psychology*, *80*(2), 160–173. http://doi.org/10.1006/jecp.2000.2625.

31. Hulme, C., Goetz, K., Gooch, D., Adams, J., & Snowling, M. J. (2007). Paired-associate learning, phoneme awareness, and learning to read. *Journal of Experimental Child Psychology*, *96*(2), 150–166. http://doi.org/10.1016/j.jecp.2006.09.002.

32. Litt, R. A., de Jong, P. F., van Bergen, E., & Nation, K. (2013). Dissociating crossmodal and verbal demands in paired associate learning (PAL): What drives the PAL-reading relationship? *Journal of Experimental Child Psychology*, *115*(1), 137–149. http://doi.org/10.1016/j.jecp.2012.11.012.

33. Litt, R. A., & Nation, K. (2014). The nature and specificity of paired associate learning deficits in children with dyslexia. *Journal of Memory and Language*, *71*(1), 71–88. http://doi.org/10.1016/j.jml.2013.10.005.

34. Coltheart, M., Davelaar, E., Jonasson, T., & Besner, D. (1977). Access to the internal lexicon. In *Attention & Performance VI*. London: Academic Press.

35. Liberman, I. Y. (1973). Segmentation of the spoken word and reading acquisition. *Annals of Dyslexia*, *23*(1), 64–77; Stanovich, K. E. (1988). Explaining the differences between the dyslexic and the garden-variety poor reader: The phonological-core variable-difference model. *Journal of Learning Disabilities*, *21*(10), 590–604.

36. A highly readable introduction to dyslexia may be found in Mark Seidenberg's wonderful book, *Language at the speed of sight* (New York: Basic Books, 2016).

37. Justice, L. M., & Pullen, P. C. (2003). Promising interventions for promoting emergent literacy skills: Three evidence-based approaches. *Topics in Early Childhood Special Education*, *23*(3), 99–113.

38. Treiman, R., & Kessler, B. (2003). The role of letter names in the acquisition of literacy. *Advances in Child Development and Behavior, 31*, 105–138.

39. Share, D. L. (2004). Knowing letter names and learning letter sounds: A causal connection. *Journal of Experimental Child Psychology, 88*(3), 213–233.

40. Ellefson, M. R., Treiman, R., & Kessler, B. (2009). Learning to label letters by sounds or names: A comparison of England and the United States. *Journal of Experimental Child Psychology, 102*, 323–341.

41. Suggate, S. P., Schaughency, E. A. & Reese, E. (2013). Children learning to read later catch up to children reading earlier. *Early Childhood Research Quarterly, 28*, 33–48.

3

Reading at a Glance

Agenda for Chapter 3

We've said that reading is a code for sound. Now we need to determine what role, if any, the look of words—that is, their spelling—plays in reading.

In Chapter 1 we explored why sound is vital to reading; the alphabetic code is one of sound, and indeed, it must be sound-based—recreating grammar in a written system is too hard, and it's much easier to simply recode what we say. In Chapter 2 we examined evidence that reading is a matter of learning and then using this sound-based code. But at the end of the chapter we saw that it is difficult to read a paragraph which *ought* to be perfectly readable based on the sound of the words ("Wunce uhpawn uh thyme"). One way to interpret this difficulty is that the typical spellings of the words help you to access the meaning. They don't seem to be *essential*—you can still work out the meaning of the paragraph—but they sure seem to help. How can this demonstration be squared with the idea that reading is sound-based?

Spelling Representations in the Mind

The visual appearance of words, not just the sound they signify, does matter. (From here on I'll use the word "spelling," rather than the clunky phrase "visual appearance of words.") Understanding the role of spelling will be clearer if we situate it in the context of what we've already talked about. Chapters 1 and 2 conceptualized reading as a way to get from

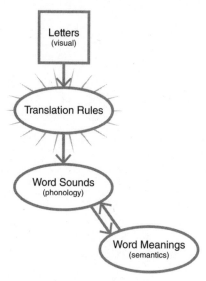

Figure 3.1. Letters, sounds, and meaning.
© Daniel Willingham

vision (seeing letters) to semantics (mental representation of meaning) via phonology (mental representations of sound) (Figure 3.1.)

This spelling-sound translation process is laborious; it consumes a lot of your attention, especially when you're first learning it. I've depicted that fact with the little lines radiating out from the oval representing the process. If you've seen a beginning reader you don't need much convincing that sounding words out takes a lot of attention. We'll return to this point, but right now let's get to spelling.

The "Wunce uhpawn uh thyme" paragraph indicates that what words look like (and not just what they sound like) matters in reading. We might also note that English has homophones: words that sound alike but are spelled differently and have different meanings like "knight" and "night" or "wholly" and "holy." We need *some* way to account for our success in reading such words, so maybe we do pay attention to spelling. That means we need another oval in our figure, to signify a mental representation of how words are spelled, what they look like on the page. (Researchers call these orthographic representations.) (Figure 3.2.)

This new set of mental representations allows a reader to go directly from printed letters to meaning, bypassing sound altogether. Just as we

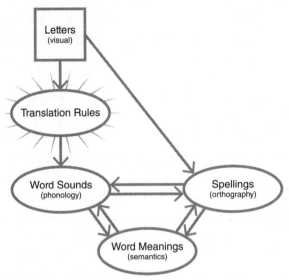

Figure 3.2. Letters, sounds, meaning, and spelling. Experienced readers can access word meaning not only through sound, but via another route that directly matches letters to knowledge of how words are spelled.
© Daniel Willingham

proposed for meaning and sound, we're proposing that spelling representations are separate, but linked.[1] That separation matches our intuition: you might know two features of a word (how to pronounce it and what it means) but not the third (how to spell it). These orthographic representations develop through reading practice, but before we consider their development, let's examine how researchers know that these spelling representations exist in the first place.

Perhaps the most persuasive evidence for readers using two routes to meaning (sound translation and the spelling route) comes from patients with brain damage. You're probably used to thinking of dyslexia as a problem in learning how to read, but there's another type of dyslexia. Some adults who were typical readers suffer some damage to the brain—usually because of a stroke—that affects their reading. For a very small number of people, the stroke is highly selective, and it happens to knock out just one of the two reading mechanisms. Thus, some people can use the letter-sound translation rules, but they cannot get to orthography directly from visual input. So when they see a word like "cake" they can read it aloud, no problem, because the translation rules work. But when presented with an irregular word like "yacht" they are stumped. They apply the translation rules and say to themselves "Yatch-ette. Hmm. I don't know that word."

Other people—again, it's rare, but it does happen—have a stroke affecting the translation process, but the spelling route works fine. So they can read "yacht" *and* they can read "cake" because there is a spelling representation for each, and that representation is linked to the sound of the word (Figure 3.2). They are stumped, however, by simple nonwords like "rilf." They can't use sound translation rules—those have been lost because of the stroke—and there's no spelling representation of "rilf" that would be linked to the sound representation.[2,3] So they cannot read "rilf" aloud.

These results indicate that both routes—the sound-based and the spelling—live side-by-side in experienced readers. The patients described can only use the single remaining route. But what about those who have not suffered a stroke? You might suppose that readers use one path or the other under different circumstances. Maybe they use the spelling path when spelling is important, like when they must differentiate "knight" and "night" and they use sound translation when sound is important, like when figuring out whether "sow" means a female pig or the act of planting. Cool idea, but that's not what happens. Both pathways operate all the time.[4]

Lots of technical experiments show that even for proficient readers, the sound-translation pathway continues to influence reading, even after the spelling path develops. (We'll get to that development shortly.) Here are three easy-to-appreciate examples. First, even skilled readers are a little slower to read words with irregular pronunciation (e.g., "foot") than words that follow translation rules (e.g., "week"). Second, people are slower to (silently) read tongue-twisters than other sentences that are just as nonsensical in meaning, but don't twist the tongue in pronunciation.[5] Third, if you ask people to proofread text, they are less likely to flag errors that have the right sound, e.g., "He said he was pleased to meat me" than errors that don't, e.g., "He said he was pleased to melt me."[6,7] So sound matters, even for experienced readers, reading silently.

This two-path model represents researchers' best guess as to how experienced readers read individual words.* In Chapter 5 we'll deal with more complex meanings like those found in sentences and paragraphs. Let's get more specific about what we mean by *orthographic knowledge*, your knowledge of how words are spelled.

What Does Spelling Knowledge Look Like?

I've been making it sound as though orthographic knowledge is rather like a list of words that we know how to spell. That's partly true but there's more to it than that. To get started, let's look at a couple of odd abilities of experienced readers.

Seeing What's Not There

Which of these looks more like a word to you: "ppes" or "sepp"? How about "nuck" or "ckun"? Now compare "fage" and "fajy." Experienced readers find this task relatively easy, but it's actually peculiar that you can do it—after all, none of these are words. What makes some more "wordy" than others?

It seems that we have some knowledge of which letters tend to go together—e.g., "fajy" looks wrong because "j" is seldom followed by "y"—and some knowledge of where in a word certain letter combinations tend to occur—e.g., double letters like "pp" tend not to occur at the beginning of words. Is this task merely a curiosity, or does it have anything to do with reading? Well, performance on tasks like this are associated with reading ability.[10-15] And evidence from other, more fine-grained laboratory tasks support the idea that we're tapping something important.

Let me describe a simple experiment, one that will help us get to the bottom of these spelling representations (and that offers another example of the peculiar abilities of readers). You sit in front of a computer monitor.

---

*A different architecture describing phonology, orthography, and semantics has been proposed by Mark Seidenberg.[8, 9] This model is influential and may well have advantages in accounting for some aspects of existing data, but the ways in which it differs would be of greater interest to specialists.

There's an asterisk on the screen and you're told that a letter will replace the asterisk, but it will appear only very briefly before it disappears and the asterisk returns. Your job is to identify the letter. Sometimes other letters appear nearby, but you can ignore them. The interesting finding is that people are more likely to correctly identify the letter if there are other letters nearby—but only if they form a word with the target. Random letters don't help.[16] (This finding is called the *word superiority effect*, by the way.)

If it's not obvious why the word superiority effect is strange, consider this. You're better at identifying the target letter if it forms a word with the neighboring letters. But how can you know that the letters form a word unless you know what the letters are? And if you've identified the letters, well, you know the letters; so identifying the letter where the asterisk was shouldn't be helped or hurt by whether or not it forms a word with the others.

This result is confusing because we assume that reading works by first identifying letters, and then putting them together to figure out what word they spell (Figure 3.3).

If we modify this simple model in two ways, it can explain the word superiority effect. First, we allow that knowledge of words can influence letter identification. Second, we assume that the process of identifying words starts before each letter is completely identified (Figure 3.4).

Figure 3.3. How one might assume words are identified. The word on the page goes into the eye, then your mind figures out the letters, and then your mind puts the letters together to figure out what word they spell.
© Daniel Willingham

Figure 3.4. How words are identified—a more complete model. The process that identifies the word can inform the process identifying letters; knowledge of what words are possible can constrain what letters might be on the page.
© Daniel Willingham

Cooperation in Identifying Letters and Words

Here's how that might work. Suppose there's a process in the mind that's figuring out which letter is in the first position of the word "ERROR." There's another process figuring out the letter in the second position, another working on the third position, and so on. Now, that assertion might seem strange—wouldn't you figure out the first letter, then the second letter and so on? It turns out we don't read letter by letter, we read in letter clumps, figuring out a few letters at a time.

Here's another surprising aspect of word-reading. It would seem logical that the visual system would identify letters, and then identify words (Figure 3.3). In other words, the visual system would be quite sure that the first letter is an "E" before passing that information to the process that figures out words. After all, if the letter-identification process jumped the gun and sent along incomplete information, how is the word-identification process supposed to do its job?

But the visual system doesn't wait. It forwards the information before identity is certain, saying (in essence): "First letter is probably an 'E' or 'F', or 'H'. Outside chance it's an 'A' or 'B'. Very unlikely it's any of the others." Meanwhile, the second letter is being analyzed and an educated guess about its identity is also forwarded ("probably a 'P', 'R', or 'B' . . .").

The process that identifies words can compare the guesses for different positions and thereby make the letter guesses better. The first letter might be "E", "F", or "H"; knowing that the second letter might be "P", "R", or "B" means that the first letter is probably *not* an "H" because there aren't any words that begin "HR" or "HP" or "HB." So the process that identifies words communicates that information back to the process that's still figuring out the identity of the letter in the first position: "probably not 'H'." In short, guesses about the identity of letters inform guesses about the identity of words, and information about what words are possible inform guesses about individual letters.

Now we can see what's behind the word superiority effect. The person is told, "identify the letter at the center of the screen and ignore the others." But the mind of a skilled reader can't ignore the others. Her mind will begin the process of identifying those neighboring letters whether she wants to or not, trying to put all the letters together as a word. And

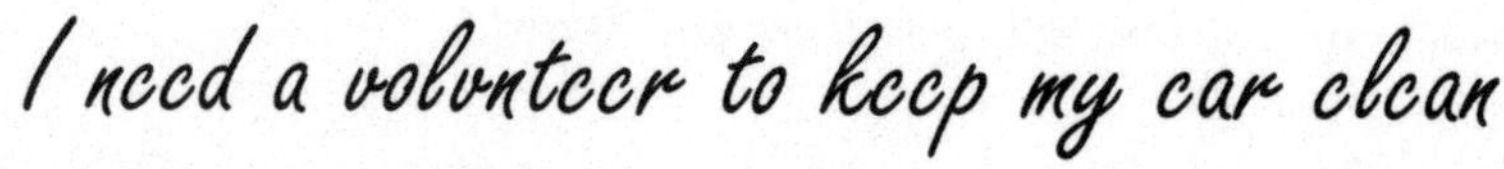

I need a volunteer to keep my car clean

Figure 3.5. Ambiguous letters. The "v" and the "u" in "volunteer" are the same shape. So are the "c" and the "e" in "clean."
© Daniel Willingham

that process that's trying to figure out the word will help identify the target letter. But that process can only help if the letters actually form a word. If they are random, knowledge of what words are possible doesn't help.

This hypothesis of how orthographic knowledge influences letter identification can also explain how ambiguous letters are interpreted, the sort of letters we saw in the Introduction (Figure 3.5).

The surrounding letters provide context that tell you that the ambiguous letter must be an "e" in "need" because "nccd" is not a word. The same shape is readily interpreted as a "c" at the start of "clean" because "elean" is not a word. It's not that you look at the ambiguous figure and consciously reason "I guess that's supposed to be a 'c.'" In context, you just read it as a "c."

But we haven't explained the phenomenon we started with. Why do we confidently say that "chim" looks more like a word than "chym"? We shouldn't have an orthographic representation of either, because neither is a word. The answer is that we have representations in memory not just of individual letters and full words, but of groups of letters. For example, we have a representation for the letter pair "im" but we don't have one for "ym" because we have seen "im" in many words, but have seldom seen "ym." The idea is that any letter string that appears frequently enough merits its own representation, whether or not it's a complete word, and even if the string is kind of long (e.g., "ould"). Words that are rated as typical-looking are those that have letter groups that appear frequently in the language, and people are able to read them a bit faster, compared to words with unusual letter groups.[17]

This notion that reading uses several levels of visual information—letters, letter groups, words—is important in demonstrations like this one, which made the rounds on Facebook a few years ago (Figure 3.6).

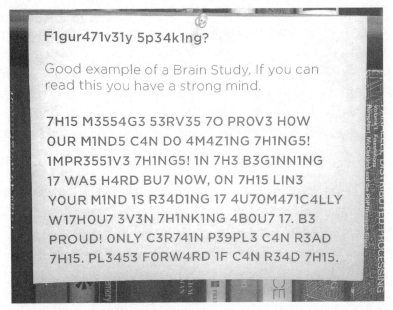

Figure 3.6. Digits can substitute for letters.
© Daniel Willingham

Being able to read this text is not a sign of a "strong mind," but it is a sign of well-developed orthographic representations. In fact, this type of writing was commonly used by teens in the 1990s when texting. Texting was available before cell phones with full keyboards were common. It was sometimes simpler to substitute digits for letters when typing on a phone. A "7" or "1" in isolation is a digit, but in the context of other letters like "7H1NK1NG" they can be evaluated as "T" and "I."

The way we've described orthographic representations also explains another Internet meme:

Aoccdrnig to a rscheearch at Cmabrigde Uinervtisy, it deosn't mttaer in waht oredr the ltteers in a wrod are, the olny iprmoatnt tihng is taht the frist and lsat ltteers be at the rghit pclae. The rset can be a toatl mses and you can sitll raed it wouthit porbelm. Tihs is bcuseae the huamn mnid deos not raed ervey lteter by istlef, but the wrod as a wlohe

This text retains the first and last letter of each word and jumbles any other interior letters. Experienced readers can manage to read it, although a good bit more slowly than they would read an un-jumbled version.[18] But the fact that they can read it at all would seem to conflict with the idea that we read by letter-sound translation or by spelling, both of which are disrupted.

But note that other texts using the same rules are tougher to read:

Abgrulay the geetasrt mteseyirs in the uresivne lie in the trehe ponud msas of clels, aplaeiorxmtpy the costiscenny of oetmaal, taht reeidss in the sulkl of ecah of us.

If you found this sentence harder, you know that "you only need the first and last letter in place" can't be right. The "Cmabrigde" text is simpler because it uses a lot of short words, so the jumbled letters are more likely to be adjacent to one another. I won't go into more detail here, but that turns out to be important—we can overcome minor errors in position,[19] especially if we can understand enough of the other words so that the possible meaning of a difficult word is constrained. (By the way, the scrambled words in the text box form the first sentence of another book I wrote: "Arguably the greatest mysteries in the universe lie in the three pound mass of cells, approximately the consistency of oatmeal, that resides in the skull of each of us").[20]

Developing orthographic knowledge—mental representations that allow you to identify letters, groups of letters, and words, by their appearance—is essential to being a good reader.[9, 21, 22] But why?

WHY ORTHOGRAPHIC REPRESENTATIONS MATTER

I said before that we need orthographic representations to read homophones correctly—"night" vs. "knight," for example. That's not their most important function, however. Orthographic representations make for better reading, in two ways.

Saving Working Memory

As shown in Figure 3.2, reading words via orthographic representations bypasses the letter-sound translation rules. Using those rules demands attention. (You'll no doubt recall my so-ingenious representation of this cost—little lines radiating from the oval representing the process.) Bypassing the translation rules makes reading faster and easier. It's so easy that it's *automatic*, a term used by psychologists to denote a process that requires very little of your working memory. Working memory is the "workspace" in which thought happens, and it is, alas, limited. You can only think of so many things at the same time. That's why driving a car is all-consuming for the beginner, who must consciously think about how far to turn the steering wheel to change lanes, how closely to follow the car ahead, and so on. Once those processes become automatic, space in working memory is freed and becomes available for other cognitive work; the driver can carry on a conversation with a passenger, for example.

Likewise, when a beginning reader uses the letter-sound translation process (i.e., sounds a word out), her working memory is occupied mostly by translation rules—"let's see, 'o' usually sounds like **aw**, but when there are two of them, 'oo,' they make a different sound. . . . what was it again?" That leaves little working memory space for the task of comprehension, for actually understanding the meaning of what she's reading. With practice, the demand on working memory imposed by translation rules is reduced. Reduced, but never completely eliminated. You very likely felt the speed impediment when you read the "Wunc uhpawn uh thyme" paragraph.

The real gain comes when orthographic representations develop. They don't require much in the way of working memory capacity at all, *and* they provide a second, supporting source of information to help you home in on the right word. I mentioned before that the spelling route and the sound route operate simultaneously in experienced readers. That sometimes slows you down a bit—for example, you're a little slower to read irregularly pronounced words like "foot" because the sound route guides you towards the wrong interpretation. But most of the time the two routes complement and support one another, making reading easier.

The savings to working memory afforded by the addition of ortho-graphic representations is important because reading is so demanding.

Reading requires figuring out the parts of speech that words will play in a sentence. It requires keeping in mind previous sentences so you can relate the current sentence to what you've read. It requires drawing information from your long-term memory that will allow you to make inferences. It's little wonder that working memory capacity is associated with reading comprehension.[23] If you'd like a concrete example of how important working memory is to reading comprehension, have someone read a random sentence from this book to you, at a pace of one word per second. That will remind you what it was like to decode words slowly.

The process of building orthographic representations happens over months and years. As he gains reading experience, the child develops a larger and larger repertoire of words he can recognize at a glance, rather than sounding out. And the representations of individual words (and letter groups) get stronger, and more reliable. As this happens, the child's reading becomes faster, smoother, and more accurate. That's called *fluency*.

It's easy to see that fluency would aid comprehension; as we've said, sound translation demands a lot of working memory space, and reducing that demand leaves more working memory space to accomplish other tasks of reading. There's just a small spelling difference between "petty" and "pretty" or between "absent" and "assent." Readers with finely tuned orthographic representations make those distinctions more quickly and reliably than readers with low-quality orthographic representations, and that makes them better readers.[24] There's also a second, somewhat more subtle way that fluency helps comprehension. Fluency actually ends up helping comprehension through sound.

Better Reading Through Sound

First, note that we can take the same set of words and change the meaning by saying them in different ways. Imagine saying "what a great party" with enthusiasm. Now imagine saying those same four words in a sarcastic voice. You can't see the difference on the page—the sound of the sentences would differ: the words that you stress, the speed of the utterance, when and where the pitch changes. These cues, collectively called *prosody*, are often referred to as the melody of speech. And this melody carries information. It helps you differentiate sarcasm from enthusiasm, but it also helps with the essential but less glamorous donkey work of comprehension; prosody helps you work out the grammatical roles that various words play.[25]

Even when you read silently, you can add prosodic information to help you comprehend. Poet Billy Collins put it more eloquently: "I think when you're reading in silence you actually hear the poem in your head because the skull is like a little auditorium."[26] Remember the passage from *Billy Bathgate* I quoted in the Introduction? "Abbadabba" Berman is said to "die of the effort" of relaying the safe combination. Most readers will put that effort and exhaustion into Berman's voice when he says, "Right. Three three. Left twice. Two seven. Right twice. Three three." And hearing a voice in our head when we read is almost irresistible if we know the person who is speaking (Figure 3.7).

Figure 3.7. Silent reading. The sense that we hear a voice in our head when we read can be very strong.
Modified by the author, original © Everett Collection / Shutterstock.com

Psychologists Stephen Kosslyn and Ann Matt gathered experimental evidence for this mental voice.[27] They had participants listen to recordings of individuals speaking either quickly or slowly. Then participants read prose allegedly written by these individuals. The researchers found that reading times were faster or slower, depending on the speaking speed of the purported author, consistent with the idea that, at least in some cases, people simulate speech as they read.

Orthographic representations make access to individual words more nearly automatic, and that means you have more working memory space to devote to working out the prosody. Indeed, some data show that it's the development of prosody, and not reading rate per se, that leads to the boosts in reading comprehension associated with fluency,[28] but this conclusion is controversial.[29]

Fluency allows for better comprehension of what you read. And fluency depends on orthographic representations. So where do orthographic representations come from?

HOW ORTHOGRAPHIC REPRESENTATIONS DEVELOP

I want to start by clarifying what might have sounded like a contradiction. In Chapter 1, I said, "a writing system wouldn't work if people had to memorize what words look like." Now I'm concluding that "people have mental representations of what words look like." But these claims don't really contradict one another. A system that requires memorizing what words look like is impractical for *learning* to read. But once you know the sound-based way to decode, your mind learns what words look like, even if you're not especially trying to do so. If the child can sound words out, then the visual experience—what the word looks like—is consistently paired with the identity of the word (determined by the sounding-out process).

This is called the *self-teaching hypothesis*.[30] Most children are taught how to sound words out, but they teach themselves (without knowing they are doing so) what letter pairs and whole words look like, based on practice distributed over months and years.[31] These visual representations build slowly, but there is a lot of practice available; even reluctant readers read 50,000 words each year (although avid readers encounter many more words—as many as 4,000,000).[26] The more frequently you encounter a word (or clump of letters), the richer the visual representation.[32, 33]

In this chapter, we've established that readers care about how words sound *and* how they look. But what about meaning? Obviously vocabulary is important to reading, and we'll examine the process of learning new word meanings in the next chapter.

Summary and Implications

Summary

- Experienced readers have distinct representations for three aspects of each word: the sound, the spelling, and the meaning. These representations are distinct, but tightly linked, so that thinking of one makes it easy to think of the other two.
- Experienced readers can access meaning from print either by sounding words out or by matching the spelling on the page to an orthographic representation in the mind.
- Experienced readers typically use both pathways to word meaning simultaneously as they read.
- Orthographic representations of words help you identify letters, even as letter identification helps you know which word you're reading; the two processes are reciprocal.
- When readers can read by spelling as well as by sound, decoding requires less attention, which leaves more attention available for the work of comprehension.
- Spelling representations develop through reading.

Implications

- It seems at least plausible that you would use the same orthographic representations to read and to write. Thus we might expect that instruction in the spelling of words would help orthographic representations develop. Indeed evidence shows that such instruction does improve reading.[34] So that's a reason to include spelling instruction in schools, even though we all use word processors with spell-checkers.
- If orthographic representations develop through self-teaching, then they won't develop as well if children don't get proper feedback. That is, if a child sees "bear" but sounds it out as **beer**,

that's going to slow progress in developing the right ortho-graphic representations. That, in turn, suggests that this aspect of reading practice will be more effective if students read aloud, rather than silently, at least until they can sound words out pretty reliably.[35,36] The quality of feedback they receive matters too—gains are larger when an adult provides feedback than when a peer does.[37]

- If spelling representations help students read with greater pros-ody, then it might be helpful for students to have a model of what prosodic reading should sound like.[38]

Discussion Questions

1. I said that the seemingly rule-less system of English spelling makes more sense if you take context into account. How many of these contextual rules do you think students are taught? Should they learn about them more explicitly, or should they learn them implicitly, as they gain experience in reading? Do you think most teachers explicitly know most of these rules?

2. How does the reciprocal nature of letter-reading and word-reading provide insight into why proofreading is so difficult?

3. People acquire all sorts of expertise that is primarily visual. For example, judges at dog shows have expertise in the desired looks of particular breeds and would notice subtle distinctions that most of us would miss. You can think of reading by orthography as a similar type of visual expertise. How do you suppose someone like a dog show judge gains their expertise? Does this make you think about teaching reading differently or confirm what you already thought?

4. What are some of the ways that writers can signal particular prosody? For example, in the sentence "Steve gave Pascual the ball," how would you signal to a reader that the important message in this sentence is that it was Steve who did this, not someone else, as the reader might have thought? Although there are some ways to signal prosody, there's nothing close to a complete system to do so. Why not? Why don't we all learn a system of marks (as some languages use accent marks) that signal changes in emphasis, tempo, and pitch?

5. I've emphasized that adding orthographic representations results in a smaller attention demand for decoding, leaving more attention available for comprehending what you're reading. What else requires attention during reading? What types of text are especially attention-demanding? What do readers choose to do as they read that draws attention away from the act of reading? How much does it matter?

References

1. Nation, K. (2009). Form-meaning links in the development of visual word recognition. *Philosophical Transactions of the Royal Society of London. Series B, Biological Sciences, 364*(1536), 3665–74. http://doi.org/10.1098/rstb.2009.0119.

2. Coltheart, M., Rastle, K., Perry, C., Langdon, R., & Ziegler, J. (2001). DRC: A dual route cascaded model of visual word recognition and reading aloud. *Psychological Review, 108*(1), 204–56. Retrieved from www.ncbi.nlm.nih.gov/pubmed/11212628/.

3. Price, C. J., & Mechelli, A. (2005). Reading and reading disturbance. *Current Opinion in Neurobiology, 15*(2), 231–238. http://doi.org/10.1016/j.conb.2005.03.003.

4. Leinenger, M., & Leinenger, M. (2014). Phonological Coding During Reading. *Psychological Bulletin, 140*(6), 1534–1555.

5. Haber, L. R., & Haber, R. N. (1982). Does silent reading involve articulation? Evidence from tongue twisters. *The American Journal of Psychology, 95*(3), 409–419. http://doi.org/10.2307/1422133.

6. Jared, D., Ashby, J., Agauas, S. J., & Levy, B. A. (2016). Phonological activation of word meanings in Grade 5 readers. *Journal of Experimental Psychology: Learning, Memory, and Cognition, 42*(4), 524–541.

7. Treiman, R., Freyd, J. J., & Baron, J. (1983). Phonological recording and use of spelling-sound rules in reading of sentences. *Journal of Verbal Learning and Verbal Behavior, 22*(6), 682–700. http://doi.org/10.1016/S0022-5371(83)90405-X.

8. Levy, B. A., Gong, Z., Hessels, S., Evans, M. A., & Jared, D. (2006). Understanding print: Early reading development and the contributions of home literacy experiences. *Journal of Experimental Child Psychology, 93*(1), 63–93. http://doi.org/10.1016/j.jecp.2005.07.003.

9. Cunningham, A. E., Perry, K. E., & Stanovich, K. E. (2001). Converging evidence for the concept of orthographic processing. *Reading and Writing, 14*, 549–568.

10. Cassar, M., & Treiman, R. (1997). The beginnings of orthographic knowledge: Children's knowledge of double letters in words. *Journal of Educational Psychology, 89*(4), 631–644. http://doi .org/10.1037//0022-0663.89.4.631.

11. Ise, E., Arnoldi, C. J., & Schulte-Körne, G. (2012). Development of orthographic knowledge in German-speaking children: A 2-year longitudinal study. *Journal of Research in Reading, 00*(00). http:// doi.org/10.1111/j.1467-9817.2012.01535.x.

12. Juel, C. (2006). The impact of early school experiences on initial reading. In D. K. Dickinson & S. B. Neuman (Eds.), *Handbook of early literacy research* (pp. 410–426). New York: Guilford.

13. Stanovich, K. E., & West, R. F. (1989). Exposure to print and orthographic processing. *Reading Research Quarterly, 24*(4), 402–433.

14. Reicher, G. M. (1969). Perceptual recognition as a function of meaningfulness of stimulus material. *Journal of Experimental Psychology, 81*(2), 275–280.

15. Farmer, T. A., Christiansen, M. H., & Monaghan, P. (2006). Phonological typicality influences on-line sentence comprehension. *Proceedings of the National Academy of Sciences, USA, 103*, 12203–12208. doi: 10.1073/pnas.0602173103.

16. Rayner, K., White, S. J., Johnson, R. L., & Liversedge, S. P. (2006). Raeding wrods with jubmled lettres: There is a cost. *Psychological Science, 17*(3), 192–193.

17. McCusker, L. X., Gough, P. B., & Bias, R. G. (1981). Word recognition inside out and outside in. *Journal of Experimental Psychology: Human Perception and Performance, 7*(3), 538–551.

18. Willingham, D. T. (2009). *Why don't students like school?* San Francisco: Jossey Bass.

19. Badian, N. A. (2001). Phonological and orthographic processing: Their roles in reading prediction. *Annals of Dyslexia, 51*(1), 177–202. http://doi.org/10.1007/s11881-001-0010-5.

20. Freebody, P., & Byrne, B. (1988). Word-reading strategies in elementary school children: Relations to comprehension, reading time, and phonemic awareness. *Reading Research Quarterly, 23*(4), 441–453.

21. Daneman, M., & Carpenter, P. A. (1980). Individual differences in working memory and reading. *Journal of Verbal Learning and Verbal Behavior, 19*(4), 450–466. http://doi.org/10.1016/S0022-5371(80)90312-6.

22. Perfetti, C. (2007). Reading ability: Lexical quality to comprehension. *Scientific Studies of Reading, 11*(4), 357–383.

23. Carlson, K. (2009). How prosody influences sentence comprehension. *Language and Linguistics Compass, 3*(5), 1188–1200. http://doi.org/10.1111/j.1749-818X.2009.00150.x.

24. Rehm, D. (2013). *Aimless love: New and selected poems.* Retrieved from http://thedianerehmshow.org/shows/2013-10-22/billy-collins-aimless-love-new-and-selected-poems/transcrip/.

25. Kosslyn, S. M., & Matt, A. M. (1977). If you speak slowly, do people read your prose slowly? Person-particular speech recoding during reading. *Bulletin of the Psychonomic Society, 9*(4), 250–252.

26. Anderson, R. C., Wilson, P. T., Fielding, L. G., Anderson, R. C., & Fielding, L. G. (1988). Growth in reading and how children spend their time outside of school. *Reading Research Quarterly, 23*(3), 285–303.

27. Rayner, K., Pollatsek, A., Ashby, J., & Clifton, C. J. (2012). *Psychology of Reading* (2nd ed.). New York: Psychology Press.

28. Share, D. L. (1995). Phonological recoding and self-teaching: Sine qua non of reading acquisition. *Cognition, 55*(2), 151–218.

29. Grainger, J., Lété, B., Bertand, D., Dufau, S., & Ziegler, J. C. (2012). Evidence for multiple routes in learning to read. *Cognition, 123*(2), 280–92. http://doi.org/10.1016/j.cognition.2012.01.003.

30. Arciuli, J., & Simpson, I. C. (2012). Statistical learning is related to reading ability in children and adults. *Cognitive Science, 36*(2), 286–304. http://doi.org/10.1111/j.1551-6709.2011.01200.x.

31. Kessler, B. (2009). Statistical learning of conditional orthographic correspondences. *Writing Systems Research, 1*(1), 19–34. http://doi.org/10.1093/wsr/wsp004.

32. Shanahan, T., & Lomax, R. G. (1986). An analysis and comparison of theoretical models of the reading–writing relationship. *Journal*

of Educational Psychology, *78*(2), 116–123. Retrieved from http://psycnet.apa.orgjournals/edu/78/2/116.

33. Chard, D. J., Vaughn, S., & Tyler, B. J. (2002). A synthesis of research on effective interventions for building reading fluency with elementary students with learning disabilities. *Journal of Learning Disabilities*, *35*(5), 386–406.

34. Kuhn, M. R., & Stahl, S. A. (2003). Fluency: A review of developmental and remedial practices. *Journal of Educational Psychology*, *95*(1), 3–21.

35. Therrien, W. J. (2004). Fluency and comprehension gains as a result of repeated reading: A meta-analysis. *Remedial and Special Education*, *25*(4), 252–261.

36. Marchand-Martella, N. E., Martella, R. C., Modderman, S. L., Petersen, H. M., & Pan, S. (2013). Key areas of effective adolescent literacy programs. *Education and Treatment of Children*, *36*(1), 161–184.

37. Harm, M. W., & Seidenberg, M. S. (2004). Computing the meanings of words in reading: Cooperative division of labor between visual and phonological processes. *Psychological Review*, *111*(3), 662–720. http://doi.org/10.1037/0033-295X.111.3.662.

38. Seidenberg, M. S., & McClelland, J. L. (1989). A distributed, developmental model of word recognition and naming. *Psychological Review*, *96*(4), 523–68. http://doi.org/10.1037/0033-295X.96.4.523.

4

WORDS, WORDS, WORDS

Agenda for Chapter 4

Chapters 2 and 3 showed how the meaning of a word can be accessed via its sound or spelling (respectively). Now we need a better understanding of how meaning is represented in the mind.

We've been building a simple model of reading since Chapter 1 and our goal has remained the same: How do you use text to access word meanings (Figure 4.1)?

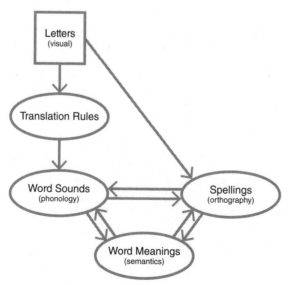

Figure 4.1. Letters, sound, spelling, and meaning.
© Daniel Willingham

But we've said next to nothing about what those word meanings in your memory actually look like, nor where they come from. We can't put that off any longer. After all, we're focusing on the aspects of cognition that lead to successful or unsuccessful reading. In that light, you would expect that vocabulary would be important—if I encounter a bunch of unknown words as I read, that can't be good for comprehension.

Researchers usually call this the *breadth* of your vocabulary and as we'll see, it matters. But we'll also see that it's only one aspect of the contribution that word representations make to reading. Another factor is vocabulary *depth*, which may matter even more. Depth implies that your knowledge of a given word is not a simple on off matter wherein you know a word or you don't; word knowledge may be shallow, deep, or somewhere in between.

Let's start by digging into what it means to know a word.

THE BAFFLING COMPLEXITY OF WORD KNOWLEDGE

As a starter, please offer a brief definition of these words:

Spill
Enjoy
Watermelon

At first blush, the question, "What does it mean to know a word?," doesn't seem that daunting. We'd guess that we have something like a mental dictionary where word meanings are stored, probably not *that* different than the paper or online dictionaries we're used to consulting. If I look up the word "spill," for example, I find these three senses of the verb:[1]

---

1. To cause or allow (something) to fall, flow, or run over the edge of a container usually in an accidental way
2. To fall or flow over the edge of a container
3. To move or spread out into a wider place or area

But the theory that mental dictionaries resemble paper dictionaries won't withstand much scrutiny because it's not hard to generate sentences that the paper dictionary says ought to work, yet our mental dictionary says don't. For example, if I wrote, "Would you mind spilling water on my plants while I'm on vacation?", that seems wrong, even though it is consistent with the second definition. And this sentence seems consistent with the third: "This sandwich would be better if I had spilled the peanut butter to the edge of the bread." This sort of lexical near-miss is familiar to teachers. Students try to enliven their writing with unusual words and, armed with a thesaurus but without detailed knowledge of definitions, they submit papers studded with rare words used in not-quite-correct ways.

Admittedly, these examples don't seem to rule out the possibility that the mental dictionary is like the paper variety. They just seem to imply that the mind's dictionary uses more precise definitions than *Merriam-Webster* does. With enough time, dictionary writers could sharpen the definition to match what's in the mind and so exclude odd usages like the peanut butter example. But that assessment is too optimistic. The real problem is that words, in isolation, are ambiguous. They derive their meaning from context. Dictionaries can't specify all contexts, and so seek to offer context-free definitions. That's why they will inevitably be incomplete.

Let's start with an easy example, the word "heavy." "Heavy" (according to *Merriam-Webster* online) means "having great weight."[2] But "great weight" depends on the noun to which "heavy" is applied. Fifty pounds is ***heavy*** if I'm describing a watermelon, but it's not ***heavy*** if I'm describing an adult human (Reminder: I'm putting quotations marks around a word as it would appear on the page; if it's boldface and italicized, that means it's the meaning of the word in your mind.) When I write, "that's a heavy watermelon," what I've actually told you is that the watermelon is heavy compared to most watermelons.

This is what I mean when I say that words take on meaning from their context: ***heavy*** becomes more meaningful when I know the word applies to ***watermelon***. And if the word ***heavy*** means less on its own than we expected, ***watermelon*** must mean more. Understanding "heavy watermelon" requires that your mental definition of ***watermelon*** cannot consist simply of something like ***sweet fruit with a juicy red flesh***. It must also include a watermelon's typical weight.

The verb *enjoy* is also ambiguous. You do different things when you enjoy a movie, or enjoy watermelon, or enjoy a friendship. The best we can do for a definition of *enjoy* without any context might be **to take pleasure in something**. But when I hear that you're enjoying a watermelon, I know more than that you're taking pleasure in it. I know you're eating it. (I suppose you could enjoy a watermelon just by looking at it or smelling it. If you tell me you're enjoying it by listening to it, we need to have a longer conversation.) To understand the word *enjoy* I must understand the function of what is being enjoyed: watermelons are for eating, movies for diversion, friendships for companionship. So again, a word (*enjoy*) turns out to be ambiguous, and so in order to make sense of it, another word (*watermelon*) must have more information stored in its definition (*edibility*) than we might have guessed.

Last example. Suppose you read this question: "Does photosynthesis contribute to the growth of a watermelon?" You can answer, of course, but it's odd that you're able to do so. Unless you happen to have studied watermelons closely at some point in school, you likely never read in a book or learned from a teacher that watermelon plants use photosynthesis. No, you successfully answer this question because you know watermelons are the fruit of a plant, and plants use photosynthesis. Again, it seems a word definition (*watermelon*) that ought to have been simple needs to have more information (*grows on plants*) crammed into it.

The meaning of *watermelon* is getting crowded, but this problem is still more extreme than I've implied. All the examples so far have shown that some words must have properties stored with them so that other, more obviously ambiguous words can have meaning. But in another sense, all words are ambiguous because all words have many different associations or features of meaning that might be important (or not). And which feature matters depends on context. Let's look at another example:

Trisha spilled her coffee, and Dan jumped up to get a rag.
Trisha spilled her coffee, and Dan jumped up to get her more.
Trisha spilled her coffee, and Dan jumped up, howling in pain.

These three examples show that even a straightforward verb you might read, like "spill," is still ambiguous in a sense. **Spill** has lots of features: spills can make a mess; when you spill something you have less of it; and that liquid spills penetrate clothing and can, depending on the liquid, injure someone. You don't know which feature is relevant upon reading "Trisha spilled her coffee," so the simple word *spill* is, outside of a particular context, somewhat ambiguous.

We've reached some sort of a tipping point. Anything I know about spilling may become relevant to how I interpret the word; it all depends on the surrounding context. We can't squeeze everything we know about watermelons and spills into their mental definitions. We need some other way to make what we know about watermelons available to shape the way we interpret the word when we encounter it.

How Words Are Organized in the Mind

Instead of packing more and more into our hypothetical mental dictionaries, we'll do the opposite. We'll minimize what's in any one entry, but we'll add lots of connections among the entries. This scheme is typically represented by showing mental concepts as nodes in a network, and adding connections or links among the nodes (Figure 4.2).

We've seen something like this network before in Chapter 2, when we discussed word identification. As before, each node in the network can have activity—think of it like energy. This time, let's add the idea that the nodes don't just turn on or off, but can be brighter or fainter, like a light bulb turned up or down with a dimmer switch. When you're conscious of a concept (thinking about **watermelon**, for example), that's synonymous with the node being fully active, the light bulb being as bright as it can be. The lines between nodes represent connections; they carry energy from one node to another. Concepts will be linked if they are attributes (watermelon has the attribute of redness) or category membership (watermelon is a type of fruit) or close semantic relationship (watermelon is similar in meaning to cantaloupe).

When the **watermelon** node is active, the energy is passed via the links to other concepts connected to **watermelon**. Characteristics of

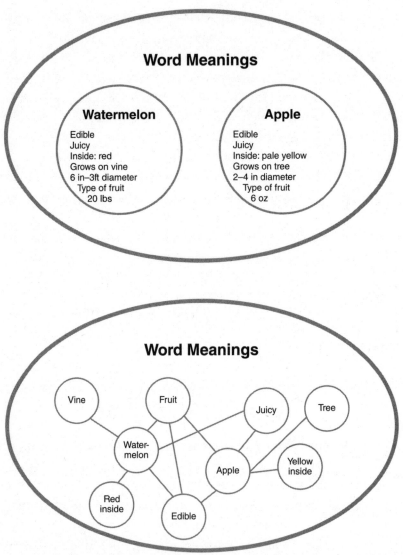

Figure 4.2. Alternative representations for word definitions. Top, how we might imagine *watermelon* and *apple* are represented in the mind. Bottom, a more workable type of representation. Note that in each case we're looking at a more detailed view of the "word meanings" component of the model from Figure 4.1.
© Daniel Willingham

watermelon and the function of watermelon and the fact that watermelons grow on plants—all of these can be related to the concept **watermelon** without having to stuff them all into the mental dictionary entry for *watermelon*.[3]

Here's why that's a big advantage. When you read the word "watermelon," the mental representation of the concept *watermelon* should have a certain promiscuity—you never know which feature of *watermelon* is going to be important, so all of them need to be available to color your interpretation of "watermelon." But they won't all be important at the same time. We need to capture the fact that your mind homes in on just the right knowledge about watermelons for the context, while ignoring all the information related to watermelons that doesn't matter for the context.

That's easy to implement in the network model. Let's look at an example using the word "spill." You read the word "spill" which activates that concept in your mind, and that activity is transmitted along the links to all the concepts connected to *spill* (Figure 4.3).

Time 1 in Figure 4.3 shows concepts in memory, connected. The solid lines show associations between concepts: *spill* is related to *oil*, to *milk*, to *mess*, and so on. When you read a word, "spill," the mental concept, *spill*, becomes active, which I've depicted by the thicker line around the *spill* concept at Time 2. Time 3 shows the state of the network perhaps two tenths of a second later. *Spill* has gained still more activity, and that activity is spreading through the network—related concepts are more active.[4]

The relationship between node activity and awareness is critical to how this model of meaning works. Lots of activity is associated with awareness—if a node is very active, you're thinking about that concept; the light bulb is very bright. But links don't convey all the activity of a node, only some of it. And that partial activation is reflected in the activity of the connected node. It's partially active—the light bulb is dimly lit. That in turn means that you're not thinking about the concept, that it's out of awareness. So when you read "spill," all the concepts linked to *spill* are somewhat active, but not enough that you're aware of them. That's the crucial idea—that just reading the word "spill" makes *all* the ideas associated with spill active, but not so active that all these varied ideas come crashing into consciousness. They are just a little more ready for cognitive

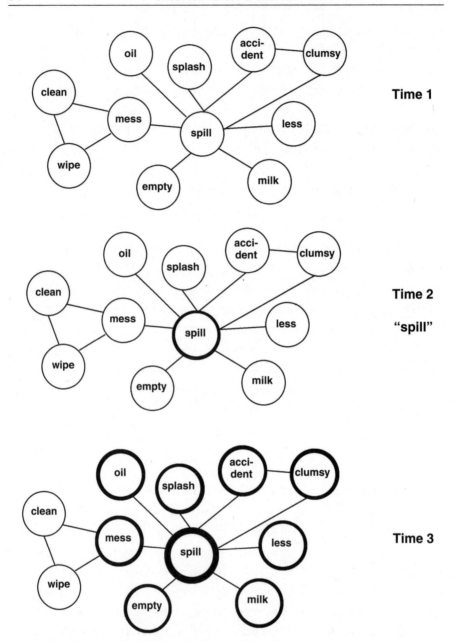

Figure 4.3. A meaning network for the concept *spill*. Such a network represents the associations between active and related concepts.
© Daniel Willingham

action—it's easier to think about the concept or read the word representing it.

Here's a classic experiment showing that claim is true. I sit you before a computer screen and I show you two buttons. Then I give you the following instructions:

On each trial you'll see two words, one above the other. Sometimes one or both won't be a real word, it will be a made-up word, like "splone." Your job is simple. If both words are real words, press the "yes" button on your left. If either is a made-up word, press the "no" button on your right.

What I don't tell you is that when both words are real, sometimes they are related, e.g., "birthday" and "party" but sometimes they are not, e.g., "nurse" and "shell." As shown in the graph, people are faster to press the "yes" button when the words are related (Figure 4.4).[5]

So when you read the first word (e.g., "bread") on the screen, the concept *bread* becomes active and related concepts—*flour, bake, oven, butter, jam*—become somewhat active. When you read the second word ("butter"), the concept (*butter*) is already somewhat active, and so the word is easier to read. Why is it easier to read? Remember that the links between a word's meaning, sound, and spelling are tight. So when the meaning becomes marginally active, so too does the sound and spelling of that word. Note that this experiment shows that the process by which

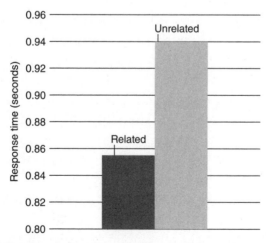

Figure 4.4. **Words activate related words.** This graph shows the time it took people to verify that each of two letter strings formed a word. Verification time was faster when the words were related, compared to when they were not.
© Anne Carlyle Lindsay based on data from Meyer & Schvanaveldt (1971)

associated words become active during reading is very rapid—it happens between the time that you've read the first word and when you start to read the second word.

Okay, so when you read a word—say, "doctor"—all the word meanings associated with **doctor** (e.g., **nurse, hospital, illness**) become somewhat active, somewhat more ready for cognitive use. Now let's consider what that implies for understanding the meaning of what you read. You read "Trisha spilled her coffee" and all the concepts related to **spill** get this half-activation we've been talking about (Figure 4.5). Then you read "Dan jumped up to get her more."

When you read the word "more" in the second sentence, the concept **more** will become active, and you'll be aware of it. Related concepts will gain a little bit of activity, but not enough that you're aware of them. But note that the concept **less** was already somewhat active because you read "spill," and **less** is associated with **spill**. Now the activation of the concept **more** will also activate the concept **less**, and that is enough to push the activation of **less** above some threshold. It enters awareness. So you're thinking of **spill** and **more** (because you read those words) and you're also thinking of **less**, even though you didn't read it. The other associations of **spill**—that a spill makes a mess, that clumsy people spill things—had the potential to be important, but nothing else in the context made those features rise to awareness. In addition, once one meaning rises to the surface, others are suppressed; in skilled readers, that process take less than a second.[6]

You can see how this model would allow for ideas to enter awareness even if the writer doesn't refer to them explicitly. If you read a bunch of words, each of which is connected to concept X, then all of those words pass activation to X, and X will pass the activation threshold of awareness. Remember the passage from the Introduction, where the dying "Abbad-abba" Berman says, "Right . . . Three three. Left twice. Two seven. Right twice. Three three." I asked how a reader knows that he's talking about a safe when the safe goes unmentioned. Now we have a model of memory that explains how that might work. Your knowledge of safes includes the ideas that the combinations use numbers between zero and 99, that the combination usually uses three numbers, that the dial is spun to the right,

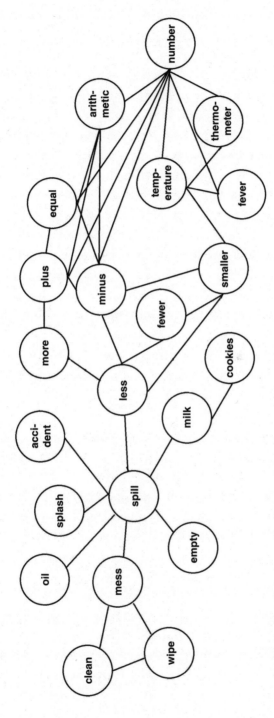

Figure 4.5. Expanded network of word meanings for *spill*.
© Daniel Willingham

then left, then right in that order, and so on. Hearing those features listed activates your memory representation for *safe*.

Naturally, the network of concepts in your mind would be enormous—I've just shown a tiny fraction of the network for illustrative purposes. The breadth of the network, and the particular connections in it are a product of an individual's experiences. In the United States, most people associate the concept *bird* with the concepts *builds a nest*, *eats bugs*, and *sings melodious songs*. Someone who grows up in an environment where most birds have different qualities will have a different network in memory. Someone who grows up in circumstances with less exposure to words, and to knowledge about the world, will have a network with fewer nodes, and with fewer connections among them.

We can also imagine that we'd need to add some features to the stripped-down architecture I've described. For example, we'd want links that don't simply pass activation, but that pass varying proportions of activation, to reflect the fact that some concepts are more closely linked than others. *Salt* should perhaps be linked to *steak* but surely the link from *salt* to *pepper* should be stronger. Come to that, we should enable links to be inhibitory too, so that if one node is active, it squelches the other. For example, if we added *pour* to the network, that concept and *spill* should mutually inhibit one another, because if something is poured, it isn't spilled, and vice versa.

We could list other niceties, but we've come far enough for the basic point to be clear. Word meanings are exquisitely sensitive to context; any concept connected to the word can influence how you interpret the word. We've made some progress in thinking through how words get their meaning from other words . . . but that points to another problem.

Coping with Missing Meanings

What happens if your network is missing a connection? A child may know that spills make a mess, but likely doesn't know that oil spills are environmental disasters. Or what if the child doesn't know what a "thermometer" is? Obviously, one possibility is that he simply doesn't understand the sentence. If someone remarks, **The Presidential candidate has**

an odd habit of catachresis, the rest of the sentence does not help me puzzle out the meaning of the rare word.

Other times the context provides significant help. Researcher Walter Kintsch offered this example: "Connors used Kevlar sails because he expected little wind."[7] Before reading this example, all I knew about Kevlar was that it had something to do with body armor. I didn't know it's a fabric (which I now assume it is), and I sure didn't know that it is used for sails. These facts are easy to infer from the context, and it's easy to infer that such sails have some property that make them suitable for calm winds although I can't tell what that property is. So what's the problem if I didn't know about Kevlar sails before reading Kintsch's example sentence?

With reading that sentence? No problem. In fact, that's one of the great pleasures of reading. You learn new things! If you had to have all of the background knowledge (and vocabulary) assumed by a writer, then it would nearly impossible to learn anything new by reading; the writer would have to be psychic, anticipating exactly what you don't know, and explaining it using only concepts you do know. So some reading is a little like problem solving, because it requires you to stop and think.

The real issue is the *amount* of problem solving you must do, because problem solving is mentally demanding and time consuming. It's not just that you have to think about what "Kevlar" might mean, it's also that doing so will interrupt the flow of the text in which you find it. You may lose the thread of the argument or story. So when there's too much problem solving to be done, reading is slower, harder, and less fun.[8]

The solution would seem obvious, especially in a school context. If a teacher assigns a text and she suspects her students lack some necessary background knowledge, she can provide it: definitions of words, historical context, functions of objects. It's certainly better to provide this information than not, but if you think about the inference mechanism described above, you can see that it's not a substitute; the relevant information is not going to be *automatically* activated because it's not well learned. Students will have to stop and think, "where did she say Rabat is, again?" And of course there is a limit to how much new information a student can absorb right before reading a text. Most of us have had the experience of reading a chapter that provides so many definitions of technical terms (or abbreviates them with acronyms) that by the middle we can no longer remember what DLPFC stands for.

Just how much unknown stuff can a text have in it before a reader will declare *mental overload!* and call it quits? This quantity surely varies depending on the reader's attitude toward reading and motivation to understand that particular text. Still, studies have measured readers' tolerance of unfamiliar vocabulary, and have estimated that readers need to know about 98% of the words for comfortable comprehension.[9–11] That may sound high, but bear in mind that that the paragraph you're reading now has about 75 unique words. So 98% familiarity means that this and every paragraph like it would have one or two words that are unfamiliar to you.

We have a pretty low tolerance for reading unknown words. And writers use a lot of words, many more than speakers do. If I'm talking about my cheap friend, I might use the word **cheap** three times within a few sentences. But writers like to mix things up, so my friend will be "frugal," "stingy," "thrifty," and "tight." Texts that students typically encounter in school have about 85,000 different words.[12] Somehow we need to ensure that children have a broad enough vocabulary so that they are not constantly colliding with unknown words.

But What Does a Word *Really* Mean?

Most of us have had this experience at one time or another. You consult a dictionary to get a word definition, perhaps "condescending." The dictionary defines it as "patronizing," which is no help because you don't know the meaning of that word, either. So you look up "patronizing," and find that it is defined as "condescending."

That's an example of a circular definition, and it's kind of funny, especially when it happens to someone else. But wait a minute. How much better is the network I introduced in the last section? Words seem defined by their features (watermelon is the red-on-the-inside, juicy, sweet fruit), but how are the features defined? By other words. So doesn't the model amount to a bunch of circular definitions, even if the circles may be bigger than the condescending-patronizing loop?[13]

The way out of this problem is to consider the possibility that some representations are grounded. That means that some mental concepts derive meaning not from other mental concepts, but more directly from experience. For example, perhaps the definition of *red* is not rooted in language. Indeed, if you look up "red" in a dictionary, the definition is pretty unsatisfying. Perhaps the mental definition of *red* should be rooted in the visual system; when you read the word "red," its referent is a memory of what it's like to actually see red.

In the last twenty years, much evidence has accumulated that some representations are grounded—they are defined, at least in part, by our senses or by how we move. For example, when you read the word "kick," the part of your brain that controls leg movements shows activity, even though you're not moving your leg. And the part of your brain that controls mouth movements is active when you read the word "lick," and that which controls finger movements is active when you read "pick."[14] Part of the mental definition of *kick*, *lick*, and *pick* is what it feels like to execute these movements.

Researchers have also gathered purely behavioral evidence (as opposed to neural evidence) for grounded representations of words. In a classic experiment, subjects were asked to keep their hand on a "home" button. A sentence appeared on a computer screen and they were to push one of two other buttons to indicate whether or not the sentence was sensible. (An example of a nonsensical sentence might be "Boil the air.") The buttons were arranged vertically, with the home button in the middle so a subject had to move his or her hand away from the body to press one of the buttons, and toward the body to press the other. For half of the subjects, the button that was closer to them signified "yes, this sentence is sensible," and for the others, the button that was farther away signified "yes."

Some of the sensible sentences described an action that would require a movement toward or away from the body, and people were slower to verify "this is a sensible sentence" if the movement they had to execute to push the button conflicted with the type of movement described in the sentence. For example, if the sentence was "Andy closed the drawer," people who had to move their hand toward their body to push the "yes" button responded more slowly than people who had to move their hand away from their body to push the "yes" button. The opposite was true when the sentence described movement toward the body, e.g., "Andy opened the drawer."[15] Part of how you represent a concept like **opening a drawer** includes the movement that would accomplish it.

No one thinks that *all* mental representations are reducible to sensations or movement plans. We can think about quite abstract concepts, e.g., **democracy**, or **genius**. Exactly how these are represented in the mind has not been worked out. Researchers have proposed different approaches, including but not limited to the obvious idea that abstract concepts might be defined by other concepts, but all must ultimately be built out of grounded concepts.[16]

Whatever their ultimate representation, a rich vocabulary matters, both in its breadth and its depth. Let's consider why.

WHY BREADTH AND DEPTH MATTER

Breadth is the easy part of vocabulary to understand. I read "bassoon" and I either know the word or I don't. There's lots of evidence that children with broader vocabularies comprehend more of what they read. Of course, that's just a correlation. It may not be true that vocabulary helps reading comprehension, but rather that people with some kind of smarts or experience have big vocabularies and also happen to be good at comprehending what they read. If we want to be confident that a broad vocabulary directly contributes to reading comprehension, we have to rule out other possible factors. So researchers apply statistical controls to remove the effect of factors like IQ, or decoding ability. When they do so, they still observe a correlation between vocabulary breadth and reading comprehension.[17] Even more persuasive, there is good evidence that teaching children new vocabulary boosts reading comprehension.[18] Again, this finding is pretty intuitive.

Vocabulary depth is a little harder to wrap one's mind around, but we've already encountered a couple of different ways that your knowledge of a word can be relatively shallow or relatively deep. One type of depth might be the density of connections between a concept and other concepts. For example, you may know that a platypus is an animal, and that it has a bill. If that's all you know, do you know the word "platypus"? Well, sure, but your knowledge of the word is pretty shallow. Deeper knowledge of the word would have it connected to concepts like *Australia*, and *mammal*, and *egg-laying*, and *venomous* and *New South Wales* (the Australian state that features the platypus on its emblem), and so on.

Why would this sort of depth matter? Recall the example sentences that highlighted different features of "spill." The concept *platypus* also has different features that can be highlighted by different contexts. So if a person who knows only that a platypus is an animal and has a bill were to read "Don't pick up a platypus, but if you must, watch out for its rear legs," he would in one sense understand. But he wouldn't have as rich an understanding as someone who knows about the venom, and who knows that platypuses deliver the venom via spurs on their hind limbs.

Research shows that depth of vocabulary matters to reading comprehension. Children identified as having difficulty in reading comprehension (but who can decode well) do not have the depth of word knowledge that typical readers do. When asked to provide a word definition, they provide fewer attributes. When asked to produce examples of categories ("name as many flowers as you can") they produce fewer. They have a harder time describing the meaning of figurative language, like the expression "a pat on the back." They are slower and more error-prone in judging if two words are synonyms, although they have no problem making a rhyming judgement.[19,20]

A second aspect of depth concerns the speed with which you can access word information. It would be helpful if the activation spreads not just to the right words, but does so quickly. Likewise, you'd like the connections between the sound of a word (phonology), the spelling of that word (orthography), and the word's meaning to be strong, and allow for quick access. Research supports this supposition. Children's knowledge of words—measured as their accuracy in judging whether word pairs are synonyms, and their accuracy in judging category membership ("rain is a type of weather")—predicts their reading comprehension. But the *speed* with which they make these judgments predicts reading comprehension over and above the accuracy of the judgments. So yes, the richness of word representations helps reading, but so too does the speed with which you can access them. And it's not just that speed of the connections matters because reading tests prize speed. Accessing word meaning quickly helps the reader make meaning because there is *other* inferential work that must be done to fully understand a text. If the word-level information can be accessed rapidly, that other work can proceed apace and is more likely to succeed.[21]

THE PROCESS OF LEARNING NEW WORDS

Learning new words doesn't seem that complicated. For example, within the last year I learned about *ropa vieja*, a Cuban dish of shredded beef. I was in a restaurant, saw someone eating it at a neighboring table, and asked the waiter about it. He told me **that is *ropa vieja***. Easy. It seems like the important factors for word learning would be whether I'm exposed to new words, the frequency of that exposure, and maybe the likelihood that I pay attention to new words.

Because we're talking about adults, we are skirting some terribly complex problems that apply to vocabulary acquisition in infants. When someone points out *ropa vieja* and says **That is ropa vieja**, I know what **that** and **is** means. I know that **ropa vieja** refers to what's on the plate, and not the plate itself, or the act of pointing at food, or what's on the plate when we talk about it in public, although a different word would be used in someone's home. Infants, presumably, know none of this.

The problem is made easier because the infant mind comes prewired with certain assumptions.[22] For example, words are assumed to refer to objects (rabbit) not object parts (the rabbit's hind leg), and words are assumed to have consistent referents—it's not called rabbit on Monday, Wednesday, and Friday, and something else on other days. Those assumptions reduce the possible referents of a word, but don't finish the job. When a parent points to a rabbit running across the lawn and exclaims **A rabbit!**, this might be referring to brownness, cuteness, furriness, the lawn, a fast-moving object, any animal, any unusual animal, and so on.

Even for adults, words can be more ambiguous than you think, especially when the referent is not present, as a plate of shredded beef is. For example, I recently heard someone referred to as a **bastion of honor** and it made me realize that my knowledge of the word ***bastion*** was shallow. I couldn't define it outside of the formulation ***bastion of X***. I recognized this must be a metaphoric use of "bastion," but I didn't know the literal meaning of the word. So I looked it up and found that it was defined as "a stronghold." Then I realized I actually had the metaphoric meaning wrong. Because bastion is a stronghold, **bastion of honor** implies **someone who would never yield on matters or honor**, whereas I had thought it meant **shining example of honor**.

Why did I have it wrong? Because I hadn't seen "bastion of X" in enough contexts to allow me to make the more fine-grained distinction between a **stronghold of a quality** and **someone who exemplifies a quality**. In other words, I'm not that different from children who try to pretty up their essays with fancy vocabulary words; I see a word in one context and think I understand it, but the meaning I've attributed is not quite right, even if that meaning is consistent with the context I saw it in. I may read "We enjoyed our ice water in the golden crepuscule of the day" and think "crepuscule" means **hottest part** or **nicest part**, rather than **twilight**. The mistake would be resolved by seeing the word in more contexts, for example, "a nasty, winter crepuscule." We would guess from this account that people who are good readers would be better at figuring out unknown words from context—they are more likely to understand everything else they are reading, and so successfully use context to figure out an unknown word, and research supports that supposition.[23,24]

This process—seeing words multiple times in different contexts to figure out what they mean—is called *statistical learning* by researchers. It is easiest to appreciate in the more extreme version that infants must do. If the child hears the word **rabbit** she can't know in any one instance if it refers to the rabbit, or brownness, or things that run fast. The child keeps a running log (unconscious, naturally) of what was happening when different words were used and eventually is able to sort out that rabbits were always present when someone said **rabbit**, brown things were always present when someone said **brown**, and so on. That sounds like an enormous bookkeeping job, and it is. Thus, word learning is a gradual process. Some researchers have even suggested that the explosive growth in vocabulary most children show around the age of two had actually been building much longer—it's only after months of exposure to instances of words that enough information about them has gradually accumulated and begins to bear fruit.

Here's an experiment showing that learning works in this gradual way, even for adults. On each trial subjects see a couple of unfamiliar objects, like odd kitchen gadgets that most people wouldn't be able to name (e.g., a nutmeg grater, a strawberry huller). The experimenter says **One of these is a blicket and the other is a timplomper**. Because there are two objects and two labels, the subject can't know which goes with which. The experimenter keeps showing objects and the labels don't change, but the pairings do; that is, you later see the strawberry huller and a garlic peeler, and the experimenter says **One of these is a blicket and the other is a wug**.[25] The experimenter is offering adults the same chance to learn that children have; the words are ambiguous each time you hear them, but if you can keep track of what you hear and what you see at the time you hear it, you can sort out which word goes with which object. Adults are able to learn the labels in this small-scale simulation of the problem that infants face.

Even more interesting, we know that they learn them gradually, not all at once. In another experiment, researchers gave adults a similar sort of word-learning task, and then tested how much subjects had learned. In this test, the experimenter said a label and then asked the subject to pick the correct object from amidst *all* the gadgets they had seen during training. The researchers noted which ones each subject got right and wrong. Then the researcher constructed a new training regimen. Half of the object-label pairs were new, and half were old, meaning they were ones that subjects had seen in the previous training, but had gotten wrong when tested. The idea is that if you missed an old item and if learning is all-or-none, well, that word is just not in your memory. In the second phase of training, you're asked to learn it, but there should be no advantage (compared to the new object-label pairs) because you didn't learn it in the first phase. But that's not what happened. People *were* faster to learn the old pairs than the new ones, consistent with the idea that learning is gradual. The first phase of the experiment yielded knowledge of the new word that was unreliable and incomplete, but it did yield something.[26]

Strong vocabulary is not all that's needed to be a strong reader. In fact, it's not all that's needed to comprehend what you read. In the next chapter, we'll consider the processes behind understanding text.

Summary and Implications

Summary

- The meaning of a word is very sensitive to the context in which it appears.
- Researchers model the organization of word knowledge with simple features of meaning that are densely interconnected.
- If you don't know the meaning of a word, sometimes (but not always) you can deduce it from the context. But people are not eager to do a lot of this work, because it's difficult and it interrupts the flow of reading.
- Words defining other words sounds circular. This problem may be partially solved through the use of grounded representations.
- It's not only important to know a lot of words (breadth) but for the words you know to have many connections, and for those connections to be strong (depth).
- New words are learned bit by bit, through exposure.

Implications

- Looking words up in a dictionary will be of limited use—not useless, but we must acknowledge that it will be just one context in which to understand the word's meaning, and it's possible that the student will misunderstand the definition.[27] Explicit instruction of new words is more likely to be successful the way teachers usually implement it, with multiple examples and with the requirement that students use each word in different contexts. There is good evidence that children do learn vocabulary this way.[28,29]
- In addition to consistent vocabulary instruction, teachers can make it more likely that students will learn words they encounter in context. They can give students pointers that will help them use context to figure out an unfamiliar word. For example, students

(continued)

can learn to use clues in the sentence about the unknown word's part of speech, to use the setting described in the text to constrain the word's meaning, and to use the tone of the text to help constrain meaning.[30]

- Students are also better able to deduce the meaning of unfamiliar words if they have had some instruction in morphology.[31,32] The definition of a morpheme is a unit of language that is meaningful on its own, and that cannot be further divided. Thus "dog" is a morpheme. The really interesting morphemes are the all-purpose ones that can be added to words—usually as prefixes or suffixes— to change their tense or inflection, or meaning. For example, the prefix "super" means *over*, the suffix "like" means *having the characteristics of*, and so on.

- Though important, direct instruction cannot account for all of children's vocabulary learning. That's because someone who stays in school up to age 18 may know as many as 20,000 word families.[33] (Word families meaning that "talk," "talks," "talked," and other obvious derivatives count just once.) If children are learning about a thousand words each year and there are about 36 weeks in a typical American school year, students would need to get instruction in about 28 words each week. That seems high, especially given that children in early elementary grades often don't get explicit vocabulary instruction.

- Much of the vocabulary we know is not the product of explicit study, but was learned incidentally, either through conversation or reading.[34,35] We would expect, however, that reading will be more useful for learning new words than conversation will be, because writers more frequently use unusual words than speakers do.

- The difference between writing and speaking in terms of the richness of vocabulary it offers becomes really important as vocabulary grows.[36] For the newborn, adult speech offers plenty of novelty, but they will obviously be most likely to learn the words that people around them most frequently use. So one way to boost student vocabulary is to prompt teachers and parents to use more unusual vocabulary words, and some research indicates that helps.[37] But that may be hard to implement for older children who already know quite a few words. For them, moderately challenging reading material will be the main way they will encounter new words. And because a single instance of exposure is not enough to learn a word—learning is, after all, gradual—it would seem that the injunction to students must not just be "Read!" but "Read a lot!"

Discussion Questions

1. I cited studies showing that people are reluctant to read texts that use unfamiliar words. How much do you think it helps to read an electronic text with a feature whereby touching a word brings up a dictionary definition?

2. For older children, what is the responsibility of teachers of subjects other than English Language Arts to provide exposure to new vocabulary? Should it just be vocabulary particular to their subject, or broader? It sounds as though it would be useful for teachers in different subjects to coordinate to be sure that students practice the same words in different subjects, but is that really practical?

3. Teachers can provide varied contexts in which students can encounter the same word, so that the meaning representation will be precise. How can someone trying to improve their vocabulary do that on their own?

4. We might propose that teachers use richer vocabulary with their students. How should this be implemented? Should teachers derive a list of words that they try to use over some period of time (say, a month) to ensure students hear repetitions of these words? Or should teachers just make a mental note to use words they know will challenge students, and to provide on-the-fly definitions?

5. Do you think most children have good morphological knowledge? How about adults? How about teachers? If a school or district were to set the goal of improving students' morphological knowledge, what would be required?

REFERENCES

1. "Spill." *Merriam-Webster*. Retrieved from www.merriam-webster.com /dictionary/spill/.

2. "Heavy." *Merriam-Webster*. Retrieved from www.merriam-webster .com/dictionary/heavy/.

3. Collins, A. M., & Loftus, E. F. (1975). A spreading-activation theory of semantic processing. *Psychological Review, 82*(6), 407–428. http://doi.org/10.1016/B978-1-4832-1446-7.50015-7.

4. Hare, M., Jones, M., Thomson, C., Kelly, S., & McRae, K. (2009). Activating event knowledge. *Cognition, 111*(2), 151–167. http://doi.org/10.1016/j.cognition.2009.01.009.

5. Meyer, D. E., & Schvaneveldt, R. W. (1971). Facilitation in recognizing pairs of words: Evidence of a dependence between retrieval operations. *Journal of Experimental Psychology, 90*(2), 227–234.

6. Gernsbacher, M. A. & Faust, M. (1995). Skilled suppression. In F. N. Dempster & C. N. Brainerd (Eds.), *Interference and inhibition in cognition* (pp. 295–327). San Diego: Academic Press.

7. Kintsch, W. (2012). Psychological models of reading comprehension and their implications for assessment. In J. Sabatini, E. Albro, & T. O'Reilly (Eds.), *Measuring up: advances in how we assess reading ability* (pp. 21–37). Plymouth, UK: Rowman & Littlefield.

8. Foertsch, J., & Gernsbacher, M. A. (1994). In search of complete comprehension: Getting "minimalists" to work. *Discourse Processes, 18*(3), 271–296. http://doi.org/10.1080/01638539409544896.

9. Carver, R. (1994). Percentage of unknown vocabulary words in text as a function of the relative difficulty of the text: Implications for instruction. *Journal of Literacy Research, 26*(4), 413–437. http://doi.org/10.1080/10862969409547861.

10. Schmitt, N., Jiang, X., & Grabe, W. (2011). The percentage of words known in a text and reading Comprehension. *The Modern Language Journal, 95*(1), 26–43. http://doi.org/10.1111/j.1540-4781.2011.01146.x.

11. Hsueh-Chao, M. H., & Nation, P. (2000). Unknown vocabulary density and reading comprehension. *Reading in a Foreign Language, 13*(1), 403–430.

12. Nagy, W. E., & Anderson, R. C. (1984). How many words are there in printed school English? *Reading Research Quarterly, 19*, 304–330.

13. Harnad, S. (1990). The symbol grounding problem. *Physica D: Nonlinear Phenomena, 42*(1-3), 335–346. http://doi.org/10.1016/0167-2789(90)90087-6.

14. Hauk, O., Johnsrude, I., & Pulvermüller, F. (2004). Somatotopic representation of action words in human motor and premotor cortex. *Neuron, 41*(2), 301–307.

15. Glenberg, A. M., & Kaschak, M. P. (2002). Grounding language in action, *Psychonomic Bulletin & Review, 9*(3), 558–565. http://doi.org /10.1109/TAMD.2011.2140890.

16. Barsalou, L. W. (2016). On staying grounded and avoiding Quixotic dead ends. *Psychonomic Bulletin & Review, 23*(4), 1122–1142. http://doi.org/10.3758/s13423-016-1028-3.

17. Ouellette, G. P. (2006). What's meaning got to do with it: The role of vocabulary in word reading and reading comprehension. *Journal of Educational Psychology, 98*(3), 554–566. http://doi.org /10.1037/0022-0663.98.3.554.

18. Elleman, A. M., Lindo, E. J., Morphy, P., & Compton, D. L. (2009). The impact of vocabulary instruction on passage-level comprehension of school-age children: A meta-analysis. *Journal of Research on Educational Effectiveness, 2*(1), 1–44. http://doi.org /10.1080/19345740802539200.

19. Nation, K. (2008). EPS Prize Lecture. Learning to read words. *Quarterly Journal of Experimental Psychology (2006), 61*(8), 1121–1133. http://doi.org/10.1080/17470210802034603.

20. Nation, K., & Snowling, M. J. (1998). Semantic processing and the development of word-recognition skills: Evidence from children with reading comprehension difficulties. *Journal of Memory and Language, 39*(1), 85–101. http://doi.org/10.1006/jmla.1998.2564.

21. Oakhill, J., Cain, K., McCarthy, D., & Nightingale, Z. (2013). Making the link between vocabulary knowledge and comprehension skill. In M. A. Britt, S. R. Goldman, & J.-F. Rouet (Eds.), *Reading: From words to multiple texts* (pp. 101–114). New York: Routledge.

22. Astuti, R., Solomon, G. E. A., & Carey, S. (2004). Constraints on conceptual development: I. Introduction. *Monographs of the Society for Research in Child Development, 69*(3), 1–24. http://doi.org/ 10.1111/j.0037-976X.2004.00297.x.

23. Cain, K., Oakhill, J. V., & Elbro, C. (2003). The ability to learn new word meanings from context by school-age children with and without language comprehension difficulties. *Journal of Child Language*, *30*(30), 681–694. http://doi.org/10.1017/S0305000903005713.

24. Cain, K., Oakhill, J., & Lemmon, K. (2004). Individual differences in the inference of word meanings from context: The influence of reading comprehension, vocabulary knowledge, and memory capacity. *Journal of Educational Psychology*, *96*(4), 671–681. http://doi.org/10.1037/0022-0663.96.4.671.

25. Yu, C., & Smith, L. (2007). Rapid word learning under uncertainty via cross-situational statistics. *Psychological Science*, *18*(5), 414–420. http://doi.org/10.1111/j.1467-9280.2007.01915.x.

26. Yurovsky, D., Fricker, D. C., Yu, C., & Smith, L. B. (2014). The role of partial knowledge in statistical word learning. *Psychonomic Bulletin & Review*, *21*(1), 1–22. http://doi.org/10.3758/s13423-013-0443-y.

27. Miller, G. A., & Gildea, P. M. (1987). How children learn words. *Scientific American*, *257*(3), 94–99.

28. Beck, I. L., Perfetti, C. A., & McKeown, M. G. (1982). Effects of long-term vocabulary instruction on lexical access and reading comprehension. *Journal of Educational Psychology*, *74*(4), 506–521. http://doi.org/10.1037/0022-0663.74.4.506.

29. McKeown, M., Beck, I., Omanson, R., & Perfetti, C. (1983). The effects of long-term vocabulary instruction on reading comprehension: A replication. *Journal of Literacy Research*, *15*(1), 3–18. http://doi.org/10.1080/10862968309547474.

30. Fukkink, R. G., & de Glopper, K. (1998). Effects of instruction in deriving word meaning from context: A meta-analysis. *Review of Educational Research*, *68*(4), 450–469. http://doi.org/10.3102/00346543068004450.

31. Bowers, P. N., Kirby, J. R., & Deacon, S. H. (2010). The effects of morphological instruction on literacy skills: A systematic review of the literature. *Review of Educational Research*, *80*(2), 144–179. http://doi.org/10.3102/0034654309359353.

32. Goodwin, A. P., & Ahn, S. (2010). A meta-analysis of morphological interventions: Effects on literacy achievement of children with literacy difficulties. *Annals of Dyslexia, 60*(2), 183–208. http://doi.org/10.1007/s11881-010-0041-x.

33. Goulden, R., Nation, P., & Read, J. (1990). How large can a receptive vocabulary be? *Applied Linguistics, 11*(4), 341–363. http://doi.org/10.1093/applin/11.4.341.

34. Nagy, W. E., & Herman, P. A. (1985). Incidental vs. instructional approaches to increasing reading vocabulary. *Educational Perspectives, 23*(1), 16–21.

35. Hayes, D. P., & Ahrens, M. G. (1988). Vocabulary simplification for children: A special case of "motherese"? *Journal of Child Language, 15*(2), 395. http://doi.org/10.1017/S0305000900012411.

36. Nation, I. S. P. (2006). How large a vocabulary is needed for reading and listening? *The Canadian Modern Language Review / La Revue Canadienne Des Langues Vivantes, 63*(1), 59–81. http://doi.org/10.1353/cml.2006.0049.

37. Schwanenflugel, P. J. (2010). Effects of a conversation intervention on the expressive vocabulary development of prekindergarten children. *Language, Speech, and Hearing Services in Schools, 41*(3), 303–313. http://doi.org/10.1044/0161-1461(2009/08-0100).

5

READING COMPREHENSION

Agenda for Chapter 5

We have reviewed how the meaning of individual words is represented in the mind. Now we need to understand how words are put together so that we understand sentences, and how we put together the meaning of multiple sentences.

O ur goal is to describe how the mind reads, which we've defined as translating ideas from the mind of the writer to the mind of the reader. We've worked through how you decode letters on the page into a sound-based or spelling-based representation of the word in the mind. Those representations are linked to a mental representation of the word's meaning, and in the last chapter we saw an account of how you can access the right sense of a word given the context—whether you should focus on the fact that spills make a mess, or that when you spill, you have less of your drink. So have we more or less accounted for how print conveys thoughts? Let's engage in a little task analysis to think through the process of reading comprehension.

TASK ANALYSIS OF READING COMPREHENSION

We can quickly discard the idea that accessing word meanings finishes the job of comprehension. Suppose you access the meanings of this set of words: biting, cat, dog, is, our, that. Obviously, there's more work to be done. You can't just have the meanings tossed into a basket, so to speak. Word order matters. In fact, different arrangements of these words express quite different ideas—"That cat is biting our dog" or "That dog is biting our cat." Word order (plus other cues) dictates the syntactic role that each word plays. Is "cat" the subject or the object of the sentence?

All right, that's one problem to be solved—we must extract ideas from sentences. If we get that right, are we done? I'm afraid not. Comprehension goes beyond the extraction of individual ideas from groups of words; these extracted ideas must be connected to one another. Consider the first two sentences from Chapter 1 of Harper Lee's *To Kill a Mockingbird*:

When he was nearly thirteen, my brother Jem got his arm badly broken at the elbow. When it healed, and Jem's fears of never being able to play football were assuaged, he was seldom self-conscious about his injury.

It's not enough to properly deploy the rules of syntax and extract the ideas from the second sentence; to comprehend it, you must tie it to the first sentence. You must perceive that "it" from the second sentence refers to "his arm" in the first sentence. And the second sentence is not meant solely to convey the three ideas it describes: elbow healed, Jem's worries assuaged, Jem seldom self-consciousness. The reader is meant to interpret those three facts *in light of* the information mentioned in the first sentence. For example, Jem's worries about never playing football again would be interpreted differently if we'd been told he was a professional player rather than a 13-year-old.

All right, let's suppose that we've extracted the ideas from each sentence, and we've appropriately connected the ideas. *Now* can we say that we've accounted for comprehension? Not yet. To get a sense of what's missing, answer this question: If you have read *To Kill a Mockingbird*, what do you remember about it? (If you haven't read it consider what you remember from the last book you read.)

I read *To Kill a Mockingbird* perhaps 30 years ago. About all I remember is the setting (the deep South, before World War II) and the basic plot: a black man is wrongly accused of a crime and is unsuccessfully defended by a white attorney. I remember that the attorney's plucky young daughter narrates the story, and I remember a few other plot fragments not worth mentioning. No doubt I could have given a better summary right after I finished the book, but certainly even then I would have forgotten many of the ideas that I had read. Right after finishing the book I doubt I remembered the bit about Jem's arm from Chapter 1.

In the same way, at the moment I read about "Abbadabba" Berman's death in *Billy Bathgate,* I had probably forgotten 90% of what I had read about him. Yet I still had an overall impression of him. That matches the pattern of what I remember of *To Kill a Mockingbird.* What you forget is not random. You lose the details, but retain the gist. So comprehension includes not only understanding the text moment by moment as you read it, but also the development of some overall sense of what the text is about. And that's what sticks with you.

So reading comprehension seems to be composed of three processes. The reader (1) extracts ideas from sentences, (2) connects these ideas to one another, and (3) builds some more general idea of what the text is about. We'll tackle each of these processes in turn, and we'll see that in each case two factors dominate mental processing. First, general rules guide the reader in making meaning. These rules—for example, rules of syntax—apply regardless of the content. Second, meaning is informed by what the reader already knows. Sometimes that's information gleaned from the text, and sometimes it's knowledge about the world gained from other sources. These two principles—meaning-free rules, plus meaningful content—will apply to all three levels: sentences, sentence connections, and gist. Let's begin with the process of understanding sentences.

EXTRACTING IDEAS FROM SENTENCES

Before we get to the process behind it, let's start with my casual claim that readers extract ideas from sentences. Maybe there's nothing to extract, per se: rather, people simply store in memory the words they read on the page. My claim, in contrast, is that readers retain the idea a sentence expresses, but discard the sentence—the particular words—once they have the idea. Occasionally, the particular wording matters—in a beautifully written quotation, for example, or jokes, which often depend on particular phrasing. But usually, the sentences "Taye wrote the essay and then had a snack" and "Taye had a snack after he wrote the essay" are interchangeable once they've been read.

Lots of research shows that people usually remember what they read, but not the way it was worded. In a typical experiment a subject reads a bunch of unconnected sentences, one at a time, such as "The little dogs were always friendly to me, even though their owner was nasty to me." An hour later the subject sees another bunch of sentences, and must say whether or not that exact sentence was presented an hour earlier. When people see a sentence with the same meaning but different phrasing (e.g., "Although their owner was nasty to me, the little dogs were always friendly"), they are likely to say that they saw it an hour ago. But if the meaning changes (e.g., "The little dogs were always friendly to me, even though their owner didn't know me"), subjects are much more likely to correctly say that sentence was not presented an hour earlier.[1]

Here's another type of experiment showing that readers discard the particular wording of sentences, and do so more or less immediately after they read each one. Subjects read a sentence on a computer screen, say, "Winters, who was pitcher, threw the white ball." When they finish reading it, subjects push a button which erases the sentence and brings up two words on the screen. Subjects push one button if both of these words appeared in the sentence they read, and another button if not. People are faster to say yes to the pair "Winters, threw" than they are to the pair "pitcher, threw." If people remember the sentence as the particular words they read, they should be really fast to affirm that "pitcher" and "threw" are both in the sentence because those words were adjacent in the sentence—they search their memory for the word "pitcher," and then when they search their memory for the word "threw" they find it right away because the words are adjacent. But that doesn't happen. Instead, they are quick to affirm that "Winters" and "threw" were in the sentence.[2] The interpretation is that people, as they read, create a mental representation of the simple ideas conveyed in a sentence. In this case the ideas would be **Winters threw the ball**, **Winters was pitcher**, and **The ball was white**. So when they search for "Winters" and find it, "threw" is closely associated with "Winters," even though it was distant from "threw" in the particular phrasing of the sentence.

We can put this process of extracting ideas from sentences (that is, comprehending them) in the context of the reading model we've been developing over the course of this book (Figure 5.1).

Now, how do readers put together words so as to understand ideas? For example, how do they know that it was Winters who did the throwing, and that what he threw was a ball? Two factors contribute. First, there are grammatical cues that offer reliable information about the role a word plays in the sentence, regardless of the sentence's meaning. For example, some words are limited in the roles they can play in a sentence because the part of speech is unambiguous: "outlet" and "car" are always nouns, and that narrows (but does not determine) the syntactic role they might play. Many words are less limited: "phone," "smoke," "bread," and "walk" can be nouns or verbs. Morphological cues might help there. When a word

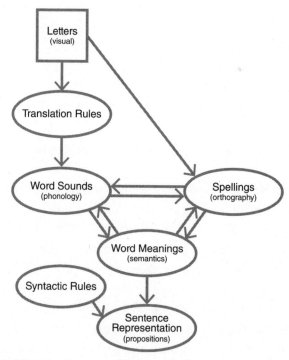

Figure 5.1. Model of reading expanded to include sentence representations. The representation of sentence meaning is based on word meanings and rules of syntax.
© Daniel Willingham

ends in "ly" it's likely an adverb, the ending "ed" signifies the past tense of a verb, a word ending with "ing" is likely a present progressive verb, and so on. These cues are what make a nonsense sentence like "Sarah nexly narped the punzer" sound grammatical. The cues converge on the interpretation that Sarah is the actor in the sentence, and she carried out an action (narping), and that the recipient of this action was the punzer.

These cues—for example, that "ed" signifies a verb in the past tense—apply irrespective of what else you've read in the text. But often grammatical cues aren't enough to specify meaning, and that's where the second factor comes in. A sentence like "They are cooking apples" is ambiguous because there are two ways of assigning syntactic roles to the words. In isolation, there is no way of knowing which meaning is intended. But a reader can use knowledge from previous sentences to make clear how the ambiguous sentence ought to be interpreted.

What type of apples did you buy?
They are cooking apples.

What are those people doing in the kitchen?
They are cooking apples.

This example may seem unusual, but many, if not most, sentences have more than one grammatically correct interpretation. A classic example is the sentence "Time flies like an arrow." Most people interpret it metaphorically—*time moves quickly, as an arrow does*. But it could also mean that *a particular type of insect (time flies) feel affection for arrows*. Or "time" could be a command, with the sentence meaning, *I want you to assess the pace of those flies, and I want you to do it in the way you would assess the pace of an arrow*. There are actually at least two other grammatically acceptable interpretations of this sentence.[3]

Grammatically acceptable, but not acceptable to common sense. There's not a variety of flies called "time flies." And who would tell someone to get out their stopwatch and time some flies in the same way they would time an arrow? Who times flies *or* arrows? Just as in the "eating apples" example, readers bring knowledge to bear on the sentence, not just grammar, to arrive at the correct interpretation. But in these examples, the knowledge is not provided in the text. The reader had to know it before reading the text.

The influence of meaning on the processing of a sentence is most obvious when grammar renders the sentences ambiguous, but meaning also has an impact on the speed and ease of processing even if the grammar is unambiguous. For example, the sentence "I cut up a slice of cooked ham" will be read more slowly when it is preceded by a few sentences describing the protagonist getting dressed, compared to a context where the protagonist was described as in a kitchen. That slowing can be avoided by adding one word at the start of the sentence: "Later, I cut up a slice of cooked ham."[4] So clearly, we're not just extracting meaning from sentences, we are coordinating the meaning of sentences with the meaning of what we've read before, and we're doing that as we process each sentence.

I've barely scratched the surface of the method by which ideas are extracted from sentences; I've just provided illustrations of the two types of information that inform this process: formal rules of grammar, and meaning-based information, either provided in the text or drawn from your memory. We will not delve further into psychologists' accounts of sentence comprehension.[5] In Chapter 1 I said that reading is too complex for us to examine all of its component cognitive processes, and we'll therefore focus on those processes that separate good readers from struggling readers. Facility in sentence comprehension appears to play a minor role in that separation.[6]

That may surprise you, but consider this. I've emphasized that humans did not evolve to be readers; reading borrows from other cognitive processes. The ability to understand written sentences piggy-backs on the ability to understand spoken sentences, and humans *did* evolve to do that. Thus, the four-year-old who understands her brother when he says **I wanted a grape lollipop, but you got me cherry**, will not have trouble comprehending this sentence when she reads it at age eight. The mental machinery will have been in place for years. That doesn't mean children don't develop in their ability to understand more complex syntax as they grow, or to appreciate more subtle uses of language, for example, irony. But slow development of these processes seems seldom to be the reason that readers struggle.

Extracting the ideas in a sentence may not pose a challenge for most readers, but connecting them often does. Let's turn our attention to how readers knit ideas together.

CONNECTING IDEAS

Suppose I read the sentence "The juice is in trunk." I extract the idea from this sentence (Figure 5.2).

Then I read another sentence, "The juice is warm." I extract that idea, and I seek a way to connect it to what I've already read (Figure 5.3).

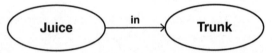

Figure 5.2. A cartoon of the mental representation of a simple sentence. Psychologists who study language use more complex (and more realistic) models of how the mind represents meaning, but this figure gives you the basic notion of simple ideas connecting.
© Daniel Willingham

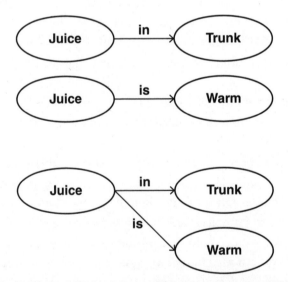

Figure 5.3. Mental representation of two sentences. The top part of the figure shows the representation of the previous sentence read (The juice in the trunk) and the new sentence just read. The bottom part of the figure shows the connection a reader would typically make. Both sentences contain the same referent, "juice," so that would be the point of connection.
© Daniel Willingham

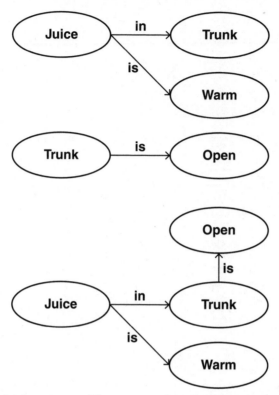

Figure 5.4. Multiple sentences. The top part of the figure shows the growing mental representation of what's been read. The bottom shows the representation of the sentence just read. The reader must find a sensible place in the representation of what's been read to connect the new sentence.
© Daniel Willingham

Then I read another sentence, "The trunk is open," and again, seek a point of connection between this new idea and what I've read before (Figure 5.4).

This the process we want to account for. As we read each sentence, we build an increasingly complex web of ideas representing the text already read. I will, with a remarkable lack of creativity, call this an *idea-web* (Figure 5.5). (Researchers actually call it a *textbase*.)

So the vital question in connecting sentences is "what principles guide the connection?" When you read a new sentence, how do you decide where to attach it to the existing idea-web?

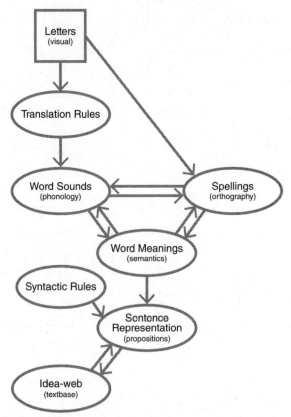

Figure 5.5. Model of reading expanded to include the idea-web. The idea-web is a representation of the ideas in the text, connected. There's an arrow going from the idea-web to the sentence representation because the idea-web—your ongoing understanding of the text—can influence how to interpret a particular sentence, as we saw in the "cut up a slice of cooked ham" example in Chapter 4.
© Daniel Willingham

Readers draw several types of connections.[7] One type depends on similar referents, just as "juice" was the common referent in the example above (Figure 5.2). In that case the referent was repeated ("The juice is warm"), but the second sentence might have used a pronoun: "It is warm." Or the second sentence might have used a different noun phrase: "The tasty treat is warm." In the case of a pronoun or different noun phrase, the reader has to figure out that the author is referring to the juice again.

Other connections are not based on a common referent. A similar method of connection applies to properties or relations; for example, these sentences seem to go together: "The juice was warm. The sandwiches were warm. The ice cream was melting." You will also readily join ideas if they share a setting, that is, they describe events occurring at the same time and place, for example: "The music was loud. There was a large buffet table. The gifts were not yet unwrapped. It was very hot in the room."

Writers can also signal the intended connections through the use of keywords. For example when you read, "but," or "however," you know that what comes next will contradict what came before that word. Other words indicate the reader should make a connection of time, e.g., "later," or "next," or "then." Still other words cue a causal connection: "because," for example, or "therefore" or "so."

When we discussed extracting ideas from sentences, we saw that you might think that rules of grammar would be the primary mechanism to put words together to make meaning. But then we saw that knowledge of the world has an impact on which grammatical interpretation we might choose for ambiguous sentences (as in the "they are cooking apples" example). And meaning impacts the speed with which sentences are interpreted, even if they are unambiguous. This same idea holds true for connecting ideas across sentences. I've described some abstract rules, for example, "connect sentences that describe the same entities, or similar properties of entities," and "connect sentences that describe things happening in the same time and place." These abstract descriptions, like a description of grammar, provide rules about connections, leaving world knowledge out of the picture. But that won't do.

The rules sometimes yield ambiguous solutions to the problem of how to connect ideas. Consider how you figure out the referent for a pronoun. Sometimes the interpretation is constrained, for example, by gender in the following sentences: "Marisol and Tom went to the party together. He had worried about going alone, so he thanked her as they left the apartment." It's unambiguous that "he" can only be Tom and "she" can only be Marisol. But now consider these sentences: "Tim beat Jerry in the race. He offered his congratulations with a smile." From the sentence alone there's no telling who "he" is. You must use your knowledge of the world—losers typically offer congratulations to winners, not the other way around—to clear up the ambiguity. Likewise, seeing that a pronoun phrase is meant to refer to an entity named earlier also requires world knowledge. If I read, "The juice was in the car trunk. So was the tool box. The tasty treat would be ruined if it was not brought in out of the heat soon," I can only connect that last sentence to the other two if I apply my knowledge that juice can be considered a tasty treat and a tool box cannot.

Causal connections usually require world knowledge to bridge the meaning of two sentences.[8] For example, consider these two sentences: "The morning precipitation had left sidewalks icy. Kayla told her children to be careful." The connection seems simple to see; the icy sidewalks caused Kayla to say that to her children. But consider all of the knowledge the reader had to bring to those sentences to make that causal connection:

The morning precipitation had left sidewalks icy.
    People walk on sidewalks.
    Ice is slippery.
    People can fall when walking on slippery surfaces.
    People can be hurt if they fall.
    Parents don't want their children to be hurt.
    People are less likely to fall if they walk carefully.
Kayla told her children to be careful.

Now of course the writer could have put that information in the text. She could have written, "The morning precipitation had left sidewalks icy. Sidewalks are for walking. Ice is slippery." And so on. The reason that writers (and speakers) omit information is plain. If they didn't, simple communication would be terribly long and boring, and readers are perfectly able to mentally add the information needed to build the causal bridge between the first and second sentence. Thus writers *always* omit a great deal of information needed to make sense of what they write. They judge what their readers already know and what must be made explicit in the text, and they write accordingly.

The reader must have the right information in memory to make the inferences that bridge the meaning of what he reads.[9] So what happens if a reader lacks that background knowledge? Obviously, he will have a harder time connecting the sentences, and may not do so at all—in short, the reader will be confused. The second sentence will seem like a non sequitur, as when you read, "The minnow swam upstream. The microwave hadn't stopped beeping."

We might note that Kayla warning her children was an instance in which the writer could have added the word "because" to provide a connection cue to the reader: "Kayla told her children to be careful because the sidewalks were icy." The word "because" signals a causal relationship between the two ideas. That would have told the reader what sort of connection to expect, but it doesn't supply the information needed to make it.[10] That is, if you knew nothing about icy sidewalks, the word "because" would help you infer that they deserve extra attention, but you wouldn't really understand the causality. Having the knowledge in memory that writers assumed you would have is ultimately more important than connection cues.[11]

If writers frequently omit information needed to build causal connections between sentences, that implies that having a lot of knowledge will be a big help in successful reading. There is reason to think that's true.[12–14] Anne Cunningham and Keith Stanovich measured the reading ability of 11th-graders with a standard reading test and also administered tests of students' knowledge of mainstream culture. There were tests of the names of artists, entertainers, military leaders, musicians, philosophers, and scientists, as well as separate tests of factual knowledge of science, history, and literature. The researchers found very robust correlations between scores on the reading test and scores on the various cultural literacy tests—correlations between 0.55 and 0.90.*

---

*If you're not used to thinking about correlations, it's a way of measuring whether two variables are related. 0.0 means there is no relationship at all, as we might expect between, say, people's shoe size and how much they like ice cream. A correlation of 1.0 means a perfect relationship—for example, the height of people measured in inches and the height measured in centimeters. To give you some perspective on what a correlation of 0.60 means, that's about the correlation of the average height of parents and their average height of their children.

The knowledge that Cunningham and Stanovich measured was highly specific—being able to recognize the term "absolute zero," for example. We expect that each bit of knowledge applies to a limited number of texts, but if you have a lot of these bits (that is, you have broad knowledge) there's a decent chance you know at least a little about the domain of most texts you happen to encounter. And in articles written for the layperson, the knowledge needed is pretty shallow because that's all that writers and editors assume in the general reader. The editors of the *New York Times*, or *National Geographic*, or any other periodical written for the intelligent layperson assume knowledge that's a million miles wide, but just a few inches deep. They will assume you know that rare postage stamps can be really valuable, for example, but they won't assume you know the going price for the 1918 Inverted Jenny.

The Situation Model

At the start of this chapter I noted that my memory for *To Kill a Mockingbird* did not include the entire idea-web. That's no surprise—people forget, and I read the book decades ago. But there's more to it than that. I suggested that readers form another memory of the text, in addition to the idea-web. That memory represents the overarching idea of the text, the overall situation it describes; hence it's called the *situation model*. You can appreciate the need for perceiving the overall idea of a text by reading one that doesn't have an overall idea:

Sally decided to go to the big market downtown. The downtown area had recently been renovated. The market included a large deli. The deli man really liked capicola ham. The deli man's wife wants a new car but she can't decide what type to get. The bank where she applied for a loan has gold carpeting.

If reading comprehension were only a matter of creating an idea-web this passage would not seem strange. Each sentence can be connected to another. But the paragraph doesn't go anywhere. There's no big picture. That big picture is the situation model. It's a representation of, well, the overall situation described in the text.

Just as you wouldn't want your memory of a sentence to be tied to the particular phrasing of the sentence, you wouldn't want your memory for a paragraph to be tied to the particular ideas in each sentence. You want something more abstract, something that allows you to think about the contents of the text from different perspectives. The situation model provides that.

Here's a classic experiment showing that people's memory for a text is, indeed, more abstract than the idea-web. Researchers asked subjects to read this very brief text: "Three turtles rested on a floating log. A fish swam beneath it."[15] Then they asked, "Were the turtles above the fish?" Subjects answered "Yes" without difficulty, but how did they do it? If all they had in memory was the idea-web based on the two sentences they had read, they'd have to combine that knowledge with some logical inference.

One sentence said that the turtles are above the log.
Therefore, I can infer the log is under the turtles.
Another sentence said that the fish is under the log.
By transitive inference, the fish must be under the turtles.
Therefore, the turtles must be above the fish.

It sure doesn't feel like you go through those steps to answer the question. Instead, it feels like you answer the question by consulting a representation of the general situation described. The situation model tells you the relative positions of the fish, log, and turtles independent of any particular description of them (Figure 5.6).

The situation model is not only more abstract than the idea web, it's less complete. As noted, your memory for *Harry Potter and the Sorcerer's Stone* can't contain every single idea in the novel, even though you might have understood each idea as you read it. But of course you don't trim the story randomly; the situation model highlights the parts of the story that are important, and omits less important details.[16]

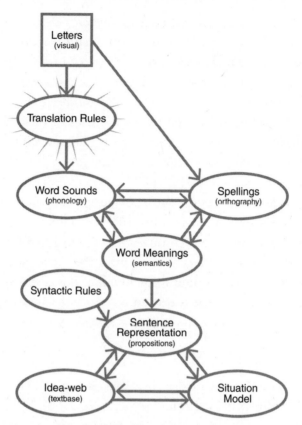

Figure 5.6. Model of reading expanded to include the situation model. The situation model is constructed from the ideas in the idea-web, but can also be updated directly from ongoing processing of sentences. The situation model can also influence the interpretation of individual sentences, as well as their place in the idea-web.
© Daniel Willingham

So how do readers decide which ideas are important enough to include in the situation model, and which can go? As with sentences and the idea-web, researchers have sought general rules that readers use to make these decisions. One influential theory posits that readers are especially concerned with keeping track of (1) what the main character is doing; (2) the timing of events; (3) the spatial relations among the elements of a story; (4) causal relations among events in the text; and (5) whether events are relevant to the main character's goals.[17]

To measure which dimensions of a text people track, researchers often use reading times. Experiments show that readers take longer to read sentences that describe greater spatial extent or a longer period of time. For example, one experiment had subjects read texts about people moving through a building; reading times were longer for sentences that described objects that were a greater distance from the protagonist.[18] Another experiment reported that readers took longer to read a sentence beginning with the phrase "A month later," compared to a sentence beginning with the phrase "A moment later . . ."[19] The idea is that, because the reader is tracking time or space, significant changes in the story on those dimensions prompt the reader to update the situation model. That takes time, and so it takes a longer time to read the sentence indicating the change.

But later work indicated that this conclusion was too hasty. It's not that readers consistently track a set of text features. Readers track different dimensions of a text depending on their goals. For example, one experiment asked subjects to read a text about a woman thinking about her upcoming exercise class.[20] Different subjects read a description of her being inside or outside the health club. A few sentences later the text described her going "outside to stretch her legs." Experimenters measured reading time for each sentence, with the expectation that readers would be slow to read the bit about the woman going outside if they had earlier read that she was already outside the health club. And that's what researchers found . . . but only if they told readers to take the perspective of the woman in the story. Without that instruction, readers seemed not to notice the inconsistency. In other words, readers didn't automatically keep track of the spatial information in the story. They did so only if it matched their goal for reading the text.

That seems to be the best generalization we can make about what goes into a situation model: it depends on the reader's goal. Most of the time we read stories to appreciate the plot and the characters. Plot is driven by causality, so we build a situation model containing a lot of causal information and a lot of personality information about characters. That's why I gasped when I read about "Abbadabba" Berman's death in *Billy Bathgate*. I surely had forgotten much of what Berman had said and done in the book, but I had a thumbnail sketch of him as a sympathetic personality in my situation model, because I attended to character as I read.

But just as was true for sentences and the idea-web, the situation model cannot be fully described by all-purpose rules like "your goals direct its construction." The content of the text matters, especially as it relates to your knowledge and expertise.

Here's one reason knowledge matters. I just said that the content of the situation model depends on the goal you set when you read. If you're quite familiar with the content, you have a good idea of what that goal ought to be, and even better, what sorts of things in the text are important to that goal. For example, when reading a text about a soccer game, both experts and novices would likely have the general idea that it's important to track events that will lead a team to win or lose—that's what sport contests are about. But the soccer expert has a much better idea than the novice about which events are likely to matter to the outcome of the game. The expert will build a better situation model.

Researchers tested this prediction by first testing elementary school children for their knowledge of soccer and for their verbal skills (that is, verbal comprehension and reasoning).[21] The experimenters separated the students into four groups, based on their soccer knowledge (high or low) and their verbal skills (high or low). Then students read a story about soccer and experimenters measured their comprehension and recall (Figure 5.7).

Verbal skill didn't matter much compared to knowledge. In other experiments reading skill does make a contribution, but it's often relatively small, and it's virtually always smaller than the importance of topic knowledge.

There's a second way that background knowledge can influence the situation model.[22] To introduce it, I'll ask you to read the following text:[23]

Carol Harris was a problem child from birth. She was wild, stubborn, and violent. By the time Carol turned eight, she was still unmanageable. Her parents were very concerned about her mental health. There was no good institution for her problem in her state. Her parents finally decided to take some action. They hired a private teacher for Carol.

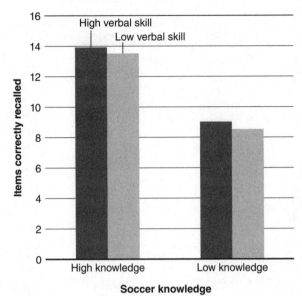

Figure 5.7. Comparison of comprehension supported by reading skills or background knowledge. The graph shows how much readers remembered of a text about soccer. Kids identified as having "high verbal skills" remembered a bit more than kids with "low verbal skills" (compare the dark and light bars). But that effect is tiny compared to the effect of knowledge of soccer.
© Anne Carlyle Lindsay, based on data from Schneider, Korkel, & Weinert (1989)

I'm wagering that you had little trouble reading this paragraph with good comprehension, and that you built a good situation model. But suppose I had told you, "By the way, the character, Carol Harris? That's actually Helen Keller. They just changed her name for the story." There's now an extra dimension to the story. You interpret statements about her wildness and violence in light of what you know about Helen Keller's blindness and deafness, and the frustration and despair it might have caused. The situation model would be different too; although the events are the same, the overall arc of the paragraph is a bit different, given your background knowledge about Helen Keller.[24]

Imagine a person reading this paragraph without knowing anything about Helen Keller. That reader would comprehend it as you did when the name Carol Harris was used. All the sentences make sense, and the paragraph as a whole hangs together. And yet an important aspect of meaning is absent. Your situation model is colored by information outside of the text, namely, other relevant knowledge from your memory. If that knowledge is missing, the situation model won't be the same.

BECOMING A BETTER READER

We've seen two types of evidence that background knowledge is important to comprehension. One type of evidence showed that reading comprehension in domain experts (for example, soccer experts) is much better when they read texts in their domain of expertise. Another type of evidence showed that having a little knowledge in many domains—but not necessarily expertise in any domain—is associated with better scores on reading comprehension tests.

But why should knowledge be so important? If you lack the relevant knowledge, can't you use the context to figure out what's missing? Sure, sometimes you can. Recall in Chapter 4 I said you could sometimes figure out the definition of unknown words from the surrounding context, as in the example "Connors used Kevlar sails because he expected little wind." The same principle applies to connecting sentences. For example, Suppose you read "Terence was perhaps the most famous of the ancient Roman playwrights. It may have been displays of verbal brilliance at a young age that prompted his master to educate him." The writer has omitted the fact that Terrence was a slave, but that may be inferred from the context.

Other times the context doesn't provide enough clues for most readers to make the intended inference. For example, consider these sentences: "The researcher noticed that the data distribution was perfectly symmetrical. She called her research assistant into her office." If you're not used to analyzing data, you could still probably guess what it means for a distribution to be symmetrical. But can you infer the causal relation between these sentences? What the writer has omitted is (1) data distributions are *never* perfectly symmetrical and (2) research assistants, not researchers, are typically responsible for data entry. So the researcher sees that something must be wrong with the data, and calls the assistant in to ask if there might have been an error in data entry.

Even in situations where you can use context to build meaning across sentences, people's patience for doing so is limited, just as they get frustrated by texts with a lot of unfamiliar words. Most readers skate along the surface of a text, satisfied with a minimal understanding and failing to coordinate meaning across sentences.[25] To get a sense of how researchers investigate this aspect of comprehension, have a look at this brief text:[26]

Superconductivity is the disappearance of resistance to the flow of electric current. Until now it has only been obtained by cooling certain materials to low temperatures near absolute zero. That made its technical applications very difficult. Many laboratories are now trying to produce superconducting alloys. Many materials with this property, with immediate technical applicability, have recently been discovered. Until now superconductivity has been achieved by considerably increasing the temperature of certain materials.

I hope you noticed that the second sentence of this paragraph directly conflicts with the last sentence; the creation of superconducting materials is initially said to require very cold temperatures, then a considerable increase in temperature. High school students were asked to read this text and then were asked whether they encountered any "difficulty" when reading it. Fully 40% of students failed to mention the direct contradiction.[26] The failure to bridge meaning across sentences and to make inferences when necessary is especially prevalent among struggling readers.[27]

Well, what would happen if we simply told readers, "you should make inferences?" You could, but a better strategy is to give the reader a goal, something to work toward that can only be completed if they build meaning across sentences, and make inferences when needed. Such a goal might be to pose and answer questions as they read, or to find the main idea of a text, or to create a graphic organizer. A great deal of research shows that these strategies are effective, especially for low-skill readers.

Skilled readers already know about and deploy such strategies as they read.[27]

The benefit readers derive from instructions to use comprehension strategies is sizable, but it seems to be a one-time gain. In other words, there's no evidence that extensive practice with these strategies yields an advantage over a brief intervention—say, 10 lessons. That may surprise you, as we are used to thinking of skills as benefiting from practice—more practice, more skill. But remembering the description of comprehension offered earlier in this chapter, it makes sense. Comprehension is a product of connecting ideas. Strategy instruction emphasizes that ideas *should be* connected, but it cannot tell a reader how to make those connections. The connections are specific to the meaning of the text. So the injunction "make inferences!" may convince a reader who has not previously done so to begin making them, but that will be a one-time improvement.[28]

We've described how readers decode text, access the meaning of words, and develop an understanding of longer texts. We've covered what needs to be in place so that students *can* read. Now we need to consider what would make them *want* to read. That is the subject of the next chapter.

Summary and Implications

Summary

- There are three levels of meaning representation: we extract ideas from sentences, we connect the ideas across sentences, and we build a general idea of what a text is about.
- At each level, there are rules about how meaning is made—rules that can be expressed independent of the content of ideas. But it's also true that meaning influences how we comprehend text at each of the three levels.
- Many readers set a low criterion when assessing whether they understand a text. They do not coordinate meaning across sentences, and thus fail to notice texts that contain contradictions.
- Teaching reading comprehension strategies that require the coordination of meaning across sentences does improve comprehension, but it seems to be a one-time improvement rather than a technique that can be practiced to continually improve reading comprehension.

Implications

- The prominent role that background knowledge plays in reading comprehension ought to make us think differently about reading tests. We might think that reading tests provide an all-purpose measure of reading ability. But we've seen that reading comprehension depends heavily on how much the reader happens to know about the topic of the text. Perhaps then, reading comprehension tests are really knowledge tests in disguise. The Cunningham and Stanovich experiment discussed in the text supports that idea.
- Teaching reading is not just a matter of teaching reading. The whole curriculum matters, because good readers have broad knowledge in civics, drama, history, geography, science, the visual arts, and so on. But the conclusion is not just "the curriculum has to have a lot of stuff in it." Sequence matters too, because students

(continued)

can only encounter so much new content at one time. They need to know most of (but not everything) the writer assumes the reader knows. Such precision in what students should know before they tackle a text calls for careful planning.

- Telling students to make inferences or teaching them reading comprehension strategies provides a one-time boost to comprehension. That implies that, when they are taught, they have no impact on some students. Students who still struggle with fluency are not able to use these strategies because decoding occupies all of their attention. Other students will have figured out on their own that comprehension requires the coordination of meaning across sentences and paragraphs. So the impact of teaching reading comprehension strategies may be larger than is commonly appreciated, but applies to only a subset of students.

- Students from disadvantaged backgrounds show a characteristic pattern of reading achievement in school; they make good progress until around fourth grade, and then suddenly fall behind.[29] The importance of background knowledge to comprehension gives us insight into this phenomenon. Reading instruction in the early grades concerns decoding, and so reading tests are basically tests of decoding ability. Kids from wealthier homes in fact do a bit better on these tests, but poorer children are still doing okay. But around fourth grade most children can decode fairly well, and so reading tests place greater weight on comprehension. The disadvantaged kids have not had the same opportunities to acquire the vocabulary and background knowledge needed to succeed on these tests and so their performance drops significantly.[30]

Discussion Questions

1. Readers usually forget the particular phrasing of what they read quite soon after reading it. Does that mean it doesn't matter much?

2. Even struggling readers seem to do a good job of coordinating meaning when they are watching a movie; they follow the plot and put together an effective situation model. Why are movies different than texts? Is there anything to be learned from movies that might help a student's reading comprehension?

3. When we learn that comprehension depends heavily on background knowledge, that naturally invites the question: "Which knowledge should children learn?" (Note that in the experiment on the relationship of background knowledge and reading, the researchers referred to knowledge as "cultural literacy." Whose culture does that literacy refer to?) Before addressing that question, I invite you to consider the *factors* that ought to contribute to your answer.

4. I noted that making inferences is sometimes possible when you lack background knowledge and vocabulary the writer assumed you have, but that doing so is mentally taxing. Much of the reading expected of students (especially in the later elementary grades and beyond) is difficult. It's not only difficult in terms of vocabulary and knowledge; they read texts with more complex structures, texts that convey more abstract and subtle ideas, and they are asked to put these texts to new purposes, like understanding the author's technique. In short, students don't do the type of reading where comprehension is smooth and there's an opportunity to be lost in the story. They mostly read in situations where reading feels like work. What impact do you think that has on students' attitudes toward reading? Do they confuse leisure reading with the reading they do for school? If so, what might be done to disabuse them of that notion?

(*continued*)

5. The account of the fourth-grade slump offered above suggests that disadvantaged children perform poorly on reading tests because they lack the background knowledge that their wealthier peers have—knowledge that is required to comprehend the texts appearing on reading tests. What texts would these children read well, likely better than middle-class children? Should such texts appear on reading tests?

References

1. Begg, I. (1971). Recognition memory for sentence meaning and wording. *Journal of Verbal Learning and Verbal Behavior, 10*(2), 176–181. http://doi.org/10.1016/S0022-5371(71)80010-5.

2. Anderson, J. R., & Bower, G. H. (1973). *Human associative memory.* Washington, DC: Winston and Sons.

3. Pinker, S. (1994). *The language instinct.* New York: Basic Books.

4. Bestgen, Y., & Vonk, W. (2000). Temporal adverbials as segmentation markers in discourse comprehension. *Journal of Memory and Language, 42*(1), 74–87.

5. For brief introductions, see Pylkkänen, L., & McElree, B. (2006). The syntax-semantic interface: On-line composition of sentence meaning. In M. Traxler & M. A. Gernsbacher (Eds.), *Handbook of psycholinguistics* (2nd ed., pp. 537–577). New York: Elsevier.

6. Long, D. L., Oppy, B. J., & Seely, M. R. (1997). Individual differences in readers' sentence-and text-level representations. *Journal of Memory and Language, 36*(1), 129–145; See also Shankweiler, D., Lundquist, E., Katz, L., Stuebing, K., Fletcher, J., Brady, S., Fowler, A., Dreyer, L., Marchione, K., Shaywitz, S., & Shaywitz, B. (1999). Comprehension and decoding: Patterns of association in children with reading difficulties. *Scientific Studies of Reading, 3,* 69–94. But see also Cain, K, & Oakhill, J. (2007). Reading comprehension difficulties: Correlates, causes, and consequences.

In Cain, K., & Oakhill, J. (Eds.), *Children's comprehension problems in oral and written language: A cognitive perspective* (pp. 41–75). New York: Guilford Press.

7. For a review, see Chapter 9, "Comprehension of discourse" in Rayner, K., Pollatsek, A., Ashby, J., & Clifton, Charles, J. (2012). *Psychology of Reading* (2nd ed., pp. 245–275). New York: Psychology Press.

8. Graesser, A. C., Singer, M., & Trabasso, T. (1994). Constructing inferences during narrative text comprehension. *Psychological Review, 101*(3), 371–395. http://doi.org/10.1037/0033-295X.101.3.371.

9. Singer, M. (2007). Inference processing in discourse comprehension. In M. G. Gaskel (Ed.), *The Oxford handbook of psycholinguistics* (pp. 343–359). New York: Oxford University Press.

10. McNamara, D. S., Louwerse, M. M., McCarthy, P. M., & Graesser, A. C. (2010). Coh-metrix: Capturing linguistic features of cohesion. *Discourse Processes, 47*(4), 292–330. http://doi.org/10.1080/01638530902959943.

11. Butcher, K. R., & Kintsch, W. (2003). Text comprehension and discourse processing. In A. F. Healy & R. W. Proctor (Eds.), *Handbook of psychology* (pp. 578–604). New York: Wiley.

12. Cunningham, A. E., & Stanovich, K. E. (1997). Early reading acquisition and its relation to reading experience and ability 10 years later. *Developmental Psychology, 33*(6), 934–945.

13. Stanovich, K. E., Cunningham, A. E., & West, R. F. (1998). *Literacy experiences and the shaping of cognition.* In S. G. Paris & H. M. Wellman (Eds.), *Global prospects for education: Development, culture, and schooling* (pp. 253–288). Washington, DC: American Psychological Association.

14. Stanovich, K. E., & Cunningham, A. E. (1993). Where does knowledge come from?: Specific associations between print exposure and information acquisition. *Journal of Educational Psychology, 85*(2), 211–229. http://doi.org/10.1037//0022-0663.85.2.211.

15. Barclay, J. R., Bransford, J. D., Franks, J. J., McCarrell, N. S., & Nitsch, K. (1974). Comprehension and semantic flexibility. *Journal of Verbal Learning and Verbal Behavior, 13*(4), 471–481. http://doi.org/10.1016/S0022-5371(74)80024-1.

16. Kintsch, W., Welsch, D., Schmalhofer, F., & Zimny, S. (1990). Sentence memory: A theoretical analysis. *Journal of Memory and Language*, *29*(2), 133–159. http://doi.org/10.1016/0749-596X(90)90069-C.

17. Zwaan, R. A., & Radvansky, G. A. (1998). Situation models in language comprehension and memory. *Psychological Bulletin*, *123*(2), 162–185.

18. Rinck, M., & Bower, G. H. (1995). Anaphora resolution and the focus of attention in situation models. *Journal of Memory and Language*, *34*(1), 110–131.

19. Zwaan, R. A. (1996). Processing narrative time shifts. *Journal of Experimental Psychology: Learning, Memory, and Cognition*, *22*(5), 1196–1207.

20. O'Brien, E. J., & Albrecht, J. E. (1992). Comprehension strategies in the development of a mental model. *Journal of Experimental Psychology: Learning, Memory, and Cognition*, *18*(4), 777–784.

21. Schneider, W., Korkel, J., & Weinert, F. E. (1989). Domain-specific knowledge and memory performance: A comparison of high- and low-aptitude Children. *Journal of Educational Psychology*, *81*(3), 306–312.

22. Anderson, R. C., Reynolds, R. E., Schallert, D. L., & Goetz, E. T. (1977). Frameworks for comprehending discourse. *American Educational Research Journal*, *14*(4), 367–381.

23. Sulin, R. A., & Dooling, D. J. (1974). Intrusion of a thematic idea in retention of prose. *Journal of Experimental Psychology*, *103*(2), 255–262. http://doi.org/10.1037/h0036846.

24. Pichert, J. W., & Anderson, R. C. (1977). Taking different perspectives on a story. *Journal of Educational Psychology*, *69*, 309–315. http://doi.org/10.1037/0022-0663.69.4.309.

25. Daneman, M., Lennertz, T., & Hannon, B. (2007). Shallow semantic processing of text: Evidence from eye movements. *Language and Cognitive Processes*, *22*(1), 83–105; Cain, K., Oakhill, J. V., Barnes, M. A., & Bryant, P. E. (2001). Comprehension skill, inference-making ability, and their relation to knowledge. *Memory & Cognition*, *29*(6), 850–859.

26. Otero, J., & Kintsch, W. (1992). Failures to detect contradictions in a text: What readers believe versus what they read. *Psychological Science*, 3(4), 229–235.

27. Ibid.

28. McNamara, D. S., & O'Reilly, T. (2009). Theories of comprehension skill: Knowledge and strategies versus capacity and suppression. In A. M. Columbus (Ed.), *Progress in Experimental Psychology Research*. Hauppauge, NY: Nova Science Publishers.

29. Ibid.

30. Willingham, D. T. & Lovette, G. (2014). Can reading comprehension be taught? *Teachers College Record*. Retrieved from www.tcrecord.org ID Number: 17701.

31. Chall, J. S., & Jacobs, V. A. (2003). The classic study on poor children's fourth-grade slump. *American Educator*, 27(1), 14–15; Sweet, A. P., & Snow, C. E. (Eds.). (2003). *Rethinking reading comprehension*. New York: Guilford.

32. Best, R. M., Floyd, R. G., & McNamara, D. S. (2008). Differential competencies contributing to children's comprehension of narrative and expository texts. *Reading Psychology*, 29(2), 137–164.

6

Becoming a Reader

Agenda for Chapter 6

In order to become a proficient reader, one must read a lot. In this chapter we will seek to understand why some people choose to read and others do not.

Chapters 1 through 5 have taken us from symbols on the page all the way to meaning in the mind, and so it would seem we've about finished our account. But we set the task of explaining reading success; what separates skilled readers from those who struggle? As we've seen, two factors have loomed especially large. First, good readers have high-quality word representations. These lexical representations have three parts—sound, spelling, and meaning—and in good readers each of these parts is robust, and the three are richly interconnected. In addition, the representation of the meaning component is connected to the meaning of other relevant words. A second factor that seems especially important for successful reading is broad knowledge about the world.

Now, why do some readers have excellent lexical representations and rich background knowledge, whereas other readers do not? The main differentiating factor seems to be the volume of reading they do.[1-3] People who read well are people who have read a lot, so if we are to account for successful reading, we need to consider why people read a lot or just a little.

ATTITUDES, MOTIVATION, AND READING

Naturally, we'd like for this focus on reading volume to affect curriculum decisions. Children should be reading a lot in school, and what they read should be carefully sequenced. Sequencing is important so that students will read texts that offer manageable doses of novel vocabulary and background knowledge. But this chapter will focus on leisure reading, not reading in school. Yes, schools vary in the volume and quality of reading they ask students to do, but there is greater variability in leisure reading. Assignments vary across schools, but one thing that doesn't vary is the requirement that the assignments be read. Leisure reading, in contrast, can vary from voluminous to nil. Leisure reading isn't required, but research shows that if children do it, their reading greatly improves.[4]

So, as is our habit, let's engage in some task analysis. What are we really trying to account for here? Why do kids read? It seems obvious; kids read a lot (or a little) in their spare time depending on how much they like it. So we're going to account for reading attitudes. That's a useful start, and certainly, children who say they like to read do so more often.[5,6] But having a positive attitude toward reading doesn't necessarily mean that you will read. For example, suppose an elementary student is in the library with her Dad. He points out an early reader novel based on the movie, *Despicable Me*. She loved the movie, and she's sure she'd love the book—her attitude is very positive. She may nevertheless turn it down because she doubts she has the skills to read it. Making the decision to act or not—in this case, read or not—is not a function of attitudes alone. The broader evaluation of whether you want to do something is generally called your *motivation*.

But even if we can account for a reader's motivation, that's still not enough to tell us whether someone will actually read. Circumstances in the environment can make an unmotivated reader read. Circumstances can also inhibit reading in someone whose motivation is high. Picture another child who borrows *Despicable Me* and is excited to read it, but lives in a crowded apartment and shares a bedroom with two brothers. His home is so noisy and bustling, it seems he can never concentrate when he tries to read.

Our job then, is threefold. We will describe attitudes (why a child likes reading or not), motivation (other factors that influence the desire to read), and environmental circumstances that make it harder or easier to act on that motivation. Bear in mind that what we *really* care about is whether the child reads. A good attitude about reading will not improve lexical representations and background knowledge. Reading will.

ATTITUDES TOWARD READING

When psychologists use the term *attitude*, they mean something close to the everyday use of the term: a belief that comes coupled with an evaluation. But psychologists differentiate among different types of attitudes.

What Is a Reading Attitude?

Some attitudes are what researchers call *cognitive*. For example, I have attitudes toward dishwasher brands, because I recently bought one and did some research on repair records, efficiency, and so on. I like Kenmore, I don't like Whirlpool, and I think Bosch is overpriced. Psychologists would call these cognitive attitudes because they came from a rational, logical analysis.[7] Cognitive attitudes are not necessarily accurate by virtue of their logical origin. It just means those were the processes that created the attitude.

Of course, we have attitudes about things where this sort of analysis is impossible, or at least much less likely. Why do you prefer Coke to Pepsi, or Old Spice to Brut? This is not a cognitive attitude. No one says, "I've looked into the matter, and research shows that Old Spice makes a man more attractive to women, and tends to make other men submissive." You use Old Spice because you like the way it smells, and perhaps equally important, you like the way it makes you feel. Psychologists call these *emotional attitudes*. Emotions also play heavily in attitudes to things that are intertwined with our values—issues like abortion, for example, or capital punishment. You could bring logical analysis to bear on such issues, and people like to think that they do. But the logical arguments are mostly post hoc, and marshaled to justify the emotionally driven opinion.[8]

Still other attitudes are derived more from your behaviors than your thoughts or feelings. For example, you might say to me, "which grocery store in town do you like most?" I consider the question for a moment and I don't really have much of an opinion. But thinking back, I seem to go to Kroger more often than others, so I figure I must like Kroger best. We seldom admit to ourselves that our attitudes are behavioral any more than we admit that they are emotional; we like to think that we do things for logical reasons. So if pressed, I'm likely to say I go to Kroger because they have the best produce, or because it's convenient to my house. It's not that I'm lying, it's that I'm scratching around for a logical reason. I probably believe what I'm telling you.

Are attitudes toward reading cognitive, emotional, or behavioral? I think it's a good bet—although there's limited research on this question—that your reading attitude is mostly emotional. It's based on whether reading seems rewarding, excites you, or interests you. It's not a reasoned judgment of its value, or an appraisal of your behavior. So where do emotional attitudes come from?

The Origins of Emotional Attitudes

The sources of some emotional attitudes are easy to appreciate. Here's Oprah Winfrey on reading: "Books were my pass to personal freedom. I learned to read at age three, and soon discovered there was a whole world to conquer that went beyond our farm in Mississippi."[9] One source—probably the primary source—of positive reading attitudes is positive reading experiences. This phenomenon is no more complicated than understanding why someone has a positive attitude toward eggplant. You taste it and like it. Oprah tasted the mental journeys reading affords, and loved them.

But we can elaborate a bit on this obvious relationship. Kids who like to read also tend to be strong readers, as measured by standard reading tests. Again, not terribly surprising—we usually like what we're good at, and vice versa. This situation yields a positive feedback loop (Figure 6.1).[10]

If you're a good reader, you're more likely to enjoy a story because reading it doesn't seem like work. That enjoyment means that you have

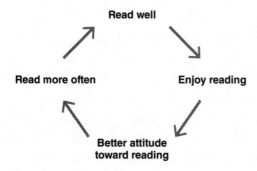

Figure 6.1. **Reading virtuous cycle.** The more you read, the more proficient a reader you are. Proficiency makes it easier to enjoy reading, and enjoying it make your attitude more positive, which prompts you to read more often.
© Anne Carlyle Lindsay

a better attitude toward reading; that is, you believe that reading is a pleasurable, valuable thing to do. A better attitude means you read more often, and more reading makes you even better at reading—your decoding gets still more fluent,[4,11] lexical representations become richer, and your background knowledge increases. We would also predict the inverse to be true: if reading is difficult you won't enjoy it, you'll have a negative attitude toward the activity, and you'll avoid it whenever possible, meaning that you'll fall still further behind your peers. This cycle has been called "The Matthew Effect"[12] from the biblical verse "For whosoever hath, to him shall be given, and he shall have more abundance; but whosoever hath not, from him shall be taken away even that he hath" (Matthew 25:29). Or more briefly, the rich get richer and the poor get poorer.[13]

Positive experiences are important, but they can't be the only source of a positive attitude. If they were, how could you explain the attitudes of people who say they love Coke, but hate Pepsi? Really, how different do they taste? (If you need proof, you'll like a study in which experimenters put Coke in a Pepsi bottle; people picked their "favorite" beverage based on the bottle label, not on the contents.)[14] The emotion in these attitudes comes not from experience of the products, but from emotional reactions to other objects that become associated with the product. Think about what Coke emphasizes in their advertising; that it tastes good, sure, but the focus is more on creating associations between Coke and things that consumers already like: young love, cute animals, Santa Claus, and (of course) attractive people.

When you spell out the psychological mechanism behind these ads, it sounds kind of creepy. It's the same as the one in Pavlov's famous experiment with the salivating dog. The dog salivates when it eats. If you ring a bell just before you feed the dog (and repeat this a few dozen times), the dog will come to salivate when it hears the bell. Advertisers are not interested in salivation but in positive emotions. A cool, funny, muscular guy in a towel prompts positive emotions in many television viewers. Pair that guy with Old Spice enough times, and Old Spice becomes associated with positive emotions.[15] It seems blatantly manipulative, and we think it wouldn't work on us, but it does.

Reading attitudes are fostered, in part, by these sorts of associations. When I see a childhood favorite in a bookstore I feel the warm glow of nostalgia. *Winnie-the-Pooh*, or *Horton Hears a Who!*, makes me think of my mother reading to me at bedtime. Seeing *Mrs. Piggle Wiggle* or a Beverly Cleary book reminds me of the pride I felt in getting my first library card and being allowed to walk to the library on my own. That warm glow is a Pavlovian emotionally conditioned response. And indeed, research shows that positive childhood experiences with books are associated with later reading.[16] (People who grow up in these circumstances are also more likely to be strong readers, so the impact of these childhood experiences on reading attitudes is calculated after the impact of being a strong reader is removed statistically.)

It's worth noting that, because reading attitudes are mostly emotional, logical appeals about the value of reading won't do much. Emotional and cognitive attitudes need not agree. For example, suppose you marshal arguments for the health benefits of broccoli, and I find them persuasive. I now have a positive cognitive attitude toward broccoli. But my emotional attitude is unmoved. I still don't like the way it tastes. And let's face it; our emotional attitudes usually win out over the cognitive.

We said that attitudes are just one contributor to motivation. So let's have a look at this broader factor.

MOTIVATION

There are several theories of motivation, and different theories apply especially well to different circumstances. For example, some theories focus on your motivation to achieve your goals.[17] Other theories concern how people interpret feedback on a task they've tried, and how that feedback impacts their motivation to try again.[18,19] Neither of those is a great fit for our concerns, as we're primarily interested in choice. Picture a student on a Sunday afternoon who has finished her homework and household chores. She has a couple of hours free until supper. How does she choose what to do?

The *expectancy-value* theory of motivation offers a useful framework to think about her choice.[20,21] The theory suggests that your motivation to choose an activity is a product of two factors: if you do it, how valuable will the outcome be? And, if you try, do you expect you'll actually get that outcome? Here some examples of different combinations of expectation and value, and the resulting motivation (Table 6.1).

Calculating Value

We would expect that attitudes ought to contribute to my judgment of the likely value of something. If my attitude toward reading is positive, that means that I think of reading as pleasurable. But there is more to "value" than my attitude, because there are varieties of value that don't promise fun. Sometimes reading serves a purpose. The daughter of a friend of mine decided that she wanted to eat vegan. She's the oldest of five kids, and my friend said, "Fine, but the whole family is not going vegan. You're going to have to cook for yourself." Her daughter, who had been an unenthusiastic reader, turned into an avid reader of vegan cookbooks and an organic gardening magazine.

We can also anticipate outcomes that build relationships. When I'm at a Chinese restaurant with a couple of friends I might agree to share the pupu appetizer platter even though I know I don't like what's on it. Here, the outcome I anticipate is making my friends happy, and enjoying the conviviality of a shared dish. For similar reasons, a teen might read a book that all of his friends are reading.

Table 6.1. Examples personal to the author of how motivation relates to the value and expectation associated with different behaviors.

Behavior	Value	Expectation	Resulting motivation to do the behavior
Buy a candy bar	High—I like candy.	Very High—If I buy it, I'm sure I'll get to enjoy it.	High
Buy a lottery ticket	Very high—the prize is millions of dollars.	Very low—I realize I'm unlikely to win.	Low
Go to a water park	Low—I don't enjoy water parks.	High—there's a small chance that bad weather will close the park, but if I go, I'll probably get to use the park.	Low
Set a world record for running the mile backward	Low—this is not the sort of recognition that excites me.	Very low—I'm out of shape and old.	Very low
Reading the instructions to do my taxes	High—I know I can get in legal trouble if I do my taxes wrong.	Moderately high— I've made mistakes on my taxes before, but I believe that I can avoid mistakes if I am careful.	High

We also need to consider costs in our calculation of value. I'm pretty sure I'd value driving a Cadillac more than my Kia, but I don't choose to because of the cost. One rather obvious way that readers must "pay up" is in the attention the book requires, which is a function of the difficulty of the text, relative to the reader's skill. We want reading material that poses a modest challenge.

These are all pretty obvious considerations, but the way you calculate value is open to many much more subtle influences. Much of the academic field called *behavioral economics* is devoted to the nuances of value calculation. Recounting them would require a book as long as this one, but to provide just one example, consider this.[22] Suppose you love ice cream, but are trying to watch your weight. Here are two scenarios in which you must choose whether or not to partake:

Scenario 1: You're in the grocery store at about noon, passing through the freezer section, and you see the ice cream section.
Scenario 2: You've just finished supper and your spouse sits down with a bowl of ice cream and says, "Oh, how thoughtless of me. I got myself ice cream and I didn't ask if you want some. Would you like this bowl?"

In each case, you're faced with similar choices: ice cream or no ice cream. I'm sure your intuition matches mine that it's easier to turn down ice cream in the first scenario. The rewarding value of ice cream (or anything) is stronger when you anticipate getting it soon after you make the decision, compared to getting it long after you make the decision. The same is true of reading. If a child learns about an interesting book from a friend, his motivation to read it is greater if he can access it immediately (perhaps by downloading it to an e-reader) than if he anticipates waiting until the weekend to borrow it from the library.

Calculating Expectancy

Our motivation to do something is not just a function of the value we attach to the outcome. We also judge the likelihood that we'll actually get the outcome we're anticipating.[21] A lottery ticket offers an extreme example: very desirable outcome, but very small odds of actually getting it. The same principle applies for the child who turned down the copy of *Despicable Me*. She assigned a high value to reading the book, but her expectation that she'd actually get to experience that value was low.[23] This factor is usually called the child's feeling of *reading self-efficacy*. Do I feel that I'm a competent reader, and, especially if I encounter difficulties when reading, that it's worth it to persevere?

The expectancy-value theory of motivation can help us understand why someone might be motivated or unmotivated to read, and it certainly helps us appreciate how complex motivation can be. But expectancy-value theory doesn't capture another factor that contributes to reading: a reading self-concept.

SELF-CONCEPT

The way psychologists conceptualize *self-concept* is pretty close to the way the term is used in everyday conversation—it's your thumbnail description of yourself. It's composed of generalizations about how you tend to act (I'm introverted, logical), and roles you fill (I'm a Cubs fan, a mother, a woodworker). Here we're focusing on one narrow aspect of the self: how you see yourself when it comes to reading.

Reading Self-Concept and Reading Attitude

Your *reading self-concept* is related to your attitude toward reading, but the two are not synonymous. You might think that reading is useful (and so your attitude is positive) and also see yourself as quite competent as a reader. But you just don't see it as an important part of who you are. Typically, however, self-concept and your attitudes are interconnected. If you see yourself as a reader, that helps you to maintain your positive attitude toward reading. Why? Well, we are all motivated to see ourselves in a positive light. If you define something as an important part of who you are, then you want to believe that thing is good.

Here's an example. A few years ago, some neighbors and I discovered that we all enjoyed bourbon. So one night we did a blind taste-testing and were surprised when a bourbon that most of us had considered good (Maker's Mark) finished last. We all felt a little sheepish (how discerning are our tastes, really?), but one friend was dumbstruck. He had the loyalty to Maker's Mark that sports fanatics have for their teams. When he learned that he had put his beloved bourbon at the bottom of the rankings he said quietly, "It's like I just found out my baby is actually ugly." Because "Maker's Mark drinker" was part of his self-concept, he was motivated to maintain a positive attitude toward it; but the facts had just showed him that he shouldn't.

This gives us insight into why Maker's Mark (and Marlborough, and Chevrolet, and many others) make it easy for us to obtain T-shirts, key chains, hats, and other gear with their logo on it. It's not just that it's free advertising, that I'm broadcasting my love of Chevrolet to others. I'm also broadcasting it to myself. I'm showing myself that I like Chevy enough to wear their shirt, and that helps create or maintain my self-image as a Chevy owner. That, in turn, motivates me to like Chevy even more.

Reading Self-Concept and Reading Behavior

Seeing yourself as a reader helps bolster positive reading attitudes. But seeing yourself as a reader influences your behavior in another, more direct way. If "reader" is part of your self-concept, reading will occur to you as a viable activity more often.[24] "What will I do on that two-hour plane trip? I could bring my iPod. Oh, I should bring my e-reader too, so I can find out what happens next in *Billy Bathgate*." And of course, the more you read, the more "reader" becomes cemented as part of your self-concept. What I do and what I think of myself reinforce one another (Figure 6.2).[25]

Conversely, the child who does not have "reader" as part of her self-concept is not likely to think of reading as an option. The child may be neutral or even mildly positive in her attitudes toward reading, but reading is not seen as "one of the things I do." Analogously, I don't make a conscious decision not to attend renaissance fairs. It never occurs to me to think about whether or not I might enjoy it.

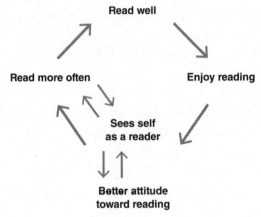

Figure 6.2. Reading virtuous cycle with self-concept added.
©Anne Carlyle Lindsay

The Origins of Self-Concept

The self-concepts of small children (ages three or four) tend to be fairly uniform and fairly hilarious.[26] Hilarious, because children tend to brim with confidence, much of it unwarranted. They usually see themselves as smart, strong, and accomplished, and they are eager to offer evidence, such as their ability to swing really high, and sing the ABC song (whether they actually know the whole thing or not). At the same time, their self-concept tends to be very concrete—being smart means being able to sing the ABC song.

By the time kids are learning to read, their self-concepts are becoming increasingly coherent. Being "smart" is not just a matter of one or another accomplishment—kids understand "smart" as something more abstract that integrates many behaviors. More important to our purposes, self-concepts are no longer a frenzy of self-congratulation. Kids begin to understand that they have some positive qualities, but lack others. Children come to this understanding via comparisons with others.[27] They see that other kids finish more books on the classroom reading wall, or that other kids don't trip over words when asked to read aloud. By the time a child hits age 11 or so, academic self-concept has more or less firmed up. But because self-image is a product of comparisons, it's open to change. Kids change their minds about who they are as they gather new information about themselves and others, and make new comparisons.[28]

Reading self-concept is rooted in reading experiences, good or bad, but it's not quite that simple. What really matters is the child's interpretation of those experiences, and parents, teachers, and peers contribute to those interpretations. One way they do that is by offering alternative explanations. For example, consider a child who is struggling with decoding. A parent might point out that he hasn't had much time to practice decoding at home due to other responsibilities, and suggest that could change. An older sibling might say that she had trouble learning to decode too; her brother is unfairly comparing his skill to his more experienced sister. In each case, a family member offers a new way to interpret what the child observes.

Family members (especially parents) also communicate to children what they consider to be family values, and that can influence a child's self-concept. Sometimes the message is quite direct. I remember visiting a friend's house when I was perhaps 10 and, spying a decorative dish in the living room, I pointed out to him that it was empty, and that it really ought to hold candy. He thought that was an excellent idea, and brought it to his mother. She said with cool derision, "We are not the type of people who put candy out in dishes." I found the comment strange even then, but the message could not have been clearer. She was communicating family values.

I think these messages are enormously important for kids. Around the age of five or six, children perceive that families differ in their habits and practices. For example, a six-year-old might visit his friend Robert's house and learn that they don't follow the rule "finish your dinner before you get dessert." The child realizes that not all adults follow this rule, that it's not a law. It dawns on the child that his parents *just made it up*.

Parents make different choices about how to run their household. Choices about things like household rules, what's displayed on the walls, the type of family stories that are repeated, who parents speak of with respect. These choices convey silent, value-laden messages to children, and by the time they are teens, they can articulate their family values. They may not accept all of them, but they are very likely to at least try them on for size. Families that display books in their homes, that speak respectfully of writers and readers, that make a habit of giving books as birthday gifts, that make a leisurely reading of the Sunday newspaper a weekly ritual—these are ways that parents communicate to children that reading is a family value, and these are the children likely to grow up with a strong reading self-concept.

Let's recap. We've looked at three factors affecting whether children choose to read: attitudes, motivation, and self-concept. We said that reading attitudes are primarily emotional, and they are a product of positive reading experiences, and a product of associating reading with other things that we like. Our motivation to undertake an activity is composed of our assessment of the value we place on the outcome, and our expectation that we can complete the task so as to obtain that outcome. That calculation of the expected value is influenced by reading attitudes, but also things like the utility of reading a particular text, or what reading it might mean to social relationships. The expectation of successful reading is based on one's sense of reading self-efficacy, and factors like whether the external environment will disrupt or support our reading. Finally, we said that our self-concept as a reader is a product of observing ourselves over time—I see that I frequently read, and I feel that reading is important to me. Comparison is an important part of that perception—I see that reading is more important to me than it appears to be to others.

This review may engender some despair. We start off asking "how can we get kids to like reading more?" but quickly learn that "liking reading" is just one part of getting kids to read, and in fact seems to be somewhat remote. One reason not to despair: reading attitudes do matter, and kids who like reading tend to read. But a more important reason for optimism is that thus far, we've assumed that the impetus to read comes from within the child and that the environment has little to do with it. That's not the case. The environment matters, and we can change the environment.

GETTING KIDS TO READ

I said at the outset that our goal is simply to get kids reading—it's reading, not positive attitudes toward reading that will make for better lexical representations and broader background knowledge. But then we saw that reading attitudes, reading self-image, and frequency of reading are interconnected (Figure 6.2). So in fact, getting kids to read will not only improve their reading, it will make them like reading more. Getting children to like reading more in order to prompt more reading is not our only option. We can reverse it—get them reading more, and that will improve reading attitudes and reading self-concept. Well then, how do we prompt a child with negative or indifferent attitudes toward reading to pick up a book?

Rewards

Adults are frequently confronted with children who don't want to do what we want them to do. A common solution is to use rewards or punishments as short-term motivators. What if I told a fourth-grader, "If you read a chapter of that book, you can have some ice cream"? The child will likely take me up on the deal and it sounds like he'd have a positive experience. And that's what we said we're aiming for, positive reading experiences.

Rewards do work, at least in the short term. If you find a reward that the child cares about, he will read in order to get it. The problem is that you don't get the attitude boost we've predicted. In fact, the attitude is often *less* positive because of the reward. The classic experiment on this phenomenon was conducted in a preschool.[29] A set of really attractive Magic Markers appeared during free play, and the researchers confirmed that kids often chose the markers from among many toys. Then the markers disappeared from the classroom. A few weeks later, researchers took kids, one at a time, into a separate room. They offered the child a fancy "good player" certificate if she would draw with the markers. Other kids were given the opportunity to draw with the markers but were not offered the certificate. A few weeks later, the Magic Markers reappeared in the classroom. The kids who got the certificate showed notably less interest in the Magic Markers than the kids who didn't get the certificate. The reward had backfired. It had made kids like the markers *less*.

The interpretation of the study rests on how kids think about their own behavior. The rewarded kids likely thought, "I drew with the markers because I was offered a reward to do so. Now here are the markers, but no reward. So why would I draw with them?" There have been many studies of rewards in academic contexts, and they often backfire in this way.[30]

We can imagine that rewarding kids for reading *could* work in certain circumstances. What if the child has such a positive experience while reading that it overwhelms his thinking that he's only reading for the sake of the reward? In other words, the child thinks, "Gosh, I only started this book to get the ice cream I was promised, but actually it's awesome. Mom was a sucker to offer me a reward!" This scenario is, of course, the fond hope of the adult who offers a reward for reading, but let's be honest, it's probably rare. If you're thinking of rewarding a child to read, that is surely a child who has not been reading recently, and whose attitude toward reading is pretty set. A massive turnaround is unlikely. If not rewards, then what?

The expectancy-value model suggests some strategies, most of them pretty intuitive. The value will be higher if the book is on a topic the child already loves, or if it's a book that a lot of his peers have read, or if it concerns a topic of practical utility to the child. The expectation of successful reading will be higher if it's at the right reading level, if it includes a lot of pictures (as a graphic novel does), if the chapters are short, or if the child already knows the story (as in a novelization of a movie she's seen). So the expectancy-value model suggests that we boost the book's value to the child, or her expectation of successful reading. What else might we try?

Make the Choice Easy

People often overlook the fact that leisure reading is a choice. A child is not deciding to read or not read. The child is choosing among competing activities: Should I read, or have a snack, or see what my friend's doing, or play a video game? When we're talking about leisure reading, it's not enough that the child like reading, and that she have a positive attitude; if she's to choose reading, it must be the most appealing activity available.

That makes our job sound terribly difficult—"good" is no longer enough; now we're shooting for "best." But bearing in mind that reading is a choice prompts some other ideas to get kids reading. One thing we can do is make reading an easy choice to make. All of us are on autopilot more often than we like to believe; we make decisions not by carefully weighing out options, but by doing what's expedient. *Expedient* often means obvious, easy. Things that are right in front of us and easy to access are more likely to be selected. For example, researchers were able to make food items at a salad bar more or less likely to be selected by moving them closer or farther from the diner—but the necessary change in distance was just 10 inches.[31]

A teacher once told me a remarkable story about the power of easy access. He had mentioned a book—Jared Diamond's *Guns, Germs, and Steel*—in the course of a high school class discussion about income inequity across nations. He enthusiastically recommended it, and mentioned that he knew the school library had two copies. There were a few murmurs of interest. The next day he checked the library and found both copies still on the shelves. He checked them out, brought them to class, and asked if anyone was interested in reading this book he had mentioned. Five students raised their hands, and he gave the copies to the two most enthusiastic students. So five students were ready to give the book a try if someone put it in their hands, but going to the school library to find it seemed like too much trouble. The library, the teacher told me, was a 30-second walk from his classroom.

The implication of these examples is that books should not just be available, but virtually falling into children's laps, or at least, visible in as many locations as possible: in the classroom, in every room of the house, in the car, and so on. If it's affordable, an e-reader is wonderful for instant access to any book that a child gets excited about. (And many books can be downloaded for free once the child has the device.)

Change the Other Choices

That leisure reading represents a choice has another implication. If a child must like reading *most* from available alternatives, parents can control the other alternatives; that is, make reading the most appealing choice around by restricting access to other activities that the parents think are less enriching. A recent survey showed that 30% of teens say they enjoy reading "a lot," but they also say they enjoy other media activities more: watching videos, engaging with friends on social media, gaming.[32] Most kids will choose screens—"screens" generically referring to video content, games, or computer applications—over a book, even a readily available one. For reasons I don't understand, moving images on a screen entrance us. We stare at them as we stare at flames or ocean waves. I've never met a parent who said, "Television? Oh yeah, she watched it a couple of times, but I just couldn't get her interested." An obvious implication is that if these other activities were unavailable, kids might read more.

A 2016 survey of parents reported that 55% say they limit teens' time online, but they also say that they are less concerned with the amount of time spent with media, and more concerned with content.[33] Content does matter, of course, but so does volume. And volume is high.

Very young children—those in their first two years of life—spend twice as much time watching television and videos as they do being read to (53 vs. 23 minutes per day). Slightly older children (ages five to eight years) watch more television than younger kids do (about two hours per day) although they read or are read to about the same amount of time (33 minutes per day). At this age, children start to use other digital devices: 90% have used a computer at least once, and 22% use a computer daily. For console video games, the figures are only slightly lower. The use of these other devices, along with greater television viewing, means that the average five- to eight-year-old is exposed to about 3 hours and forty-five minutes of various media each day.[34] By the time kids are in their late teens, average media exposure approaches *11 hours per day*.[35]

My guess is that very few parents are happy that their teens spend so much time with digital devices. I'm also guessing those parents didn't see it coming when their kids were toddlers. But as any parent knows, it's easier to limit something at an early age than to wait until it's a problem and then try to change course. Obviously some video content is more enriching than others—*Sesame Street* is not equivalent to *Tom and Jerry* cartoons—but if children are to choose reading, controlling the content of screen time won't do it. The amount must be controlled as well. But again, that alone probably won't be enough. It must be coupled with ensuring ready access to reading material that kids will value.

Digital technologies came up for both good and ill in this chapter— good in the easy access e-reader can provide to texts, and ill in the mesmerizing appeal of most screen-based content. In the next chapter we'll consider the possibility that new digital technologies may have changed the reading landscape more broadly.

Summary and Implications

Summary

- Reading attitudes are largely emotional. They are derived from past reading experiences and from the emotions connected to things associated with reading. Motivation to read is a product of the value one expects to derive from reading, and the expectation that that value will actually be obtained if one reads. Reading self-concept comes from the sense that you read more than your peers.
- To change reading attitudes, reading motivation, or reading self-concept, kids must read. That sounds like a catch-22. But there are ways of getting kids to read even if they do not currently have positive reading attitudes, motivation, or self-concepts.
- Rewards should not be the first strategy to get reluctant kids to read, because they have the potential to depress reading attitudes once the rewards stop.
- Changes to the environment that can boost reading include: making books *very* readily available—that is, visible in the environment—and restricting access to other choices, especially screen-based entertainment.

Implications

- We tend to focus on getting kids to want to read for the *pleasure* of reading, but that's just one positive outcome the child might expect. Another is *utility*. Parents and teachers can try to exploit situations where reading is useful to the child. Young children can help parents in ways that call for reading: sorting household mail, reading a recipe, helping to find a store by reading signs. When an older child wants something—to be allowed to try out for a sports team, or to own a pet—parents can require they learn something about it by reading first.
- Because reading attitudes are emotional, there's not much point in haranguing children with logical reasons to read (for example,

saying that it will help them later in life). Sure, it's worth mentioning because children should know it's true and you think it's important, but don't expect it to influence what kids do.

- Communicating that reading is a family value is not just about parents modeling good reading habits, although that is, of course, important. It's about intellectual hunger; being the sort of family that likes to learn new things, and likes to have new experiences, for their own sake.
- As much as access to books should be easy for kids, it should also be easy for parents. Sure, libraries are great, and parents may really intend to visit them, but it's not always easy to find time. Putting books directly into the hands of parents may help, but research indicates it's especially important that parents follow up with kids by encouraging them to read the books and by discussing them.[36]
- If positive associations can rub off one object or activity and onto another (as in the Old Spice example), that offers an opportunity to improve reading attitudes, even in the absence of reading. Books (and other reading material) can be associated with birthdays, Christmas, and other happy occasions via gifts. New reading material can be a regular part of vacations. And if there is a time that reading already holds positive association in the child's mind—for example, if the child enjoys being read to before bed, or the child has a cozy spot where she reads the same book again and again—that positive association probably shouldn't be disrupted through parental badgering. For example, a parent might be tempted to practice reading during that bedtime book, or to nag the child to read something else in her cozy chair. Pick another time for these encouragements, and let a happy reading child stay happy.

Discussion Questions

1. Research indicates that children's attitudes toward reading are positive in first grade, but drop every year thereafter.[6] Attitudes level off in high school, settling around "indifference." That's a correlation, of course, and we don't *know* that experiences in school are making attitudes toward reading less positive. What's your take? What do you think contributes to reading attitudes becoming less positive?

2. We elect to do something (or not) based on our estimate of the value of the outcome of making the choice, and the probability that we think we'll get the outcome. We typically focus on personal pleasure as the main contributor to the value of the outcome, but as I mentioned, sometimes the social concerns play a role—I might read a book because all my friends are reading it. Teens, as we know, are hyper-social. What might parents and schools do to leverage teens' social awareness to promote reading?

3. Children are sensitive to the family values their parents communicate, but they are also sensitive to values communicated by other people they respect. Which people in the public eye do students pay attention to? Would they be credible as promotors of reading? Would they be willing to take on the job?

4. Some parents are not interested in reading and do not consider it a family value. Do policymakers or educators have a right to try to persuade them otherwise? Should anyone be in the business of telling parents how to parent?

References

1. Chateau, D., & Jared, D. (2000). Exposure to print and word recognition processes. *Memory & Cognition, 28*(1), 143–153. http://doi.org/10.3758/bf03211582.

2. Cunningham, A. E., & Stanovich, K. E. (1991). Tracking the unique effects of print exposure in children: Associations with vocabulary, general knowledge, and spelling. *Journal of Educational Psychology, 83*(2), 264–274. http://doi.org/10.1037//0022-0663.83.2.264.

3. Sparks, R. L., Patton, J., & Murdoch, A. (2014). Early reading success and its relationship to reading achievement and reading volume: Replication of "10 years later." *Reading and Writing, 27*(1), 189–211. http://doi.org/10.1007/s11145-013-9439-2.

4. Lee, J. (2014). Universal factors of student achievement in high-performing Eastern and Western countries. *Journal of Educational Psychology, 106*(2), 364–374. http://doi.org/10.1037/a0035609.

5. Baker, L., & Wigfield, A. (2012). Dimensions of children's motivation for reading and their relations to reading activity and reading achievement. *Reading Research Quarterly, 34*(4), 452–477.

6. Mckenna, M. C., Kear, D. J., & Ellsworth, R. A. (1995). Children's attitudes toward reading: A national survey. *Reading Research Quarterly, 30*(4), 934–956.

7. Aronson, E., Wilson, T. D., & Akert, R. M. (2012). *Social psychology* (8th ed.). New York: Pearson.

8. Haidt, J. (2001). The emotional dog and its rational tail: A social intuitionist approach to moral judgment. *Psychological Review, 108*(4), 814–834. http://doi.org/10.1037/0033-295X.108.4.814.

9. Blaydes, J. (2003). *The educator's book of quotes* (p. 9). Thousand Oaks, CA: Corwin.

10. Mol, S. E., & Bus, A. G. (2011). To read or not to read: A meta-analysis of print exposure from infancy to early adulthood. *Psychological Bulletin, 137*(2), 267–296. http://doi.org/10.1037/a0021890.

11. Clark, C., & DeZoysa, S. (2011). *Mapping the interrelationships of reading enjoyment, attitudes, behaviour and attainment: An exploratory investigation.* London: National Literacy Trust.

12. Stanovich, K. E. (1986). Matthew Effects in reading: Some consequences of individual differences in the acquisition of literacy. *Reading Research Quarterly, 21*, 360–407.

13. Morgan, P. L., & Fuchs, D. (2007). Is there a bidirectional relationship between children's reading skills and reading motivation? *Exceptional Children, 73*(2), 165–183.

14. Woolfolk, M. E., Castellan, W., & Brooks, C. I. (1983). Pepsi versus Coke: Labels, not tastes, prevail. *Psychological Reports, 52*, 185–186.

15. Stuart, E. W., Shimp, T. A., & Engle, R. W. (1984). Classical conditioning of consumer attitudes: four experiments in an advertising context. *Journal of Consumer Research, 14,* 334–349.

16. Baker, L., Scher, D., & Mackler, K. (1997). Home and family influences on motivations for reading. *Educational Psychologist, 32*(2), 69–82. http://doi.org/10.1207/s15326985ep3202_2.

17. Dweck, C. S., & Leggett, E. L. (1988). A social-cognitive approach to motivation and personality. *Psychological Review, 95*(2), 256–273. http://doi.org/10.1037/0033-295X.95.2.256.

18. Heider, F. (1958). *The psychology of interpersonal relations.* New York: Wiley.

19. Weiner, B. (2000). Intrapersonal and interpersonal theories of motivation from an attribution perspective. *Educational Psychology Review, 12*(1), 1–14. Retrieved from http://link.springer.com/chapter/10.1007/978-1-4615-1273-8_2/.

20. Eccles, J. S., Adler, T. F., Futterman, R., Goff, S. B., Kaczala, C. M., Meece, J. L., & Midgley, C. (1983). Expectancies, values, and academic behaviors. In J. T. Spence (Ed.), *Achievement and achievement motivation* (pp. 75–146). San Francisco: Freeman.

21. Wigfield, A., & Eccles, J. S. (2000). Expectancy-value theory of achievement motivation. *Contemporary Educational Psychology, 25,* 68–81.

22. da Matta, A., Gonçalves, F. L., & Bizarro, L. (2012). Delay discounting: Concepts and measures. *Psychology & Neuroscience, 5*(2), 135–146.

23. Cloer, T. J., & Ross, S. Y. (1997). The relationship of standardized reading scores to children's self-perception as readers. In K. Camperel, B. L. Hayes, & R. Telfer (Eds.), *Yearbook of the American Reading Forum* (pp. 93–104). Logan, UT: American Reading Forum.

24. Hall, L. A. (2012). The role of reading identities and reading abilities in students' discussions about texts and comprehension strategies. *Journal of Literacy Research, 44*(3), 239–272. http://doi.org/10.1177/1086296X12445370.

25. Retelsdorf, J., Köller, O., & Möller, J. (2014). Reading achievement and reading self-concept: Testing the reciprocal effects model.

Learning and Instruction, *29*, 21–30. http://doi.org/10.1016/j. learninstruc.2013.07.004.

26. Harter, S. (1999). *The cognitive and social construction of the developing self.* New York: Guilford.

27. Ruble, D. N., & Frey, K. S. (1991). Changing patterns of comparative behavior as skills are acquired: A functional model of self-evaluation. In J. Suls & T. A. Wills (Eds.), *Social comparison: Contemporary theory and research* (pp. 79–113). Hillsdale, NJ: Erlbaum.

28. Grotevant, H. D. (1987). Toward a process model of identity formation. *Journal of Adolescent Research*, *2*(3), 203–222. http://doi. org/10.1177/074355488723003.

29. Lepper, M. R., Greene, D., & Nisbett, R. E. (1973). Undermining children's intrinsic interest with extrinsic reward: A test of the "overjustification" hypothesis. *Journal of Personality and Social Psychology*, *28*(1), 129–137. Retrieved from http://psycnet.apa.orgjournals/psp/28/1/129.

30. Deci, E. L., Koestner, R., & Ryan, R. M. (1999). A meta-analytic review of experiments examining the effects of extrinsic rewards on intrinsic motivation. *Psychological Bulletin*, *125*(6), 627–668. Retrieved from http://psycnet.apa.orgjournals/bul/125/6/627.

31. Rozin, P., Scott, S., & Dingley, M. (2011). Nudge to nobesity I: Minor changes in accessibility decrease food intake. *Judgement and Decision Making*, *6*(4), 323–332. http://doi.org/10.1111/j.1753-4887.2009.00206.x.

32. Rideout, V. J. (2015). *The common sense census: media use by tweens and teens.* San Francisco: Common Sense Media.

33. Anderson, M. (2016). *Parents, teens and digital monitoring.* Washington, DC: Pew Research Center.

34. Rideout, V. J. (2011). *Zero to eight: Children's media use in America.* San Francisco: Common Sense Media.

35. Rideout, V. J., Foehr, U. G., & Roberst, D. F. (2010). *Generation M2: Media in the lives of 8- to 18-year-olds.* Menlo Park, CA: Kaiser Foundation.

36. Kim, J. S., & White, T. G. (2008). Scaffolding voluntary summary reading for children in Grades 3 to 5: An experimental study. *Scientific Studies of Reading*, *12*(1), 1–23.

7

READING AFTER THE DIGITAL REVOLUTION

Agenda for Chapter 7

Much of what we do and how we do it has changed in the last 20 years, due to the omnipresence of digital technologies. In this chapter we will examine how they have affected the teaching and practice of reading.

We're nearing the end of our cognitive account of reading, having covered two varieties of decoding (auditory and visual), vocabulary, comprehension, and motivation. In this chapter we consider whether digital technologies change any of these processes. "Digital technologies" will include video gaming, computer use (especially surfing the Web), text messaging, and consumption of music and video content. Children listened to music and watched video before digital devices became available, but new technologies greatly increased their access to these activities.

We'll look at three ways that digital technologies might have prompted a revolution in reading. First, we'll examine how digital tools have been brought to bear on reading itself. Does reading from a screen change the core processes we've examined? Second, we'll consider the possibility that digital technologies promote activities that have an indirect effect on reading. For example, perhaps the increased information available on the Internet has changed the way that background knowledge contributes to reading comprehension. Third, we'll evaluate the evidence that digital technologies are having a broad impact not just on the way we read, but on thinking as a whole. I will conclude that the changes the digital revolution has brought to reading are actually quite modest.

DIGITAL TOOLS FOR READING

We'll begin with a narrow focus—how software developers have applied digital technologies to the teaching of reading, and the process of reading itself.

Reading Instruction

Digital technologies would seem ideally suited to instruction. For example, a computer application might titrate instruction to the child's performance. A child learning letter-sound pairings can receive more practice for the material that gives her the most trouble and less for that which she's mastered. Animation and sound could make the lesson more interesting, and voice recognition technology offers the promise of evaluating student oral responses individually. You can't do any of that with a worksheet, and a teacher can't do it with a whole class simultaneously.

Scores of studies have examined the impact of educational technology on learning to read, and several research reviews have summarized this work. Researchers have concluded that technology has a modest positive effect on reading outcomes.[1] "Modest" means researchers estimate that technology interventions, on average, would move a student at the 50th percentile of reading up to perhaps the 55th or 65th percentile—the estimates vary.

Nice to know that technology helps, but really? With all the power we attribute to technology, that seems like a pretty wimpy effect. But the modest impact is actually typical for educational technology interventions, whether they concern math, science, history, whatever.[2,3] More disturbing is a point made by researcher John Hattie: *any* intervention you try usually yields a modest boost—at least, any intervention that ends up reported in an academic journal. That may be a publishing bias (that is, journal editors don't publish reports of interventions that didn't work), or it may be a real effect; an intervention may have some beneficial side effect, for example, prompting teachers to rethink their practice. The conclusion I'm emphasizing here is that educational technology interventions in general (and those targeting reading in particular) have been less successful than we would have expected.

But, you might protest, "does technology improve reading achievement?" is a dumb question. Surely there is variation in the quality of technology applications. I think that point is exactly right. It was *possible* that the advantages of digital technology were so powerful that virtually any tool you developed would be pretty good. In fact, you still hear people talk this way. They point out (as I just did) that technology enables self-paced learning, that it enables the integration of other media like sound and video, and that it enables individualized feedback. These advantages are displayed on the table, so to speak, and we are invited to take it as self-evident that technology will be a boon.

The research shows, on the contrary, that these features can be implemented poorly or well. Embedded video may distract rather than illuminate, or the algorithm meant to adapt to a student's reading level may be faulty. And if we're just making a case based on what *ought* to happen, we should note that teaching reading with technology also brings some potential drawbacks. Most notable is that it does not capitalize on the student's relationship with the teacher, a factor known to be important in early reading.[4] In addition, broken or lost devices, software glitches, and compatibility problems are frequent headaches in many tech-heavy environments.

Here's the challenge. A new program meant to teach reading comes as a package, with all the pieces intertwined: the materials used; their sequence; the graphics; the assessment; the decision rules for continuing to new material or reviewing old material; whether kids are meant to work alone or with a teacher; and so on. The program is successful or not as a consequence of all of these features working together. Two programs might be equally successful for very different reasons, but we have no way of seeing what they are.

Researchers have learned one thing over the last 15 years or so. Technology alone doesn't do much. So researchers must move on to the next job: sorting out which features of reading instruction software help, hinder, or have no effect on reading achievement. They must also sort out the (likely complex) interactions among these features. That will be no small job.

Thus the current bland conclusion is that some tech products meant to teach reading are good, some bad, and some indifferent. Obvious, but at least we know that we shouldn't make a panicky decision to buy a reading program merely out of fear that we will be left behind the times. I know a decision made on that basis sounds foolish, but ask around and you'll meet plenty of teachers who will tell you that their school or district has made technology purchasing decisions on just that basis: "we don't want our kids to be left behind."

Screen vs. Paper

Marshall McLuhan famously said, "the medium is the message." By this he meant the way you receive a message influences the content. Does that apply to reading? Do we understand better, worse, or differently when reading on a screen compared to paper?

For stories aimed at young children, there doesn't seem to be an enormous difference. Studies have compared children listening to an audio version of a book with reading a paper book or ebook with a parent. The outcome measures might be story comprehension, or improvements in phonological awareness, or knowledge of letters. Some studies show that e-readers are superior to paper, some show them as inferior, and some show no difference.[5–12] Some studies indicate that parents and children interact differently when reading an electronic book together, although the impact is not consistently good or bad for the child.[13]

Why are the data all over the place? Very likely for the same reason that data on digital reading instruction are all over the place. Electronic books for children have many features that can take different forms. For example, suppose that when the child touches a picture of an animal, an audible voice spells the label. That might boost letter awareness if the phonograms are simple and regular ("dog"), but not if they are irregular (e.g., "jaguar"). This interactive feature might contribute to story comprehension if drawing attention to the animal made sense at that moment, and if the interactive feature helped the child understand something about the narrative. If not, it might be a distraction that detracts from comprehension.

What about adults? Would the process of reading *Billy Bathgate* have been different if I had read it on paper rather than my Kindle? Experiments investigating this question have mostly examined the types of texts students would encounter in school—an expository text describing the function of the heart, for example—but have in some cases included narratives as well. Most studies have shown that reading from paper holds a small edge over reading from a screen either in reading comprehension or reading speed.[14–16] People often report that reading from a screen feels more effortful,[14,15,17] although at least one study shows no difference when more objective measures of effort were used.[18]

Why would reading on a screen be different? Small changes in design can prompt small changes in comprehension. For example, comprehension is better if you navigate a book by flipping virtual pages, compared to scrolling.[19] And clickable links (hyperlinks) incur a cost to comprehension, even if you don't click them.[20] Because you can see that they are clickable, you still need to make a decision about whether or not to click. That draws on your attention, and so carries a cost to comprehension. Although it has not been fully investigated yet, researchers suspect that the three-dimensionality of paper books may be important—it's easier to remember an event as occurring at the end of a book with the spatial cue that it happened on a page near the back of the book. These small effects seem to add up to a slight knock to comprehension when reading from a screen.

If comprehension is compromised when reading on a screen, why do people love their Kindles? There are a couple of possibilities. First, it may be that the deficit to comprehension is smaller when reading narratives and light nonfiction (which is what people mostly read on e-readers) than it is when reading the sort of challenging material found in textbooks. Second, the deficit may be equivalent for these two types of material, but people don't much care if they don't understand every last bit of a novel they read, whereas they know they must master details of textbooks. And indeed, people may like Kindles, but surveys show that consistent majorities of students prefer paper textbooks to their electronic counterparts.

Digital Literacy

Perhaps the use of digital technologies does not make it easier to learn decoding or to read, but surely it leads to greater knowledge of digital technologies. And that, some have suggested, should be considered a new type of literacy. The ability to create, navigate, and evaluate information on various digital platforms is generically called *digital literacy*.

Different aspects of digital literacy should be evaluated separately. First, take the idea of a general tech-savviness. I think there's little doubt that exposure to and practice with digital technologies will teach kids certain conventions one finds across these technologies: menu systems, hierarchical file structures, and the like. This knowledge is important exactly because these conventions are respected across applications and across devices. But they are pretty easy to learn. Software is engineered to be easy to use, and so the skills needed are not that deep, and kids learn them rapidly. Some adults like to joke about how helpless they are in the face of these newfangled gadgets, compared to kids who seem such naturals. But actually, kids vary widely in their tech knowledge, and age-related differences, when they exist, are not due to limited learning abilities on the part of oldsters; they are due to youngsters' greater motivation and opportunities to learn from their peers.[21,22]

A second important aspect of digital literacy is the ability to evaluate information. The Web is often praised for its effect in democratizing publishing. Twenty years ago, the owners of newspapers, magazines, and book publishing companies were gatekeepers of information. My comprehensive knowledge of, say, rare animal species in the Pacific Northwest would be hidden from others if I could not persuade the gatekeepers to publish something I wrote. Now I can publish whatever I like and let consumers decide whether or not it's valuable. That's great, but the gatekeepers did serve a function; most had an interest in ensuring some quality control. On the Web, the reader must take greater responsibility for evaluating the reliability of what she encounters.

In the mid-2000s the need for greater student education in evaluating Web content gained publicity through a website describing the fictitious "endangered Northwest Tree Octopus" (Figure 7.1).

Figure 7.1. Tree octopus. A screenshot from the website describing the fictitious tree octopus.

http://zapatopi.net/treeoctopus/

The website deftly mimics the prose used in science textbooks. ("Because of the moistness of the rainforests and specialized skin adaptations, they are able to keep from becoming desiccated for prolonged periods of time.") Aside from the absurdity of a cephalopod living out of water, there are hints scattered throughout the site that it's a hoax—for example, the octopus's main predator is said to be the sasquatch, and the website is endorsed by the organization "Greenpeas."

Yet when researchers at the University of Connecticut asked 25 seventh-graders to evaluate the site—seventh-graders nominated for the study by their schools as their most proficient online readers—every single one fell for the hoax.[23] When they were told that it was false, most struggled to find evidence that could have told them that, and some even insisted that the website was legitimate. Other research has shown that students rarely critically evaluate information they find on the Web, and if they do try to evaluate the credibility of a website, they are likely to focus more on the look of the site than source characteristics.[24-27] When they look for information via Google, they are much more influenced by the position of the site in the search results than by who authored the site, which organization sponsored the site, or anything else. It's as though they thought Google was evaluating trustworthiness for them.[28]

In the last few years there have been greater efforts to teach students how to be critical readers of information on the Web. Students learn techniques like evaluating the author's credentials, tracing the domain to evaluate whether the website is commercial or originates in the education community, checking how recently the Web page was updated, and looking for other websites that have linked back to it. Teaching students these evaluation skills is still in its infancy, but there is some indication of promise. Several studies show that interventions can help students understand the need to evaluate the veracity of information found on the Web, and some interventions seem to help them make these evaluations.[29-32]

INDIRECT EFFECTS

In the last section we considered digital applications that were designed to facilitate reading or the teaching of reading. Digital technologies may also have indirect consequences for reading. Just as nursery rhymes help children learn speech sounds (which prepares them to learn to read), some activities facilitated by new technologies may help or harm reading even though they seem unrelated.

Now you might protest that it's impossible to generalize about such indirect effects, because there is no telling what kids are doing with digital technologies. Are they using the Web to read a Shakespeare concordance or pornographic Harry Potter fan fiction? Are they using social media to stay in touch with their grandmother in Europe, or to bully the child down the street?

Even though we can say with wide-eyed innocence, "Hey, they *could* be reading Shakespeare," we suspect otherwise. One wag put it this way: "I possess a device, in my pocket, that is capable of accessing the entirety of information known to man. I use it to look at pictures of cats and get

Table 7.1. Children's report of time spent per day on activity with media.

	Tweens	Teens
Video content	2:26	2:38
Gaming	1:19	1:21
Music content	0:51	1:54
Reading	0:29	0:28
Social media	0:16	1:11
Other computer/mobile	0:13	0:32
Browsing Web	0:12	0:36
Video-chatting	0:06	0:13
Going to movies	0:02	0:03
Total screen time	4:36	6:40

in arguments with strangers."[33] We do have *some* idea of the media lives of tweens and teens, shown from a 2015 survey in Table 7.1.[34]

We can't generalize to every child, but on average kids clearly spend a lot of time consuming video and music content, and playing video games. Older children also browse websites and use social media. This survey did not ask about texting, but we'll take that on shortly.

How might these activities affect reading?

Information and Reading Comprehension

Okay, maybe students aren't reading Shakespeare online, but they certainly can access information about Shakespeare with ease, should the need or impulse arise. We can quickly dispose of the suggestion that this ready access will have a marked impact on reading comprehension. As we noted in Chapters 4 and 5, looking up information is a poor substitute for knowing that information when you're reading: first, it's often difficult to find the right bit of information the author intended, and second, it turns reading into problem solving and so incurs a significant cognitive cost.

Still, perhaps digital technologies have a positive effect on reading by making information easier to learn by virtue of its greater availability. Information has been made cheap—cheap in the sense that it's abundant and omnipresent. If the digital age provides a fire hose of information, couldn't kids be learning incidentally from this continuous stream?

They could, and there's good evidence that they do, at least from certain sources. Toddlers and preschoolers who watch educational television really do learn about numbers and letters, as well as social lessons, e.g., about sharing.[35] But overall, kids learn less from video than you'd think. Kids don't learn much from videos that are supposed to make them smart, like "Baby Einstein."[36,37] That may be because the videos are not as well designed as some broadcast shows, or because the effects of the latter are usually assessed after kids have been watching for at least several months, whereas videos are often assessed after a few weeks. But another factor is that infants and toddlers seem to have a harder time learning from video than from a live person, a well-established phenomenon called the "video deficit."[38,39]

Mostly, the idea that new technologies leave people more knowledgeable goes unsupported—it might be right, but at the moment it's unsupported. For older kids the relationship between television viewing and academic achievement is negative, not positive; but note, that effect is really due to the heavy viewers. Kids who watch only a little TV show no academic cost. And for all kids, TV content, not just volume, matters.[35,40] More generally, kids who report being heavy users of all media (television, music, gaming, et al.) also report getting lower grades—but the relationship of grades and leisure reading is positive.[41]

It's striking when we see a student use the Internet to teach himself a new skill, or pursue an academic interest. Those uses should be encouraged and celebrated, of course. But as I've mentioned, teens mostly use computers for gaming, watching videos, and social networking. There's just not much evidence that the digital age has prompted an intellectual renaissance among kids.

Reading Volume and Comprehension or Fluency

Although reading is commonly thought to be in decline, kids today actually read more than previous generations did. A 2009 study at the University of California, San Diego examined the number of words to which the average American is exposed, per day (Figure 7.2).[42]

The volume of words received via computer is enormous. And although "via computer" includes words read and words heard, in 2008, when the data were collected, most Americans did not have Internet access speed adequate for video content. Most of the words would have been written. These data were collected from adults, and they are now several years old. Still, I think it's reasonable to suggest that kids do an enormous amount of incidental reading on digital platforms, especially via text messages, which this study did not include. So does all this reading make them better readers?

We don't really know, but our theories of reading would predict little benefit. Reading improves comprehension through the acquisition of broader background knowledge and better representations of words, but most of what the average kid reads on screens is not content-rich because

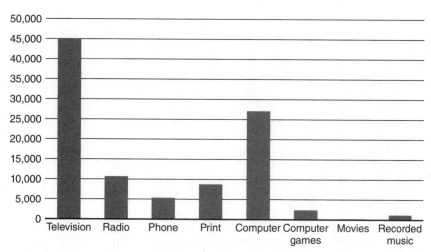

Figure 7.2. Graph of word consumption. These are based on a national sample of adults. Note that the measure is "words," so they might be spoken, sung, or written.
© Anne Carlyle Lindsay

most of it is not ebooks. It's information within games, text messages, social network updates, and the like. But even that sort of reading should (according to theory) have a positive effect on fluency. Practice improves fluency, and the content of what kids read during this practice doesn't matter much. To my knowledge, the relationship between use of digital technologies and the development of fluency has not been investigated.

Texting and Writing

About 90% of teens have smartphones, and of those, 90% text via the messaging service provided by their phone carrier. Many others also use messaging apps like Kik or WhatsApp. A typical teen sends and receives about 30 messages per day.[43] It's difficult to estimate the time devoted to messaging, partly because messages vary in length and complexity, and partly because messaging comes in unpredictable bursts; the time estimate ought to include the time lost by the interruption, but that's hard to calculate.

Observers are usually less concerned with the time spent on texting and more concerned with *textese*—the habit of omitting unnecessary words, capitalization, and punctuation in text messages; for example, typing "b4" instead of "before" or "pix" instead of "pictures." Would frequent use of textese constitute practicing bad habits, and leave the texter less able to use proper spelling and grammar when needed?

Research on this issue has produced some conflicting results, but the best studies (which examine actual texts people send, rather than asking about texting habits) indicate that there could be a problem. Greater use of textese is associated with less successful word reading and spelling. Among college students this relationship is statistically significant, but small.[44] Interestingly, it reverses for younger children;[45] more textese is associated with better spelling and reading. It may be that knowing what can be omitted while still communicating the intended message is a sign of relatively good literacy skills for kids this age (around 10 years old).

None of this research will support causal conclusions—that is, we don't know whether textese causes poor spelling, whether kids who don't spell well are more likely to use textese, or whether some third factor (for example, generally thinking that details are important) is responsible for both. In truth, this matter is likely of decreasing importance. Textese is on the decline. People used textese because it made typing easier, but now messaging systems routinely include autocorrection and text anticipation features, thus reducing the benefit of textese.[46]

THE AGE OF DISTRACTION

In this final section I consider what I'm guessing worries people most about reading and the digital age: that the activities afforded by digital technologies either (1) change our brains so that we can't concentrate long enough to read anything; or (2) consume so much time that there's none left for reading. Let's look at the evidence for each.

Concentration Lost

People probably read ebooks and paper books with the same purpose, namely, a straightforward reading of the prose. That's not how we read material on the Web. There, we are much more likely to scan contents, read snippets, seek a quick summary, and most importantly, get distracted from our purpose by other content. Sure, you scan a paper newspaper, but once you find an article you like, you'll probably read a substantial part of it. Most of us feel that's less true when we read on the Web.

Some observers—including prominent reading researcher MaryAnn Wolf—have suggested that habitual Web reading, characterized by caroming from one topic to another and skimming when one alights, changes one's ability to read deeply.[47] Nick Carr popularized this sinister possibility with the question: "Is Google Making Us Stoopid?"[48] In that article (and in a follow-up book, *The Shallows*), Carr argued that something had happened to his brain.[49] Years of quick pivots in his thinking prompted by Web surfing had left him unable to read a serious novel or long article.

We've all been there. You flick from a document to a website to check a fact. A few minutes later you're three sites away, watching a video of a donkey eating a burrito (and perhaps, in a moment of clarity, asking "what am I doing with my life?"). The consequences of inveterate rapid attention shifts are an actual change in the wiring of the brain that renders us incapable of focusing attention—or so the argument goes. This does sound similar to the mental change many teachers feel they have seen in their students in the last decade or two; they can't pay attention, and teachers feel they must do a song and dance to engage them.[50]

I doubt kids' brains have changed for the worse, and although a formal poll has not been taken, I suspect most cognitive psychologists are in my camp.* First of all, sure, video games and surfing the Web change the brain. So does reading this book, buying gasoline, or seeing a stranger smile. The brain is adaptive, so it's always changing.

Well, if it's adaptive, couldn't that mean that it would adapt to the need for constant shifts in attention, and maybe thereby lose the ability to sustain attention to one thing? I don't think so because the basic architecture of the mind probably can't be completely reshaped. Cognitive systems (vision, attention, memory, problem solving) are too interdependent. If one system changed in a fundamental way—such as attention losing the ability to stay focused on one object—that change would cascade through the entire cognitive system, affecting most or all aspects of thought. I suspect the brain is too conservative in its adaptability for that to happen, and if it had happened, I think the results would be much more obvious. The consequences wouldn't be limited to our interest in reading longer texts; reading comprehension would drop, as would problem-solving ability, math achievement, and a host of higher cognitive functions that depend on attention and working memory.

More important, I don't know of any good evidence that young people are worse at sustaining attention than their parents were at their age. They can sustain attention through a three-hour movie like *Titanic,* just as their parents did. They are capable of reading a novel they enjoy, like *The Perks of Being a Wallflower.* So I doubt that they can't sustain attention. But being *able* to sustain attention is only half of the equation. You also have to deem something worthy of your attention, and that is where I think digital technologies may have their impact. They may change expectations.

---

*Steven Pinker and Roger Schank have both written in this vein. See: Pinker, S. (2010, January). Not at all. Retrieved from http://edge.org/q2010/q10_10.html#pinker. See also: Schank, R. (2010, January). The thinking process hasn't changed in 50,000 years. Retrieved from www.edge.org/response-detail/11519/.

I'm bored. Fix it.

Despite the diversity of activities afforded by digital technologies, I think many have two characteristics in common. Specifically, I think whatever experience the technology offers, you get it immediately—no waiting. Furthermore, producing this experience costs you very little—minimal effort. For example, if you're watching a YouTube video and don't like it, you can switch to another. In fact, the website makes it simple by displaying a list of suggestions. If you get tired of videos, you can check Snapchat. If that's boring, look for something funny on theonion.com. Television has the same characteristics: cable offers a few score of channels, but if nothing appeals, get something from Netflix. When it comes to gaming, the carefully staircased pattern of challenge and reward is often pointed to as essential to a successful gaming experience. If the staircase is too steep, the game fails. Perhaps most important, those who own smartphones have sources of entertainment at all times. There is never a reason to be bored.

The consequence of long-term experience with digital technologies is not an inability to sustain attention. It's impatience with boredom. It's an expectation that I should always have something interesting to listen to, watch, or read, and that creating an interesting experience should require little effort. In Chapter 6, we said that a child's choice to read or not should be seen in context of what else the child might do. The mind-boggling availability of experiences afforded by digital technologies means there is *always* something right at hand that one might do. Unless we're really engrossed, we have the continuous, nagging suspicion: *There's a better way to spend my time than this.* That's why, when a friend sends me a video titled "Dog goes crazy over sprinkler—FUNNY!," I find myself impatient if it's not funny within the first 10 seconds. That's why my nephew checks his phone at red lights, even when he's not expecting any messages. That's why teachers feel they must sing and dance to keep students' attention. We're not distractible. We just have a very low threshold for boredom.

If I'm right, there's good news; the distractibility we're all seeing is addressable. It's not due to long-term changes in the brain that represent a fundamental (and unwanted) overhaul in how attention operates.

It's due to beliefs—beliefs about what is worthy of sustained attention, and about what brings rewarding experiences. Beliefs are difficult to change, true, but the prospect intimidates less than repairing a perhaps permanently damaged brain.

Some people focus less on cognitive changes wrought by digital technologies and more on behavior, specifically the raw amount of time they consume. How can one have time for anything else, including reading? Isn't it *inevitable* that people will read less if they devote more time to things other than reading?

The Displacements

There's no time for reading! This idea is called the *displacement hypothesis*, and though it comes in several varieties, the basic idea is that when a new activity (like browsing the Web) becomes available, it takes the place of something else we typically do (like reading). Evaluating whether that has happened is actually pretty tricky because lots of factors go into our choices of how we spend our time. For example, if you simply ask, "are people browsing the Web when they could be reading?," you're expecting a negative correlation: more Web time goes with less reading, and less Web time goes with more reading. But the wealthier you are, the more leisure time you have, so you can spend more time reading and more time browsing the Web. Thus, even if Web browsing does bite into reading time, we may not see the data pattern we expect, simply because both activities are facilitated by free time.

Researchers in the 1950s who wanted to study the impact of television tackled this problem as follows.[51,52] They would find a community that did not yet have access to television, but would get it soon. Then they asked people to record their daily activities, and they examined whether reading and listening to the radio declined once television became available. The data showed that both reading and radio use dropped, but not uniformly. People read less light fiction (as offered by magazines like *Colliers* and the *Saturday Evening Post*), but they still read newspapers. As for radio, evening programs suffered more than daytime programs. This pattern of data led to the *functional equivalence* hypothesis: an activity is most likely to displace another if it serves the same function. In its early days, television offered light drama so audiences turned away from magazine fiction, but people thought television news was thin, so they continued to read newspapers. And families began to gather in the evening to watch television programs together, as they had used to gather around the radio. But during the day people had been more likely to listen to the radio on their own, and they continued to do so.

So has reading been displaced by digital technologies? Many researchers have investigated this question, and on balance, the answer seems to be "No." Unfortunately, most studies could not use the technique of waiting until a technology was poised for introduction into a community because availability has always been uneven, based on personal choice. (Even we restrict "technology" to mean the Internet, "access" meant buying a modem.) So researchers have examined simple correlations between time spent on the Internet and time spent reading, controlling for the other variables (like overall amount of leisure time) as well as could be done. The correlation in most studies seems to be nil or slightly positive. (That is, in the direction opposite that predicted by the displacement hypothesis.) Research on television viewing does indicate that heavy viewing (more than four hours each day) is associated with less reading.[53,54]

Given the enormous amount of time devoted to digital technologies—recent estimates for teen use are eight hours each day or more—how is it possible that they don't shove reading aside? One answer is that most people already read so little there wasn't much to be shoved aside when new technologies became available. In 1999, when they had no access to digital technologies (outside of gaming), children (ages eight to 18) spent an average of just 21 minutes per day reading books.[55] In 2009, when access was much greater, they averaged 25 minutes.[41] In 2015, it was about 28 minutes.[34]

Most people don't read much, but most people were not readers before the digital revolution either. And for people who were, the functional equivalence idea may be relevant. Reading provides a sort of pleasure that digital technologies don't replace. Notably, magazine and newspaper reading did drop during the 2000s, arguably because that sort of reading can be done on the Internet; indeed, virtually all magazines and newspapers have some presence on the Web.

So I'm offering a mixed message. Good news: I doubt digital activities are "changing kids' brains" in a scary way, and I don't think they soak up reading time. Bad news: I think they are leading kids to expect full-time amusement, and for some kids, reading time isn't soaked up only because there's little to soak up. It's already dry as a sun-bleached Saltine.

Summary and Implications

Summary

- Software designed to teach reading has been variable in its success. Some applications work well, others do not. Advantages that software could theoretically bring to the teaching of reading have been harder to exploit than anticipated.
- There is a small cost to reading on a screen compared to reading on paper. That cost will likely decline and may well disappear in the coming years, as engineers find better ways to design ebooks.
- Students can access information at unprecedented scale and with unprecedented speed, but there is little evidence that this access is influencing reading or learning.
- There's also little evidence that students today cannot concentrate as they used to. I speculate that there may have been a change in children's threshold for boredom.
- There's also little evidence that digital gadgets have displaced reading in students' lives, but that may mostly be because students have never read much.

Implications

- Although the comprehension cost associated with e-textbooks is modest, it's large enough that most students don't want to use them. Schools and districts should be cautious in adopting them until they improve.
- "Digital literacy" (defined as learning how to navigate common applications) seems to be mostly overblown. Common applications and platforms are written to be easy to use, and most students gain familiarity with them at home. The exception is disadvantaged students who do not have the access to digital technologies that wealthier student do. For these students, the idea of gaining this sort of digital literacy at school makes sense.

(*continued*)

- Although there's little evidence that digital amusements are displacing reading, I still favor limits on screen time. I believe the lack of evidence is due to what statisticians call a "floor effect"; reading didn't decline with the introduction of digital technologies because it couldn't go much lower. Limiting screen time will not only make time for reading, it removes a choice from the environment for part of a kid's day, and that may make reading the most attractive choice available, as described in Chapter 6.

- If I'm right about children today having a lower threshold for boredom than children a generation ago, then limits on screen time might help. If children are more often left to entertain themselves, we would expect they will not only learn to do so, they will learn that sometimes one is bored for a while before there's a payoff. Sometimes a book starts slowly, but builds in excitement. A flower or an ant hill initially may seem mundane, but sustained attention reveals more there than was first appreciated. There are, so far as I know, no data on whether this supposition is true.

Discussion Questions

1. Many parents I speak to express a sense of helplessness about screen time. They feel the digital revolution makes technology ubiquitous and they cannot keep their children removed from it. What would you say to such a parent?

2. As noted, students are often too trusting of information they find on the Web. Researchers are trying to develop training regimens to help students learn the skills to evaluate what they find, but progress has been halting. What should parents and teachers do? Limit the sites that students visit for research to a list of trusted sources? Let students roam the Web, but follow them and provide feedback?

3. Data indicate that children spend most of their digital time on activities we would not say are especially enriching: Instagramming selfies, shooting zombies in virtual worlds, and so on. Most parents would prefer they were getting some fresh air, or seeing friends face to face. The obvious strategy is to limit screen time. But doing so surrenders the possibility that children will take advantage of other great opportunities a computer affords to learn, or to build, or to meaningfully connect with others. Is there not a strategy by which we can nudge students toward doing more of the digital activities we think are enriching, rather than just cutting them off entirely?

4. I suggested that children today read more than ever, but the big increase comes from texting, reading within computer games, and the like. I noted that this type of reading is unlikely to improve comprehension, but could improve fluency. There's no data on whether or not it would actually work, but would you be willing to take the plunge? Should increased access to text-heavy gaming be a routine part of reading instruction (presumably used as children are developing fluency)?

5. Have you ever cut yourself off from digital devices for a significant period of time, say, 48 hours or more? How did you react? Did you feel differently in the 48th hour compared to the first hour? Would this be a useful exercise for students?

REFERENCES

1. Cheung, A. C. K., & Slavin, R. E. (2011, May). The effectiveness of education technology for enhancing reading achievement: A meta-analysis, 1–48. Downloaded November 15, 2015, from http://files.eric.ed.gov/fulltext/ED527572.pdf.

2. Hattie, J. (2009). *Visible learning.* London: Routledge.

3. Tamim, R. M., Bernard, R. M., Borokhovski, E., Abrami, P. C., & Schmid, R. F. (2011). What forty years of research says about the impact of technology on learning: A second-order meta-analysis and validation study. *Review of Educational Research, 81*(1), 4–28. http://doi.org/10.3102/0034654310393361.

4. Mashburn, A. J., Pianta, R. C., Hamre, B. K., Downer, J. T., Barbarin, O. A., Bryant, D., Burchinal, M., Early, D. M., & Howes, C. (2008). Measures of classroom quality in prekindergarten and children's development of academic, language, and social skills. *Child Development, 79*(3), 732–49. http://doi.org/10.1111/j.1467-8624.2008.01154.x.

5. Korat, O., & Shamir, A. (2007). Electronic books versus adult readers: Effects on children's emergent literacy as a function of social class. *Journal of Computer Assisted Learning, 23*(3), 248–259. http://doi.org/10.1111/j.1365-2729.2006.00213.x.

6. Segal-Drori, O., Korat, O., Shamir, A., & Klein, P. S. (2009). Reading electronic and printed books with and without adult instruction: Effects on emergent reading. *Reading and Writing, 23*(8), 913–930. http://doi.org/10.1007/s11145-009-9182-x.

7. de Jong, M. T., & Bus, A. G. (2002). Quality of book-reading matters for emergent readers: An experiment with the same book in a regular or electronic format. *Journal of Educational Psychology, 94*(1), 145–155. http://doi.org/10.1037//0022-0663.94.1.145.

8. Matthew, K. (1997). A comparison of the influence of interactive CD-ROM storybooks and traditional print storybooks on reading comprehension. *Journal of Research on Computing in Education, 29*, 1–13.

9. Trushell, J., Burrell, C., & Maitland, A. (2001). Year 5 pupils reading an "interactive storybook" on CD-ROM: Losing the plot? *British Journal of Educational Technology, 32*(4), 389–401.

10. de Jong, M. T., & Bus, A. G. (2004). The efficacy of electronic books in fostering kindergarten children's emergent story understanding. *Reading Research Quarterly, 39*(4), 378–393. http://doi.org/10.1598/RRQ.39.4.2.

11. Korat, O., & Or, T. (2010). How new technology influences parent–child interaction: The case of e-book reading. *First Language, 30*(2), 139–154. http://doi.org/10.1177/0142723709359242.

12. Korat, O., & Shamir, A. (2007). Electronic books versus adult readers: Effects on children's emergent literacy as a function of social class. *Journal of Computer Assisted Learning, 23*(3), 248–259. http://doi.org/10.1111/j.1365-2729.2006.00213.x.

13. Parish-Morris, J., Mahajan, N., Hirsh-Pasek, K., & Golinkoff, R. M. (2011). Once upon a time: Parent–child dialogue and storybook reading in the electronic era. *Mind, Brain, and Education, 7*(3), 200–211.

14. Connell, C., Bayliss, L., & Farmer, W. (2012). Effects of ebook readers and tablet computers on reading comprehension. *International Journal of Instructional Media, 39*(2), 131–139.

15. Daniel, D. B., & Woody, W. D. (2013). E-textbooks at what cost? Performance and use of electronic v. print texts. *Computers & Education, 62*, 18–23. http://doi.org/10.1016/j.compedu.2012.10.016.

16. Jeong, H. (2012). A comparison of the influence of electronic books and paper books on reading comprehension, eye fatigue, and perception. *The Electronic Library, 30*(3), 390–408. http://doi.org/https://doi.org/10.1108/09564230910978511.

17. Ackerman, R., & Lauterman, T. (2012). Taking reading comprehension exams on screen or on paper? A metacognitive analysis of learning texts under time pressure. *Computers in Human Behavior, 28*(5), 1816–1828. http://doi.org/10.1016/j.chb.2012.04.023.

18. Kretzschmar, F., Pleimling, D., Hosemann, J., Füssel, S., Bornkessel-Schlesewsky, I., et al. (2013). Subjective impressions do not mirror online reading effort: Concurrent EEG-eyetracking evidence from the reading of books and digital media. *PLoS ONE 8*(2): e56178. doi: 10.1371/journal.pone.0056178.

19. Sanchez, C. A., & Wiley, J. (2009). To scroll or not to scroll: Scrolling, working memory capacity, and comprehending complex texts. *Human Factors: The Journal of the Human Factors and Ergonomics Society, 51*(5), 730–738. http://doi.org/10.1177/0018720809352788.

20. DeStefano, D., & LeFevre, J.-A. (2007). Cognitive load in hypertext reading: A review. *Computers in Human Behavior, 23*(3), 1616–1641. http://doi.org/10.1016/j.chb.2005.08.012.

21. Bennett, S., Maton, K., & Kervin, L. (2008). The "digital natives" debate: A critical review of the evidence. *British Journal of Educational Technology, 39*(5), 775–786. http://doi.org/10.1111/j.1467-8535.2007.00793.x.

22. Margaryan, A., Littlejohn, A., & Vojt, G. (2011). Are digital natives a myth or reality? University students' use of digital technologies. *Computers & Education, 56*(2), 429–440. http://doi.org/10.1016/j.compedu.2010.09.004.

23. Leu, D. J., & Castek, J. (2006). What skills and strategies are characteristic of accomplished adolescent users of the Internet? In *Annual Conference of the American Educational Research Association.* San Francisco, CA.

24. Barzilai, S., & Zohar, A. (2012). Epistemic thinking in action: Evaluating and integrating online sources. *Cognition and Instruction, 30*(1), 39–85. http://doi.org/10.1080/07370008.2011.636495.

25. Killi, C., Laurinen, L., & Marttunen, M. (2008). Students evaluating Internet sources: From versatile evaluators to uncritical readers. *Journal of Educational Computing Research, 39*(1), 75–95.

26. Kuiper, E., Volman, M., & Terwel, J. (2008). Integrating critical Web skills and content knowledge: Development and evaluation of a 5th grade educational program. *Computers in Human Behavior, 24*(3), 666–692. http://doi.org/10.1016/j.chb.2007.01.022.

27. Macedo-Rouet, M., Braasch, J. L. G., Britt, M. A., & Rouet, J. F. (2013). Teaching fourth and fifth graders to evaluate information sources during text comprehension. *Cognition and Instruction*, *31*(2), 204–226. http://doi.org/10.1080/07370008.2013.769995.

28. Wineburg, S., & McGrew, S. (2016, November 1). Why students can't Google their way to the truth. *Education Week*. http://www.edweek.org/ew/articles/2016/11/02/why-students-cant-google-their-way-to.html

29. Braasch, J. L. G., Bråten, I., Strømsø, H. I., Anmarkrud, Ø., & Ferguson, L. E. (2013). Promoting secondary school students' evaluation of source features of multiple documents. *Contemporary Educational Psychology*, *38*(3), 180–195. http://doi.org/10.1016/j.cedpsych.2013.03.003.

30. Mason, L., Junyent, A. A., & Tornatora, M. C. (2014). Epistemic evaluation and comprehension of Web-source information on controversial science-related topics: Effects of a short-term instructional intervention. *Computers and Education*, *76*, 143–157. http://doi.org/10.1016/j.compedu.2014.03.016.

31. Walraven, A., Brand-Gruwel, S., & Boshuizen, H. P. A. (2010). Fostering transfer of websearchers' evaluation skills: A field test of two transfer theories. *Computers in Human Behavior*, *26*(4), 716–728. http://doi.org/10.1016/j.chb.2010.01.008.

32. Zhang, S., & Duke, N. K. (2011). The impact of instruction in the WWWDOT framework on students' disposition and ability to evaluate Web sites as sources of information. *The Elementary School Journal*, *112*(1), 132–154. http://doi.org/10.1086/660687.

33. Nusername. (2013). AskReddit. Retrieved from User "nusernamed" on the entertainment site Reddit: www.reddit.com/r/AskReddit/comments/15yaap/if_someone_from_the_1950s_suddenly_appeared_today/c7qyp13?context=5#c7qyp13/.

34. Rideout, V. J. (2015). *The common sense census: Media use by tweens and teens*. San Francisco: Common Sense Media.

35. Anderson, D. R., Huston, A. C., Schmitt, K. L., Linebarger, D. L., Wright, J. C., & Larson, R. (2001). Childhood television viewing and adolescent behavior: The recontact study. *Monographs of the Society for Research in Child Development*, *66*(1), 1–154.

36. DeLoache, J. S., Chiong, C., Sherman, K., Islam, N., Vanderborght, M., Troseth, G. L., Strouse, G. A. & O'Doherty, K. (2010). Do babies learn from baby media? *Psychological Science, 21*(11), 1570–4. http://doi.org/10.1177/0956797610384145.

37. Richert, R., Robb, M. B., Fender, J. G., & Wartella, E. (2010). Word learning from baby videos. *Archives of Pediatrics & Adolescent Medicine, 164*(5), 432–7. http://doi.org/10.1001/archpediatrics.2010.24.

38. Deocampo, J. A., & Hudson, J. A. (2005). When seeing is not believing: Two-year-olds' Use of video representations to find a hidden toy. *Journal of Cognition and Development, 6*(2), 229–258. http://doi.org/10.1207/s15327647jcd0602_4.

39. Troseth, G. L., Saylor, M. M., & Archer, A. H. (2006). Young children's use of video as a source of socially relevant information. *Child Development, 77*(3), 786–99. http://doi.org/10.1111/j.1467-8624.2006.00903.x.

40. Guernsey, L. (2007). What's educational about "educational" TV. In *Into the minds of babes: How screen time affects children from birth to age five* (pp. 113–134). New York: Basic Books.

41. Rideout, V. J., Foehr, U. G., & Roberst, D. F. (2010). *Generation M2: Media in the lives of 8- to 18-year-olds*. Menlo Park, CA: Henry J. Kaiser Family Foundation.

42. Bohn, R. E., & Short, J. E. (2009). *How much information? 2009 report on American consumers*. San Diego: Global Information Center, University of California.

43. Lenhart, A. (2015). *Teens, social media & technology overview 2015*. Washington, DC: Pew Research Center.

44. Drouin, M., & Driver, B. (2012). Texting, textese and literacy abilities: A naturalistic study. *Journal of Research in Reading, 37*(3), 250–267. http://doi.org/10.1111/j.1467-9817.2012.01532.x.

45. van Dijk, C. N., van Witteloostuijn, M., Vasić, N., Avrutin, S., & Blom, E. (2016). The influence of texting language on grammar and executive functions in primary school children. *Plos ONE, 11*(3), 1–22. http://doi.org/10.1371/journal.pone.0152409.

46. Ouellette, G., & Michaud, M. (2016). Generation text: Relations among undergraduates' use of text messaging, textese, and language and literacy skills. *Canadian Journal of Behavioural Science / Revue Canadienne Des Sciences Du Comportement*, *48*(3), 217–221. http://doi.org/10.1037/cbs0000046.

47. Rosenwald, M. S. (2014, April 6). Serious reading takes a hit from online scanning and skimming, researchers say. *Washington Post*. Retrieved from www.washingtonpost.com/local/serious-reading-takes-a-hit-from-online-scanning-and-skimming-researchers-say/2014/04/06/088028d2-b5d2-11e3-b899-20667de76985_story.html/.

48. Carr, N. (2008). Is Google making us stupid? *Yearbook of the National Society for the Study of Education*, *107*(2), 89–94. http://doi.org/10.1111/j.1744-7984.2008.00172.x

49. Carr, N. (2011). *The shallows: What the Internet is doing to our brains*. New York: Norton.

50. Richtel, M. (2012, November 1). For better and for worse, technology use alters learning styles, teachers say. *New York Times*, A18.

51. Coffin, T. E. (1955). Television's impact on society. *American Psychologist*, *10*(10), 630–641. http://doi.org/10.1037/h0039880.

52. Szalai, A. (1972). *The use of time: Daily activities of urban and suburban populations in twelve countries*. Den Haag, Netherlands: Moton.

53. Koolstra, C. M., & van der Voort, T. H. A. (1996). Longitudinal effects of television on children's leisure-time reading: A test of three explanatory models. *Human Communication Research*, *23*(1), 4–35.

54. Neuman, S. B. (1988). The displacement effect: Assessing the relation between television viewing and reading performance. *Reading Research Quarterly*, *23*(4), 414–440.

55. Roberts, D. F., Foehr, U. G., Rideout, V. J., Brodie, M. (1999). Kids and Media at the New Millennium. Menlo Park, CA: Kaiser Family Foundation. Available at http://kff.org/hivaids/report/kids-media-the-new-millennium/.

CONCLUSION

The Utility of Theory

At the start of this book I set the task of explaining the mental processes required to read a brief passage from *Billy Bathgate*. We've seen how my mind organized black marks on a white screen into letters and words, and how the correct meaning of the homonym "right" was accessed in my memory. We've examined how my comprehension of the passage required very local and very global thinking at the same time: local such as the deduction that Berman was describing the combination to a safe; global in that my immediate reaction to Berman's death was determined by my view of his character, an amalgamation of his actions throughout the novel. We've considered why I and some others on that airplane chose to read when we might have done something else, and we've surveyed evidence showing that my experience was no more than a little different because I read from a screen rather than paper. I hope you have found this account interesting. Here, at the book's end, I'd like to reconsider its utility for practitioners and policymakers.

PRACTITIONERS

You'll recall that I commented on the relationship of basic science and education in the Introduction, and I took a fairly cautious stance. Basic science differs fundamentally from the enterprise of educating children. Scientists seek to describe the world as it is. Indeed, that's the goal I set in the Introduction, to describe the mind as an experienced reader reads. Educators, in contrast, don't seek to describe what happens, but to *make* something happen. Seeking to make a reader out of a child who does not read is an educational goal, not a scientific one.

This difference in goals drives differences in the practices of basic scientists and those who seek to make practical use of science.[1] Here I'll focus on just one. Scientists must simplify. When we study complex systems, we start with simple cases. Galileo didn't try to describe how a leaf falls from a tree in a windstorm; he started with a sphere rolling down an inclined plane. Likewise, scientists usually study reading in simple situations, for example, a child reading a short text with no distractions. But children don't always read short texts in quiet environments. That difference limits the implications of research in two ways.

First, we must ask if the research finding will hold in a different environment. Classrooms offer more distractions than a laboratory environment, for example. Then too, the child may be less motivated to read in a classroom, compared to a laboratory situation where she agreed to participate in the study, and so feels she ought to give it her best. Do these differences matter materially to the findings?

There's a second problem. Scientific findings often apply to just part of the complex process of reading. The implication you draw to address one part of reading might have a negative impact on some *other* cognitive process. For example, I might learn that background knowledge is important to reading comprehension and conclude that students ought to memorize long lists of facts, so as to acquire background knowledge. That sounds like it would be terrible for motivation. (Lists are also a terrible way to learn new facts, by the way.)

So a basic scientist like me faces a dilemma. On the one hand, we know that the applications of our knowledge are limited. On the other hand, we also know that practitioners are confronted with snake-oil salesmen at every turn, who are only too happy to claim scientific backing for their products. If scientists won't step forward and say, "we think research supports *this* practice," then we yield the stage to the mountebanks.

My choice in this dilemma is plain—I ended each chapter with a section labeled "Implications." You'll note that the implications I drew were usually accompanied by research citations. So it wasn't the case that I just looked at the science-of-reading findings and said, "Huh. You know what I bet would work?" I was tying theory to other research in which people had actually tested a hypothesis, or tried an intervention in a classroom.

But if that's true, how is the basic science helping? For example, in Chapter 4 I concluded (based on laboratory studies) that morphology is an important cue to help readers deduce the meaning of unfamiliar words, and then I cited studies showing that teaching morphology to kids helps them work out the definition of unfamiliar words. Why did I need the first bit at all? If teaching morphology helps, then it helps, whatever the scientific theory of reading says. What's gained by going into the theory? Why not just stick with the practice?

To get some purchase on this challenge, let's quickly review the conclusions I drew (Table C.1).

Table C.1. Conclusions drawn.

Mental process or structure	What scientific research indicates is needed	Implications for practical action
Decoding by sound	Automatic letter-sound translation.	Reading. Phonemic awareness activities. Hearing children's literature. Explicit phonics instruction.
Decoding by sight	Lots of orthographic representations of words and letter "clumps."	Reading practice. (Self-teaching hypothesis.) Spelling instruction.
Broad vocabulary	Familiarity with lots of word meanings.	Reading. Hanging around people who use rare words. Explicit vocabulary instruction. Instruction in morphology. Instruction in using context to deduce word meaning.

(continued)

Table C.1.   (*Cont'd*)

Mental process or structure	What scientific research indicates is needed	Implications for practical action
Deep vocabulary	Efficient representation and interconnection of sound, spelling, and meaning. Connection of meaning with other, related word meanings.	Reading.
Comprehension	Broad background knowledge to aid inferences and construction of the situation model.	Reading. Other activities that promote background knowledge, e.g., watching serious television programming, conversations with knowledgeable people. Exposure to a school curriculum that is knowledge-rich and carefully sequenced. Instruction in the need to make inferences.
Attitudes toward reading	Positive emotional attitudes.	Positive reading experiences. Association of reading with things the child already likes.

Table C.1. *(Cont'd)*

Mental process or structure	What scientific research indicates is needed	Implications for practical action
Motivation to read	Evaluation that reading is worthy, and that reading will be successful.	Many factors—most important are previous reading experiences which lead you to conclude that reading is valuable, and that you usually succeed in reading tasks. Practical utility or social utility of a particular reading task.
Choosing to read	An environment that facilitates reading.	An environment in which choosing to read is easy, and in which reading is the most attractive choice. Very easy access to books.
Reading self-image	The child sees herself as a reader.	Living in a house where reading is value: reading is modeled as is enjoyment of learning new things.

Reviewing the actions that promote reading (according to our cognitive analysis) shows that basic science is useful in that it generates intervention ideas we might not have come up with otherwise. For example, research highlights the role of spelling instruction in reading, the importance of wordplay for young children, and the importance of parents emphasizing not just reading, but openness to new intellectual experiences. Research also helps refine some ideas we might have intuited, but used too bluntly. For example, it seems obvious that easy access to books might encourage kids to read; it will help more if kids are virtually tripping over books.

Research has also revealed the importance of timing. Parents who promote reading at home do so in advance of when these actions actually pay off, even though that's probably not by design. Think about it this way. The importance of different components of reading becomes apparent at different times. The importance of decoding is obvious in Kindergarten, when children are first taught letters and their associated sounds. Kids from reading homes will be prepared for decoding via months or years of activities that promote phonemic awareness, like read-alouds from children's books and chanting nursery rhymes.

The importance of comprehension becomes obvious around fourth grade. That's when most children can decode fairly fluently, and the expectations for comprehension greatly increase. Kids from reading homes will be prepared with rich background knowledge to help make inferences in these more challenging texts; that knowledge (and rich vocabulary) was building for years, but the contribution to reading remained hidden while children were learning to decode.

The importance of motivation becomes apparent in middle school, when time pressure mounts and leisure reading tends to get dropped. Kids from reading homes will have been thinking of themselves as readers for many years, and reading will be more likely to retain a place in their lives. Thus research has not only suggested ways to promote reading, it has clarified when problems are likely to arise, and highlighted the importance of taking steps to prevent problems far in advance of their emergence.

We might also question the necessity of the reading model we've laboriously built over the course of this book (Figure C.1). If we know what to do to guide action in the classroom or home, and we know the basic science behind the action, why fool with orthographic representations, idea-webs, situation models, and all the rest?

The model does two things. First, it provides a deeper level of understanding as to why classroom practices are effective (or not). For example, at the shallowest level of understanding, we might simply know that children who play phonemic awareness games learn to read more easily than

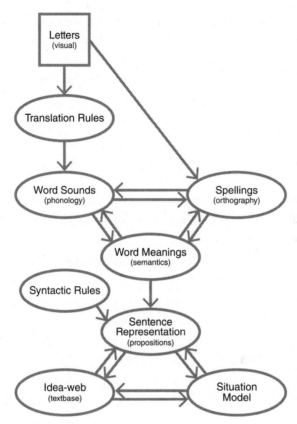

Figure C.1. Model of reading.

those who don't. At a deeper level of understanding, we can explicate the role of phonemic awareness in the learning of the alphabetic principle and letter-sound pairings. But it's still more satisfying to have that knowledge coordinated with knowledge about the other components of reading. Knowing what to do and knowing there's research behind it is like comprehending the story about Carol Harris without knowing it's really about Helen Keller. There's "why" and then there's "big-picture why." The latter makes things hang together and gives you insight into some details that you would otherwise miss.

If we think the model of reading that we've built over the course of this book as comparable to a situation model in reading, we see utility beyond the satisfaction of knowing why things work. A situation model affords better inferences. If an educator has a model of reading in her head, like a complex clockwork, she can predict what will happen to the system as a whole when a part of it changes in some way. Having this model in memory can serve as a summary of important mental processes and their relationships, to be called on when thinking through instructional decisions and anticipating their outcomes.

POLICYMAKERS

And what about policymakers? Do cognitive psychologists have anything of value to offer them? Cognitive psychologists are (or ought to be) chary indeed of commenting on policy. We understand something about the individual mind, and that knowledge becomes less applicable when the mind is situated in a classroom with 30 other minds. How relevant is that knowledge to principles of action by governments and other organizations that influence people from a distance? Not very. Still, if education policymakers set out to influence reading in schools and homes, knowing something about the reading mind might help. So here I set out a handful of very big-picture principles of reading I think ought to interest policymakers, one or two for each of the three abilities on which successful reading depends: fluent decoding, comprehension, and motivation. Reading is analogous to a three-legged stool, in that if any one of these abilities is missing, reading falls on its behind.

Children are most likely to grow into fluent decoders if they have received explicit instruction in the letter-sound code (that is, phonics instruction) and if they practice reading. The idea of practice—reading helps you become a better reader—has not been controversial. Phonics instruction has been, but there are few topics in educational psychology that have been more thoroughly studied, and for which the data are clearer.[2] For educators on the ground, the picture might be foggier, because the amount of explicit phonics instruction that children need varies; it depends on their phonemic awareness coming into school, the quality and quantity of oral language to which they've been exposed at home, and other factors. But it's clear that virtually all kids benefit from explicit instruction in the code, and that such instruction is crucial for children who come to school with weak oral language skills.

In Chapters 4 and 5, we saw that comprehension occurs at four levels: individual words (that is, depth and breadth of vocabulary), understanding sentences, connecting sentences, and deriving a situation model. We also saw that for each level there are formal rules we can describe about how to make meaning: ways to use context to understand an unknown vocabulary word, syntactic rules that describe roles that words play in a sentence, principles by which sentences are connected, and features of texts that guide the construction of a situation model. We also saw that these content-free mechanisms are not a complete description of comprehension, and that knowing something about the topic of a text has a big impact on comprehension at every level.

Policymakers should bear in mind the importance of background knowledge to reading comprehension. But it's not enough to say, "It's good to know things." That principle suggests a lots-of-stuff curriculum, and that's insufficient. The curriculum must be sequenced, planned. If student comprehension depends on some familiarity with the topic, then educators must select texts that have the right balance of familiar and new content, so that students are continually exposed to and challenged by new ideas, but not overwhelmed. Teachers already do that, of course, but the importance of background knowledge to reading suggests that this planning must span years. Another reason that's true was not discussed in this book, but it's rooted in an intuitive feature of human memory. People forget. If you want students to remember content, it needs to be repeated in one form or another, across years. That requires curricular planning across years.

The third leg of the stool is motivation. I include motivation because a glance at Table C.1 shows that "reading" is often among the activities that leads to reading improvement. That's coupled with research discussed earlier in the book showing that excellent readers read a lot, and although the relationship between "reading excellence" and "reading" is doubtless reciprocal (that is, people choose to read more if they are good at it), at least part of the way they got to be good readers is by reading. Hence, reading motivation matters.

Two factors in motivation could be considered "big ideas," ones that policymakers should know about. First, reading attitudes are emotional. Trying to persuade children to read with rational appeals—it's the best way to succeed in school, for example—simply won't work. They are not ineffective because kids may have a long history of doubting that school is valuable to them, although they may, and that's important for other reasons. They are ineffective because reading attitudes are emotional, not cognitive. Persuading kids reading makes you smart is comparable to persuading me that broccoli is healthy. I believe you, but I still won't eat it. It's the emotional tenor of children's reading experiences that ought to matter to adults.

That's challenging, because getting kids to have a positive reading experience requires that they do some reading in the first place. Still, other methods of persuasion may help, by tying reading to things that students value *now*, rather than appealing to what we hope they will value in the future. For example, researchers were able to improve teen eating habits by making rejection of junk food seem an act of rebellion, of resisting manipulation by corporate authority.[3] Young men in Texas were persuaded to think differently about littering after an advertising campaign framed the improper disposal of trash as "messing with Texas."[4] There's no reason to think that a similarly innovative method could not be found to foster positive reading attitudes.

In addition to considering the nature of reading attitudes, policymakers must recognize that liking reading is not enough. Leisure reading is a choice, which means children must like reading more than whatever else is available to them at the time. Hence, we cannot think about reading in isolation. We must think about the child's entire environment, all of the choices that are available, and how to shape that environment so that reading is most likely to be the activity selected.

One final observation on the application of basic scientific principles to education policy for reading. I offered basic principles that apply to fluent decoding, comprehension, and motivation—principles that I suggested be borne in mind. But these suggestions presuppose a particular goal, a particular type of reader one is hoping children will grow into. My assumption has been that the goal is the intelligent layreader; someone who can pick up the *Washington Post* or *Scientific American* and read almost any article with understanding. Furthermore, it's the type of reader who might *want* to read magazines and newspapers in his or her spare time.

Are there not adults who are "good readers" by a different definition? Suppose someone were an engineer, never read in her spare time, didn't have broad background knowledge, and so probably couldn't read everything in the *Washington Post* with good comprehension. But this engineer has deep background knowledge in her domain of expertise and so can easily read technical material related to work, and is happy enough with her reading. I offer this example to highlight that education is a goal-driven enterprise, and before one starts discussing how to apply findings from basic science to make education better, one needs to be clear about what "better" means. And science will be silent on that matter. The goals one sets for educating children reflect personal and community values, not scientific truths.

ON THE BEAUTY OF THEORY

Americans generally think that science has practical utility and that funding scientific research is a good idea.[5] The notion that public investment in basic science brings benefits to society has been part of our collective consciousness since World War II. Before that, government expenditure on science was trivial. Elected officials assumed that industries should fund scientific research, should they need it. High-profile scientific successes during World War II, including the development of the atom bomb and the production of antibiotics at scale, changed that. Policymakers came to believe that investments in basic science brought long-term benefits to society. Economists verified that the investment in basic science more than paid for itself in increased economic productivity.[6]

When the occasion arises, I'm quick to point out the successes of my own field in making life better. Cognitive psychologists can help people learn things more efficiently,[7] they can make software and other products easier to use,[8] they can make athletes more mentally tough,[9] they can help people make better financial decisions,[10] and they can even help people create better PowerPoint presentations.[11] And I think we can help children develop into great readers. Naturally, there's satisfaction in the thought that the work you do might in some way contribute to public good.

But in truth, these altruistic concerns played a small part in my decision to make psychology my life's work, and selfish thoughts loomed large. I simply find it fascinating. Upon my first exposure to the subject (during my freshman year of college), I was dumbstruck by the fact that most thought is unconscious. Not furtive lust for your mother as envisioned by Freud, or wily manipulations of your buying behavior as advertisers naively hope for, but the bulk of what the mind is set up to do: seeing, moving your body, using language. In each case we are aware of the result of thought—what we see, how we move—but not the mental computations behind it. Some testimony to their complexity is that it required a book to explicate just 10 seconds worth of just one behavior: my reading that brief passage of *Billy Bathgate*.

Thirty-five years later, I still find the explication of these abilities fascinating. I hope I have conveyed some of that feeling. My fondest hope for this book was that the contents not only would be useful, but that you would, in the words of the epigraph, "gasp not only at what you read but at the miracle of its being readable."

References

1. For a more extended discussion, see Willingham, D. T. (2012). *When can you trust the experts?* San Francisco, CA: Jossey-Bass.

2. National Reading Panel (US), National Institute of Child Health, & Human Development (US). (2000). Report of the National Reading Panel: Teaching children to read: An evidence-based assessment of the scientific research literature on reading and its implications for reading instruction: Reports of the subgroups. Washington, DC: National Institute of Child Health and Human Development, National Institutes of Health.

3. Bryan, C. J., Yeager, D. S., Hinojosa, C. P., Chabot, A., Bergen, H., Kawamura, M., & Steubing, F. (2016). Harnessing adolescent values to motivate healthier eating. *Proceedings of the National Academy of Sciences, 113*(39), 10830–10835.

4. Thaler, R. H., & C. R. Sunstein. (2008). *Nudge: Improving decisions about health, wealth and happiness.* New Haven: Yale University Press.

5. National Science Board. (2014). *Science and engineering indicators 2014.* Chapter 7, "Science and technology: Public attitudes and understanding." Arlington, VA: National Science Foundation (NSB 10-01). Retrieved from www.nsf.gov/statistics/seind14/index.cfm/chapter-7/c7h.htm/.

6. Committee on Prospering in the Global Economy of the 21st Century. (2007). *Rising above the gathering storm: Energizing and employing America for a brighter economic future.* Washington, DC: National Academies Press.

7. Brown, P. C., Roediger, H. L. III, & McDaniel, M. A. (2014). *Make it stick.* Cambridge, MA: Harvard University Press.

8. Norman, D. (2013). *The design of everyday things.* New York: Basic Books.

9. Beilock, S. (2010). *Choke: What the secrets of the brain reveal about getting it right when you have to.* New York: Free Press.

10. Kahneman, D. (2011). *Thinking, Fast and slow.* New York: Basic Books.

WORKS CITED

Introduction

Doctorow, E. L. (1989). *Billy Bathgate.* New York: Harper & Row.

Liversedge, S. P., White, S. J., Findlay, J. M., & Rayner, K. (2006). Binocular coordination of eye movements during reading. *Vision Research, 46*(15), 2363–2374.

Rayner, K., Pollatsek, A., Ashby, J. & Clifton, C. (2012). *The psychology of reading.* New York: Psychology Press.

Willingham, D. T. (2012). *When can you trust the experts?* San Francisco: Jossey-Bass.

Chapter 1

Bell, L. C., & Perfetti, C. A. (1994). Reading skill: Some adult comparisons. *Journal of Educational Psychology, 86*(2), 244–255.

Dick, F., Bates, E., Wulfeck, B., Utman, J. A., Dronkers, N., & Gernsbacher, M. A. (2001). Language deficits, localization, and grammar: Evidence for a distributive model of language breakdown in aphasic patients and neurologically intact individuals. *Psychological Review, 108*(4), 759–788.

Gernsbacher, M. A., Varner, K. R., & Faust, M. E. (1990). Investigating differences in general comprehension skill. *Journal of Experimental Psychology: Learning, Memory, and Cognition, 16*(3), 430–445.

Herodotus. *The histories.* Available at http://perseus.uchicago.edu/perseus-cgi/citequery3.pl?dbname=GreekFeb2011&query=Hdt.%204.131.2&getid=1/.

Marr, D. (1982). *Vision.* New York: Freeman.

National Institute of Child Health and Human. (2000). National Reading Panel. Teaching children to read: An evidence-based assessment of the scientific research literature on reading and its implications for reading instruction. Report of the subgroups. Washington, DC. Retrieved from www.nichd.nih.gov/research/supported/Pages/nrp.aspx/.

Perfetti, C. A. (2003). The universal grammar of reading. *Scientific Studies of Reading, 7*(1), 3–24. http://doi.org/10.1207/S1532799XSSR0701_02.

"Review of Kavanagh, a Tale by Henry Wadsworth Longfellow." (1849, July). *The North American Review, 69*(144), 207.

Robinson, A. (2007). *The story of writing* (2nd ed.). London: Thames & Hudson.

Schmandt-Besserat, D., & Erard, M. (2008). Origins and forms of writing. In C. Bazerman (Ed.), *Handbook of research on writing* (pp. 7–22). New York: Erlbaum.

Chapter 2

Anthony, J. L., & Francis, D. J. (2005). Development of phonological awareness. *Current Directions in Psychological Science, 14*(5), 255–259. http://doi.org/10.1111/j.0963-7214.2005.00376.x.

Backman, J. (1983). The role of psycholinguistic skills in reading acquisition: A look at early readers. *Reading Research Quarterly, 18*(4), 466–479.

Bradley, L., & Bryant, P. E. (1983). Categorizing sounds and learning to read: A causal connection. *Nature, 301*, 419–421.

Bus, A. G., & van Ijzendoorn, M. H. (1999). Phonological awareness and early reading: A meta-analysis of experimental training studies. *Journal of Educational Psychology, 91*(3), 403–414.

Calfee, R. C., Lindamood, P., & Lindamood, C. (1973). Acoustic-phonetic skills and reading: Kindergarten through twelfth grade. *Journal of Educational Psychology, 64*(3), 293–298. Retrieved from www.ncbi.nlm.nih.gov/pubmed/4710951.

Changizi, M. A., Zhang, Q., Ye, H., & Shimojo, S. (2006). The structures of letters and symbols throughout human history are selected to match those found in objects in natural scenes. *The American Naturalist, 167*(5), E117–E139, Figure 6b. http://doi .org/10.1086/502806.

Coltheart, M., Davelaar, E., Jonasson, T., & Besner, D. (1977). Access to the internal lexicon. In *Attention & performance VI*. London: Academic Press.

Courrieu, P., & De Falco, S. (1989). Segmental vs. dynamic analysis of letter shape by preschool children. *European Bulletin of Cognitive Psychology, 9*(2), 189–198.

Cunningham, A. E., & Zibulsky, J. (2014). *Book smart*. New York: Oxford University Press.

Ehri, L. C., Nunes, S. R., Stahl, S. A., & Willows, D. M. (2001). Systematic phonics instruction helps students learn to read: Evidence from the National Reading Panel's meta-analysis. *Review of Educational Research, 71*(3), 393–447. http://doi.org/10.3102/ 00346543071003393.

Ellefson, M. R., Treiman, R., & Kessler, B. (2009). Learning to label letters by sounds or names: A comparison of England and the United States. *Journal of Experimental Child Psychology, 102,* 323–341.

Grainger, J., Rey, A., & Dufau, S. (2008). Letter perception: From pixels to pandemonium. *Trends in Cognitive Sciences, 12*(10), 381–387. http://doi.org/10.1016/j.tics.2008.06.006.

Hanson, V. L., Liberman, I. Y., & Shankweiler, D. (1984). Linguistic coding by deaf children in relation to beginning reading success. *Journal of Experimental Child Psychology, 37*(2), 1984.

Hanson, V. L., Goodell, E. W., & Perfetti, C. A. (1991). Tongue-twister effects in the silent reading of hearing and deaf college students. *Journal of Memory and Language, 30,* 319–330.

Holden, M. H., & MacGinitie, W. H. (1972). Children's conceptions of word boundaries in speech and print. *Journal of Educational Psychology, 63*(6), 551–557. Retrieved from http://psycnet.apa .orgjournals/edu/63/6/551.

Hu, C.-F., & Catts, H. W. (1998). The role of phonological processing in early reading ability: What we can learn from Chinese. *Scientific Studies of Reading, 2*(1), 55–79.

Hubel, D., & Wiesel, T. (1962). Receptive fields, binocular interaction and functional architecture in the cat's visual cortex. *The Journal of Physiology, 160*(1), 106–154. Retrieved from http://onlinelibrary .wiley.com/doi/10.1113/jphysiol.1962.sp006837/full/.

Hulme, C., Goetz, K., Gooch, D., Adams, J., & Snowling, M. J. (2007). Paired-associate learning, phoneme awareness, and learning to read. *Journal of Experimental Child Psychology, 96*(2), 150–166. http:// doi.org/10.1016/j.jecp.2006.09.002.

Justice, L. M., & Pullen, P. C. (2003). Promising interventions for promoting emergent literacy skills: Three evidence-based approaches. *Topics in Early Childhood Special Education, 23*(3), 99–113.

Liberman, I. Y. (1973). Segmentation of the spoken word and reading acquisition. *Annals of Dyslexia, 23*(1), 64–77.

Liberman, I. Y., Shankweiler, D., Orlando, C., Harris, K. S., & Berti, F. B. (1971). Letter confusions and reversals of sequence in the beginning reader: Implications for Orton's Theory of Developmental Dyslexia. *Cortex, 7*(2), 127–142. http://doi.org/10.1016/S0010-9452(71)80009-6.

Litt, R. A., de Jong, P. F., van Bergen, E., & Nation, K. (2013). Dissociating crossmodal and verbal demands in paired associate learning (PAL): What drives the PAL-reading relationship? *Journal of Experimental Child Psychology, 115*(1), 137–149. http://doi.org/10.1016/j.jecp .2012.11.012.

Litt, R. A., & Nation, K. (2014). The nature and specificity of paired associate learning deficits in children with dyslexia. *Journal of Memory and Language, 71*(1), 71–88. http://doi.org/10.1016/ j.jml.2013.10.005.

Melby-Lervåg, M., Lyster, S. A. H., & Hulme, C. (2012). Phonological skills and their role in learning to read: A meta-analytic review. *Psychological Bulletin, 138*(2), 322–52. http://doi.org/10.1037/ a0026744.

Morais, J., Luz, G., Alegria, J., & Bertels, P. (1979). Does awareness of speech as a sequence of phones arise spontaneously? *Cognition*, *7*, 323–331.

Morford, J. P., Wilkinson, E., Villwock, A., Piñar, P., & Kroll, J. F. (2011). When deaf signers read English: Do written words activate their sign translations? *Cognition*, *118*(2), 286–292. http://doi.org/10.1016/j.cognition.2010.11.006.

Nodine, C. F., & Lang, N. J. (1971). Development of visual scanning strategies for differentiating words. *Developmental Psychology*, *5*(2), 221–232. http://doi.org/10.1037/h0031428.

Rodriguez, E. T., & Tamis-Lemonda, C. S. (2011). Trajectories of the home learning environment across the first 5 years: Associations with children's vocabulary and literacy skills at prekindergarten. *Child Development*, *82*(4), 1058–1075. http://doi.org/10.1111/j.1467-8624.2011.01614.x.

Seidenberg, Mark (2016). *Language at the speed of sight*. New York: Basic Books.

Share, D. L. (2004). Knowing letter names and learning letter sounds: A causal connection. *Journal of Experimental Child Psychology*, *88*(3), 213–233.

Stanovich, K. E. (1988). Explaining the differences between the dyslexic and the garden-variety poor reader: The phonological-core variable-difference model. *Journal of Learning Disabilities*, *21*(10), 590–604.

Storch, S. A., & Whitehurst, G. J. (2002). Oral language and code-related precursors to reading: Evidence from a longitudinal structural model. *Developmental Psychology*, *38*(6), 934–947. http://doi.org/10.1037//0012-1649.38.6.934.

Suggate, S. P., Schaughency, E. A., & Reese, E. (2013). Children learning to read later catch up to children reading earlier. *Early Childhood Research Quarterly, 28*, 33–48.

Traxler, C. B. (2000). The Stanford Achievement Test, 9th edition: National norming and performance standards for deaf and hard-of-hearing students. *Journal of Deaf Studies and Deaf Education*, *5*(4), 337–348. http://doi.org/10.1093/deafed/5.4.337.

Treiman, R., & Broderick, V. (1998). What's in a name: Children's knowledge about the letters in their own names. *Journal of Experimental Child Psychology, 70*(2), 97–116. http://doi.org/10.1006/jecp.1998.2448.

Treiman, R., & Kessler, B. (2003). The role of letter names in the acquisition of literacy. In *Advances in child development and behavior* (Vol. *31,* pp. 105–138).

Treiman, R., Kessler, B., & Pollo, T. C. (2006). Learning about the letter name subset of the vocabulary : Evidence from US and Brazilian preschoolers. *Applied Psycholinguistics, 27,* 211–227.

Treiman, R., Levin, I., & Kessler, B. (2012). Linking the shapes of alphabet letters to their sounds: The case of Hebrew. *Reading and Writing, 25*(2), 569–585. http://doi.org/10.1007/s11145-010-9286-3.

Vaughn, J. S. (1902, August). Our strange language. *The Spectator, 187.*

Vellutino, F. R., Smith, H., Steger, J. A., & Kaman, M. (1975). Reading disability: Age differences and the perceptual-deficit hypothesis. *Child Development, 46*(2), 487–493. Retrieved from www.jstor.org/stable/1128146.

Windfuhr, K. L., & Snowling, M. J. (2001). The relationship between paired associate learning and phonological skills in normally developing readers. *Journal of Experimental Child Psychology, 80*(2), 160–173. http://doi.org/10.1006/jecp.2000.2625.

Ziegler, J. C., Stone, G. O., & Jacobs, A. M. (1997). What is the pronunciation for -ough and the for computing spelling for /u /? A database for computing feedforward and feedback consistency in English. *Behavior Research Methods, Instruments, & Computers, 29*(4), 600–618.

CHAPTER 3

Anderson, R. C., Wilson, P. T., Fielding, L. G., Anderson, R. C., & Fielding, L. G. (1988). Growth in reading and how children spend their time outside of school. *Reading Research Quarterly, 23*(3), 285–303.

Arciuli, J., & Simpson, I. C. (2012). Statistical learning is related to reading ability in children and adults. *Cognitive Science, 36*(2), 286–304. http://doi.org/10.1111/j.1551-6709.2011.01200.x.

Badian, N. A. (2001). Phonological and orthographic processing: Their roles in reading prediction. *Annals of Dyslexia, 51*(1), 177–202. http://doi.org/10.1007/s11881-001-0010-5.

Carlson, K. (2009). How prosody influences sentence comprehension. *Language and Linguistics Compass, 3*(5), 1188–1200. http://doi.org/10.1111/j.1749-818X.2009.00150.x.

Cassar, M., & Treiman, R. (1997). The beginnings of orthographic knowledge: Children's knowledge of double letters in words. *Journal of Educational Psychology, 89*(4), 631–644. http://doi.org/10.1037//0022-0663.89.4.631.

Chard, D. J., Vaughn, S., & Tyler, B. J. (2002). A synthesis of research on effective interventions for building reading fluency with elementary students with learning disabilities. *Journal of learning disabilities, 35*(5), 386–406.

Coltheart, M., Rastle, K., Perry, C., Langdon, R., & Ziegler, J. (2001). DRC: A dual route cascaded model of visual word recognition and reading aloud. *Psychological Review, 108*(1), 204–56. Retrieved from www.ncbi.nlm.nih.gov/pubmed/11212628.

Cunningham, A. E., Perry, K. E., & Stanovich, K. E. (2001). Converging evidence for the concept of orthographic processing. *Reading and Writing, 14*, 549–568.

Daneman, M., & Carpenter, P. A. (1980). Individual differences in working memory and reading. *Journal of Verbal Learning and Verbal Behavior, 19*(4), 450–466. http://doi.org/10.1016/S0022-5371(80)90312-6.

Farmer, T. A., Christiansen, M. H., & Monaghan, P. (2006). Phonological typicality influences on-line sentence comprehension. *Proceedings of the National Academy of Sciences, USA, 103*, 12203–12208. doi: 10.1073/pnas.0602173103.

Freebody, P., & Byrne, B. (1988). Word-reading strategies in elementary school children: Relations to comprehension, reading time, and phonemic awareness. *Reading Research Quarterly, 23*(4), 441–453.

Grainger, J., Lété, B., Bertand, D., Dufau, S., & Ziegler, J. C. (2012). Evidence for multiple routes in learning to read. *Cognition, 123*(2), 280–92. http://doi.org/10.1016/j.cognition.2012.01.003.

Haber, L. R., & Haber, R. N. (1982). Does silent reading involve articulation? Evidence from tongue twisters. *The American Journal of Psychology, 95*(3), 409–419. http://doi.org/10.2307/1422133.

Harm, M. W., & Seidenberg, M. S. (2004). Computing the meanings of words in reading: Cooperative division of labor between visual and phonological processes. *Psychological Review, 111*(3), 662–720. http://doi.org/10.1037/0033-295X.111.3.662.

Ise, E., Arnoldi, C. J., & Schulte-Körne, G. (2012). Development of orthographic knowledge in German-speaking children: A 2-year longitudinal study. *Journal of Research in Reading, 37*(3), 233–249. http://doi.org/10.1111/j.1467-9817.2012.01535.x.

Jared, D., Ashby, J., Agauas, S. J., Levy, B. A. (2016). Phonological activation of word meanings in Grade 5 readers. *Journal of Experimental Psychology: Learning, Memory, and Cognition, 42*(4), 524–541.

Juel, C. (2006). The impact of early school experiences on initial reading. In D. K. Dickinson & S. B. Neuman (Eds.), *Handbook of early literacy research* (pp. 410–426). New York: Guilford.

Kessler, B. (2009). Statistical learning of conditional orthographic correspondences. *Writing Systems Research, 1*(1), 19–34. http://doi.org/10.1093/wsr/wsp004.

Kosslyn, S. M., & Matt, A. M. (1977). If you speak slowly, do people read your prose slowly? Person-particular speech recoding during reading. *Bulletin of the Psychonomic Society, 9*(4), 250–252.

Kuhn, M. R., & Stahl, S. A. (2003). Fluency: A review of developmental and remedial practices. *Journal of Educational Psychology, 95*(1), 3–21.

Leinenger, M., & Leinenger, M. (2014). Phonological Coding During Reading. *Psychological Bulletin, 140*(6), 1534–1555.

Levy, B. A., Gong, Z., Hessels, S., Evans, M. A., & Jared, D. (2006). Understanding print: Early reading development and the contributions of home literacy experiences. *Journal of Experimental*

Child Psychology, 93(1), 63–93. http://doi.org/10.1016/j.jecp.2005 .07.003.

Marchand-Martella, N. E., Martella, R. C., Modderman, S. L., Petersen, H. M., & Pan, S. (2013). Key areas of effective adolescent literacy programs. *Education and Treatment of Children, 36*(1), 161–184.

McCusker, L. X., Gough, P. B., & Bias, R. G. (1981). Word recognition inside out and outside in. *Journal of Experimental Psychology: Human Perception and Performance, 7*(3), 538–551.

Nation, K. (2009). Form-meaning links in the development of visual word recognition. *Philosophical Transactions of the Royal Society of London. Series B, Biological Sciences, 364*(1536), 3665–3674. http:// doi.org/10.1098/rstb.2009.0119.

Perfetti, C. (2007). Reading ability: Lexical quality to comprehension. *Scientific Studies of Reading, 11*(4), 357–383.

Price, C. J., & Mechelli, A. (2005). Reading and reading disturbance. *Current Opinion in Neurobiology, 15*(2), 231–238. http://doi .org/10.1016/j.conb.2005.03.003.

Rayner, K., Pollatsek, A., Ashby, J., & Clifton, C. J. (2012). *Psychology of reading* (2nd ed.). New York: Psychology Press.

Rayner, K., White, S. J., Johnson, R. L., & Liversedge, S. P. (2006). Raeding wrods with jumbled lettres: There is a cost. *Psychological Science, 17*(3), 192–193.

Rehm, D. (2013). *Aimless love: New and selected poems.* Retrieved from http://thedianerehmshow.org/shows/2013-10-22/billy-collins-aimless-love-new-and-selected-poems/transcrip/.

Reicher, G. M. (1969). Perceptual recognition as a function of meaningfulness of stimulus material. *Journal of Experimental Psychology, 81*(2), 275–280.

Seidenberg, M. S., & McClelland, J. L. (1989). A distributed, developmental model of word recognition and naming. *Psychological Review, 96*(4), 523–68. http://doi.org/10.1037/0033-295X.96.4.523.

Shanahan, T., & Lomax, R. G. (1986). An analysis and comparison of theoretical models of the reading–writing relationship. *Journal of Educational Psychology, 78*(2), 116–123. Retrieved from http:// psycnet.apa.orgjournals/edu/78/2/116.

Share, D. L. (1995). Phonological recoding and self-teaching: Sine qua non of reading acquisition. *Cognition, 55*(2), 151–218.

Stanovich, K. E., & West, R. F. (1989). Exposure to print and orthographic processing. *Reading Research Quarterly, 24*(4), 402–433.

Therrien, W. J. (2004). Fluency and comprehension gains as a result of repeated reading: A meta-analysis. *Remedial and Special Education, 25*(4), 252–261.

Treiman, R., Freyd, J. J., & Baron, J. (1983). Phonological recording and use of spelling-sound rules in reading of sentences. *Journal of Verbal Learning and Verbal Behavior, 22*(6), 682–700. http://doi.org/10.1016/S0022-5371(83)90405-X.

Willingham, D. T. (2009). *Why don't students like school?* San Francisco: Jossey Bass.

Chapter 4

"Spill." *Merriam-Webster*. Retrieved from www.merriam-webster.com/dictionary/spill/.

"Heavy." *Merriam-Webster*. Retrieved from www.merriam-webster.com/dictionary/heavy/.

Astuti, R., Solomon, G. E. A., & Carey, S. (2004). Constraints on conceptual development: I. *Introduction. Monographs of the Society for Research in Child Development, 69*(3), 1–24. http://doi.org/10.1111/j.0037-976X.2004.00297.x.

Barsalou, L. W. (2016). On staying grounded and avoiding Quixotic dead ends. *Psychonomic Bulletin & Review, 23*(4), 1122–1142. http://doi.org/10.3758/s13423-016-1028-3.

Beck, I. L., Perfetti, C. A., & McKeown, M. G. (1982). Effects of long-term vocabulary instruction on lexical access and reading comprehension. *Journal of Educational Psychology, 74*(4), 506–521. http://doi.org/10.1037/0022-0663.74.4.506.

Bowers, P. N., Kirby, J. R., & Deacon, S. H. (2010). The effects of morphological instruction on literacy skills: A systematic review of the literature. *Review of Educational Research*, *80*(2), 144–179. http://doi.org/10.3102/0034654309359353.

Cain, K., Oakhill, J. V., & Elbro, C. (2003). The ability to learn new word meanings from context by school-age children with and without language comprehension difficulties. *Journal of Child Language*, *30*(30), 681–694. http://doi.org/10.1017/S0305000903005713.

Cain, K., Oakhill, J., & Lemmon, K. (2004). Individual differences in the inference of word meanings from context: The influence of reading comprehension, vocabulary knowledge, and memory capacity. *Journal of Educational Psychology*, *96*(4), 671–681. http://doi.org/10.1037/0022-0663.96.4.671.

Carver, R. (1994). Percentage of unknown vocabulary words in text as a function of the relative difficulty of the text: Implications for instruction. *Journal of Literacy Research*, *26*(4), 413–437. http://doi.org/10.1080/10862969409547861.

Collins, A. M., & Loftus, E. F. (1975). A spreading-activation theory of semantic processing. *Psychological Review*, *82*(6), 407–428. http://doi.org/10.1016/B978-1-4832-1446-7.50015-7.

Elleman, A. M., Lindo, E. J., Morphy, P., & Compton, D. L. (2009). The impact of vocabulary instruction on passage-level comprehension of school-age children: A meta-analysis. *Journal of Research on Educational Effectiveness*, *2*(1), 1–44. http://doi.org/10.1080/19345740802539200.

Foertsch, J., & Gernsbacher, M. A. (1994). In search of complete comprehension: Getting "minimalists" to work. *Discourse Processes*, *18*(3), 271–296. http://doi.org/10.1080/01638539409544896.

Fukkink, R. G., & de Glopper, K. (1998). Effects of instruction in deriving word meaning from context: A meta-analysis. *Review of Educational Research*, *68*(4), 450–469. http://doi.org/10.3102/00346543068004450.

Gernsbacher, M. A. & Faust, M. (1995). Skilled suppression. In F. N. Dempster & C. N. Brainerd (Eds.), *Interference and inhibition in cognition* (pp. 295–327). San Diego: Academic Press.

Glenberg, A. M., & Kaschak, M. P. (2002). Grounding language in action. *Psychonomic Bulletin & Review, 9*(3), 558–565. http://doi.org/10.1109/TAMD.2011.2140890.

Goodwin, A. P., & Ahn, S. (2010). A meta-analysis of morphological interventions: Effects on literacy achievement of children with literacy difficulties. *Annals of Dyslexia, 60*(2), 183–208. http://doi.org/10.1007/s11881-010-0041-x.

Goulden, R., Nation, P., & Read, J. (1990). How large can a receptive vocabulary be? *Applied Linguistics, 11*(4), 341–363. http://doi.org/10.1093/applin/11.4.341.

Hare, M., Jones, M., Thomson, C., Kelly, S., & McRae, K. (2009). Activating event knowledge. *Cognition, 111*(2), 151–167. http://doi.org/10.1016/j.cognition.2009.01.009.

Harnad, S. (1990). The symbol grounding problem. *Physica D: Nonlinear Phenomena, 42*(1–3), 335–346. http://doi.org/10.1016/0167-2789(90)90087-6.

Hauk, O., Johnsrude, I., & Pulvermüller, F. (2004). Somatotopic representation of action words in human motor and premotor cortex. *Neuron, 41*(2), 301–307.

Hayes, D. P., & Ahrens, M. G. (1988). Vocabulary simplification for children: A special case of "motherese"? *Journal of Child Language, 15*(02), 395. http://doi.org/10.1017/S0305000900012411.

Hsueh-Chao, M. H., & Nation, P. (2000). Unknown vocabulary density and reading comprehension. *Reading in a Foreign Language, 13*(1), 403–430.

Kintsch, W. (2012). Psychological models of reading comprehension and their implications for assessment. In J. Sabatini, E. Albro, & T. O'Reilly (Eds.), *Measuring up: advances in how we assess reading ability* (pp. 21–37). Plymouth, UK: Rowman & Littlefield.

McKeown, M., Beck, I., Omanson, R., & Perfetti, C. (1983). The effects of long-term vocabulary instruction on reading comprehension: A replication. *Journal of Literacy Research, 15*(1), 3–18. http://doi.org/10.1080/10862968309547474.

Meyer, D. E., & Schvaneveldt, R. W. (1971). Facilitation in recognizing pairs of words: Evidence of a dependence between retrieval operations. *Journal of Experimental Psychology, 90*(2), 227–234.

Miller, G. A., & Gildea, P. M. (1987). How children learn words. *Scientific American, 257*(3), 94–99.

Nagy, W. E., & Anderson, R. C. (1984). How many words are there in printed school English? *Reading Research Quarterly, 19*, 304–330.

Nagy, W. E., & Herman, P. A. (1985). Incidental vs. instructional approaches to increasing reading vocabulary. *Educational Perspectives, 23*(1), 16–21.

Nation, I. S. P. (2006). How large a vocabulary is needed for reading and listening? *The Canadian Modern Language Review / La Revue Canadienne Des Langues Vivantes, 63*(1), 59–81. http://doi.org/10.1353/cml.2006.0049.

Nation, K. (2008). EPS Prize Lecture. Learning to read words. *Quarterly Journal of Experimental Psychology (2006), 61*(8), 1121–1133. http://doi.org/10.1080/17470210802034603.

Nation, K., & Snowling, M. J. (1998). Semantic processing and the development of word-recognition skills: Evidence from children with reading comprehension difficulties. *Journal of Memory and Language, 39*(1), 85–101. http://doi.org/10.1006/jmla.1998.2564.

Oakhill, J., Cain, K., McCarthy, D., & Nightingale, Z. (2013). Making the link between vocabulary knowledge and comprehension skill. In M. A. Britt, S. R. Goldman, & J.-F. Rouet (Eds.), *Reading: From words to multiple texts* (pp. 101–114). New York: Routledge.

Ouellette, G. P. (2006). What's meaning got to do with it: The role of vocabulary in word reading and reading comprehension. *Journal of Educational Psychology, 98*(3), 554–566. http://doi.org/10.1037/0022-0663.98.3.554.

Schmitt, N., Jiang, X., & Grabe, W. (2011). The percentage of words known in a text and reading comprehension. *The Modern Language Journal, 95*(1), 26–43. http://doi.org/10.1111/j.1540-4781.2011.01146.x.

Schwanenflugel, P. J. (2010). Effects of a conversation intervention on the expressive vocabulary development of prekindergarten children. *Language, Speech, and Hearing Services in Schools, 41*(3), 303–313. http://doi.org/10.1044/0161-1461(2009/08-0100).

Yu, C., & Smith, L. (2007). Rapid word learning under uncertainty via cross-situational statistics. *Psychological Science, 18*(5), 414–420. http://doi.org/10.1111/j.1467-9280.2007.01915.x.

Yurovsky, D., Fricker, D. C., Yu, C., & Smith, L. B. (2014). The role of partial knowledge in statistical word learning. *Psychonomic Bulletin & Review, 21*(1), 1–22. http://doi.org/10.3758/s13423-013-0443-y.

CHAPTER 5

Anderson, J. R., & Bower, G. H. (1973). *Human associative memory.* Washington, DC: Winston and Sons.

Anderson, R. C., Reynolds, R. E., Schallert, D. L., & Goetz, E. T. (1977). Frameworks for comprehending discourse. *American Educational Research Journal, 14*(4), 367–381.

Barclay, J. R., Bransford, J. D., Franks, J. J., McCarrell, N. S., & Nitsch, K. (1974). Comprehension and semantic flexibility. *Journal of Verbal Learning and Verbal Behavior, 13*(4), 471–481. http://doi.org/10.1016/S0022-5371(74)80024-1.

Begg, I. (1971). Recognition memory for sentence meaning and wording. *Journal of Verbal Learning and Verbal Behavior, 10*(2), 176–181. http://doi.org/10.1016/S0022-5371(71)80010-5.

Best, R. M., Floyd, R. G., & McNamara, D.S. (2008). Differential competencies contributing to children's comprehension of narrative and expository texts. *Reading Psychology, 29*(2), 137–164.

Bestgen, Y., & Vonk, W. (2000). Temporal adverbials as segmentation markers in discourse comprehension. *Journal of Memory and Language, 42*(1), 74–87.

Butcher, K. R., & Kintsch, W. (2003). Text comprehension and discourse processing. In A. F. Healy & R. W. Proctor (Eds.), *Handbook of psychology* (pp. 578–604). New York: Wiley.

Cain, K., & Oakhill, J. (2007). Reading comprehension difficulties: Correlates, causes, and consequences. In K. Cain, & J. Oakhill (Eds.), *Children's comprehension problems in oral and written language: A cognitive perspective* (pp. 41–75). New York: Guilford.

Cain, K., Oakhill, J. V., Barnes, M. A., & Bryant, P. E. (2001). Comprehension skill, inference-making ability, and their relation to knowledge. *Memory & Cognition, 29*(6), 850–859.

Chall, J. S., & Jacobs, V. A. (2003). The classic study on poor children's fourth-grade slump. *American Educator, 27*(1), 14–15.

Cunningham, A. E., & Stanovich, K. E. (1997). Early reading acquisition and its relation to reading experience and ability 10 years later. *Developmental Psychology, 33*(6), 934–945.

Daneman, M., Lennertz, T., & Hannon, B. (2007). Shallow semantic processing of text: Evidence from eye movements. *Language and Cognitive Processes, 22*(1), 83–105.

Graesser, A. C., Singer, M., & Trabasso, T. (1994). Constructing inferences during narrative text comprehension. *Psychological Review, 101*(3), 371–395. http://doi.org/10.1037/0033-295X.101.3.371.

Kintsch, W., Welsch, D., Schmalhofer, F., & Zimny, S. (1990). Sentence memory: A theoretical analysis. *Journal of Memory and Language, 29*(2), 133–159. http://doi.org/10.1016/0749-596X(90)90069-C.

Long, D. L., Oppy, B. J., & Seely, M. R. (1997). Individual differences in readers' sentence-and text-level representations. *Journal of Memory and Language, 36*(1), 129–145.

McNamara, D. S., Louwerse, M. M., McCarthy, P. M., & Graesser, A. C. (2010). Coh-Metrix: Capturing linguistic features of cohesion. *Discourse Processes, 47*(4), 292–330. http://doi.org/10.1080/01638530902959943.

McNamara, D. S., & O'Reilly, T. (2009). Theories of comprehension skill: Knowledge and strategies versus capacity and suppression. In A. M. Columbus (Ed.), *Progress in experimental psychology research.* Hauppauge, NY: Nova Science Publishers.

O'Brien, E. J., & Albrecht, J. E. (1992). Comprehension strategies in the development of a mental model. *Journal of Experimental Psychology: Learning, Memory, and Cognition, 18*(4), 777–784.

Otero, J., & Kintsch, W. (1992). Failures to detect contradictions in a text: What readers believe versus what they read. *Psychological Science, 3*(4), 229–235.

Pichert, J. W., & Anderson, R. C. (1977). Taking different perspectives on a story. *Journal of Educational Psychology, 69*, 309–315. http://doi.org/10.1037/0022-0663.69.4.309.

Pinker, S. (1994). *The language instinct.* New York: Basic Books.

Pylkkänen, L., & McElree, B. (2006). The syntax-semantic interface: On-line composition of sentence meaning. In M. Traxler & M.A. Gernsbacher (Eds.), *Handbook of psycholinguistics* (2nd ed., 537–577). New York: Elsevier.

Rayner, K., Pollatsek, A., Ashby, J., & Clifton, C. J. (2012). *Psychology of reading* (2nd ed., pp. 245–275). New York: Psychology Press.

Rinck, M., & Bower, G. H. (1995). Anaphora resolution and the focus of attention in situation models. *Journal of Memory and Language, 34*(1), 110–131.

Schneider, W., Korkel, J., & Weinert, F. E. (1989). Domain-specific knowledge and memory performance : A comparison of high- and low-aptitude children. *Journal of Educational Psychology, 81*(3), 306–312.

Shankweiler, D., Lundquist, E., Katz, L., Stuebing, K., Fletcher, J., Brady, S., Fowler, A., Dreyer, L., Marchione, K., Shaywitz, S., & Shaywitz, B. (1999). Comprehension and decoding: Patterns of association in children with reading difficulties. *Scientific Studies of Reading, 3*, 69–94.

Singer, M. (2007). Inference processing in discourse comprehension. In M. G. Gaskel (Ed.), *The Oxford handbook of psycholinguistics* (pp. 343–359). New York: Oxford University Press.

Stanovich, K. E., & Cunningham, A. E. (1993). Where does knowledge come from? Specific associations between print exposure and information acquisition. *Journal of Educational Psychology, 85*(2), 211–229. http://doi.org/10.1037//0022-0663.85.2.211.

Stanovich, K. E., Cunningham, A. E., & West, R. F. (1998). Literacy experiences and the shaping of cognition. In S. G. Paris & H. M.

Wellman (Eds.), *Global prospects for education: Development, culture, and schooling* (pp. 253–288). Washington, DC: American Psychological Association.

Sulin, R. A., & Dooling, D. J. (1974). Intrusion of a thematic idea in retention of prose. *Journal of Experimental Psychology, 103*(2), 255–262. http://doi.org/10.1037/h0036846.

Sweet, A. P., & Snow, C. E. (Eds.). (2003). *Rethinking reading comprehension*. New York: Guilford.

Willingham, D. T., & Lovette, G. (2014). Can reading comprehension be taught? *Teachers College Record.* Retrieved from www.tcrecord.org. ID Number: 17701.

Zwaan, R. A. (1996). Processing narrative time shifts. *Journal of Experimental Psychology: Learning, Memory, and Cognition, 22*(5), 1196–1207.

Zwaan, R. A., & Radvansky, G. A. (1998). Situation models in language comprehension and memory. *Psychological Bulletin, 123*(2), 162–185.

CHAPTER 6

Anderson, M. (2016). *Parents, teens and digital monitoring*. Washington, DC: Pew Research Center.

Aronson, E., Wilson, T. D., & Akert, R. M. (2012). *Social psychology* (8th ed.). New York: Pearson.

Baker, L., Scher, D., & Mackler, K. (1997). Home and family influences on motivations for reading. *Educational Psychologist, 32*(2), 69–82. http://doi.org/10.1207/s15326985ep3202_2.

Baker, L., & Wigfield, A. (2012). Dimensions of children's motivation for reading and their relations to reading activity and reading achievement. *Reading Research Quarterly, 34*(4), 452–477.

Blaydes, J. (2003). *The educator's book of quotes* (p. 9). Thousand Oaks, CA: Corwin.

Chateau, D., & Jared, D. (2000). Exposure to print and word recognition processes. *Memory & Cognition, 28*(1), 143–153. http://doi.org/10.3758/bf03211582.

Clark, C., & DeZoysa, S. (2011). *Mapping the interrelationships of reading enjoyment, attitudes, behaviour and attainment: An exploratory investigation.* London: National Literacy Trust.

Cloer, T. J., & Ross, S. Y. (1997). The relationship of standardized reading scores to children's self-perception as readers. In K. Camperel, B. L. Hayes, & R. Telfer (Eds.), *Yearbook of the American Reading Forum* (pp. 93–104). Whitewater, WI: American Reading Forum

Cunningham, A. E., & Stanovich, K. E. (1991). Tracking the unique effects of print exposure in children: Associations with vocabulary, general knowledge, and spelling. *Journal of Educational Psychology, 83*(2), 264–274. http://doi.org/10.1037//0022-0663.83.2.264.

da Matta, A., Gonçalves, F. L., & Bizarro, L. (2012). Delay discounting: Concepts and measures. *Psychology & Neuroscience, 5*(2), 135–146.

Deci, E. L., Koestner, R., & Ryan, R. M. (1999). A meta-analytic review of experiments examining the effects of extrinsic rewards on intrinsic motivation. *Psychological Bulletin, 125*(6), 627–668. Retrieved from http://psycnet.apa.orgjournals/bul/125/6/627.

Dweck, C. S., & Leggett, E. L. (1988). A social-cognitive approach to motivation and personality. *Psychological Review, 95*(2), 256–273. http://doi.org/10.1037/0033-295X.95.2.256.

Eccles, J. S., Adler, T. F., Futterman, R., Goff, S. B., Kaczala, C. M., Meece, J. L., & Midgley, C. (1983). Expectancies, values, and academic behaviors. In J. T. Spence (Ed.), *Achievement and Achievement Motivation* (pp. 75–146). San Francisco: Freeman.

Grotevant, H. D. (1987). Toward a process model of identity formation. *Journal of Adolescent Research, 2*(3), 203–222. http://doi.org/10.1177/074355488723003.

Haidt, J. (2001). The emotional dog and its rational tail: A social intuitionist approach to moral judgment. *Psychological Review, 108*(4), 814–834. http://doi.org/10.1037/0033-295X.108.4.814.

Hall, L. A. (2012). The role of reading identities and reading abilities in students' discussions about texts and comprehension strategies. *Journal of Literacy Research, 44*(3), 239–272. http://doi.org/10.1177/1086296X12445370.

Harter, S. (1999). *The cognitive and social construction of the developing self.* New York: Guilford.

Heider, F. (1958). *The psychology of interpersonal relations.* New York: Wiley.

Kim, J. S., & White, T. G. (2008). Scaffolding voluntary summary reading for children in Grades 3 to 5: An experimental study. *Scientific Studies of Reading, 12*(1), 1–23.

Lee, J. (2014). Universal factors of student achievement in high-performing Eastern and Western countries. *Journal of Educational Psychology, 106*(2), 364–374. http://doi.org/10.1037/a0035609.

Lepper, M. R., Greene, D., & Nisbett, R. E. (1973). Undermining children's intrinsic interest with extrinsic reward: A test of the "overjustification" hypothesis. *Journal of Personality and Social Psychology, 28*(1), 129–137. Retrieved from http://psycnet.apa.orgjournals/psp/28/1/129.

Mckenna, M. C., Kear, D. J., & Ellsworth, R. A. (1995). Children's attitudes toward reading: A national survey. *Reading Research Quarterly, 30*(4), 934–956.

Meyer, D. E., & Schvanaveldt, R. (1971) Facilitation in recognizing pairs of words: Evidence of a dependence between retrieval operations. *Journal of Experimental Psychology, 90*(2), 227–234.

Mol, S. E., & Bus, A. G. (2011). To read or not to read: A meta-analysis of print exposure from infancy to early adulthood. *Psychological Bulletin, 137*(2), 267–296. http://doi.org/10.1037/a0021890.

Morgan, P. L., & Fuchs, D. (2007). Is there a bidirectional relationship between children's reading skills and reading motivation? *Exceptional Children, 73*(2), 165–183.

Retelsdorf, J., Köller, O., & Möller, J. (2014). Reading achievement and reading self-concept: Testing the reciprocal effects model. *Learning and Instruction, 29,* 21–30. http://doi.org/10.1016/j.learninstruc.2013.07.004.

Rideout, V. J. (2015). *The common sense census: Media use by tweens and teens.* San Francisco: Common Sense Media.

Rideout, V. J. (2011). *Zero to eight: Children's media use in America.* San Francisco: Common Sense Media.

Rideout, V. J., Foehr, U. G., & Roberst, D. F. (2010). *Generation M2: Media in the lives of 8- to 18-year-olds.* Menlo Park, CA: Kaiser Foundation.

Rozin, P., Scott, S., & Dingley, M. (2011). Nudge to nobesity I : Minor changes in accessibility decrease food intake. *Judgement and Decision Making, 6*(4), 323–332. http://doi.org/10.1111/j.1753-4887.2009.00206.x.

Ruble, D. N., & Frey, K. S. (1991). Changing patterns of comparative behavior as skills are acquired: A functional model of self-evaluation. In J. Suls & T. A. Wills (Eds.), *Social comparison: Contemporary theory and research* (pp. 79–113). Hillsdale, NJ: Erlbaum.

Sparks, R. L., Patton, J., & Murdoch, A. (2014). Early reading success and its relationship to reading achievement and reading volume: Replication of "10 years later." *Reading and Writing, 27*(1), 189–211. http://doi.org/10.1007/s11145-013-9439-2.

Stanovich, K. E. (1986). Matthew Effects in reading: Some consequences of individual differences in the acquisition of literacy. *Reading Research Quarterly, 21*, 360–407.

Stuart, E. W., Shimp, T. A., & Engle, R. W. (1984). Classical conditioning of consumer attitudes : Four experiments in an advertising context. *Journal of Consumer Research, 14*, 334–349.

Weiner, B. (2000). Intrapersonal and interpersonal theories of motivation from an attribution perspective. *Educational Psychology Review, 12*(1), 1–14. Retrieved from http://link.springer.com/chapter/10.1007/978-1-4615-1273-8_2.

Wigfield, A., & Eccles, J. S. (2000). Expectancy-value theory of achievement motivation. *Contemporary Educational Psychology, 25*, 68–81.

Woolfolk, M. E., Castellan, W., & Brooks, C. I. (1983). Pepsi versus Coke: Labels, not tastes, prevail. *Psychological Reports, 52*, 185–186.

Chapter 7

Ackerman, R., & Lauterman, T. (2012). Taking reading comprehension exams on screen or on paper? A metacognitive analysis of learning texts under time pressure. *Computers in Human Behavior*, *28*(5), 1816–1828. http://doi.org/10.1016/j.chb.2012.04.023.

Anderson, D. R., Huston, A. C., Schmitt, K. L., Linebarger, D. L., Wright, J. C., & Larson, R. (2001). Childhood television viewing and adolescent behavior: The recontact study. *Monographs of the Society for Research in Child Development*, *66*(1), 1–154.

Barzilai, S., & Zohar, A. (2012). Epistemic thinking in action: evaluating and integrating online sources. *Cognition and Instruction*, *30*(1), 39–85. http://doi.org/10.1080/07370008.2011.636495.

Bennett, S., Maton, K., & Kervin, L. (2008). The "digital natives" debate: A critical review of the evidence. *British Journal of Educational Technology*, *39*(5), 775–786. http://doi.org/10.1111/j.1467-8535.2007.00793.x.

Bohn, R. E., & Short, J. E. (2009). *How much information? 2009 report on American consumers*. San Diego: Global Information Center, University of California.

Braasch, J. L. G., Bråten, I., Strømsø, H. I., Anmarkrud, Ø., & Ferguson, L. E. (2013). Promoting secondary school students' evaluation of source features of multiple documents. *Contemporary Educational Psychology*, *38*(3), 180–195. http://doi.org/10.1016/j.cedpsych.2013.03.003.

Carr, N. (2008). Is Google making us stupid? *Yearbook of the National Society for the Study of Education*, *107*(2), 89–94. http://doi.org/10.1111/j.1744-7984.2008.00172.x.

Carr, N. (2011). *The Shallows: What the Internet is doing to our brains*. New York: Norton.

Cheung, A. C. K., & Slavin, R. E. (2011, May). The effectiveness of education technology for enhancing reading achievement: A meta-analysis, 1–48. Retrieved from http://files.eric.ed.gov/fulltext/ED527572.pdf.

Coffin, T. E. (1955). Television's impact on society. *American Psychologist, 10*(10), 630–641. http://doi.org/10.1037/h0039880.

Connell, C., Bayliss, L., & Farmer, W. (2012). Effects of ebook readers and tablet computers on reading comprehension. *International Journal of Instructional Media, 39*(2), 131–139.

Daniel, D. B., & Woody, W. D. (2013). E-textbooks at what cost? Performance and use of electronic v. print texts. *Computers and Education, 62,* 18–23. http://doi.org/10.1016/j.compedu.2012.10.016.

de Jong, M. T., & Bus, A. G. (2002). Quality of book-reading matters for emergent readers: An experiment with the same book in a regular or electronic format. *Journal of Educational Psychology, 94*(1), 145–155. http://doi.org/10.1037//0022-0663.94.1.145.

de Jong, M. T., & Bus, A. G. (2004). The efficacy of electronic books in fostering kindergarten children's emergent story understanding. *Reading Research Quarterly, 39*(4), 378–393. http://doi.org/10.1598/RRQ.39.4.2.

DeLoache, J. S., Chiong, C., Sherman, K., Islam, N., Vanderborght, M., Troseth, G. L., Strouse, G. A. & O'Doherty, K. (2010). Do babies learn from baby media? *Psychological Science, 21*(11), 1570–4. http://doi.org/10.1177/0956797610384145.

Deocampo, J. A., & Hudson, J. A. (2005). When seeing is not believing: Two-year-olds' use of video representations to find a hidden toy. *Journal of Cognition and Development, 6*(2), 229–258. http://doi.org/10.1207/s15327647jcd0602_4.

DeStefano, D., & LeFevre, J.-A. (2007). Cognitive load in hypertext reading: A review. *Computers in Human Behavior, 23*(3), 1616–1641. http://doi.org/10.1016/j.chb.2005.08.012.

Drouin, M., & Driver, B. (2012). Texting, textese and literacy abilities: A naturalistic study. *Journal of Research in Reading, 37*(3), 250–267. http://doi.org/10.1111/j.1467-9817.2012.01532.x.

Guernsey, L. (2007). What's educational about "educational" TV. In *Into the minds of babes: How Screen time affects children from birth to age five* (pp. 113–134). New York: Basic Books.

Hattie, J. (2009). *Visible learning.* London: Routledge.

Jeong, H. (2012). A comparison of the influence of electronic books and paper books on reading comprehension, eye fatigue, and perception. *The Electronic Library, 30*(3), 390–408. http://doi.org/https://doi .org/10.1108/09564230910978511.

Mashburn, A. J., Pianta, R. C., Hamre, B. K., Downer, J. T., Barbarin, O. A., Bryant, D., Burchinal, M., Early, D. M, & Howes, C. (2008). Measures of classroom quality in prekindergarten and children's development of academic, language, and social skills. *Child Development, 79*(3), 732–49. http://doi.org/10.1111/j.1467-8624.2008.01154.x.

Matthew, K. (1997). A comparison of the influence of interactive CD-ROM storybooks and traditional print storybooks on reading comprehension. *Journal of Research on Computing in Education, 29*, 1–13.

Killi, C., Laurinen, L., & Marttunen, M. (2008). Students evaluating Internet sources: From versatile evaluators to uncritical readers. *Journal of Educational Computing Research, 39*(1), 75–95.

Koolstra, C. M., & van der Voort, T. H. A. (1996). Longitudinal effects of television on children's leisure-time reading: A test of three explanatory models. *Human Communication Research, 23*(1), 4–35.

Korat, O., & Or, T. (2010). How new technology influences parent–child interaction: The case of e-book reading. *First Language, 30*(2), 139–154. http://doi.org/10.1177/0142723709359242.

Korat, O., & Shamir, A. (2007). Electronic books versus adult readers: Effects on children's emergent literacy as a function of social class. *Journal of Computer Assisted Learning, 23*(3), 248–259. http://doi .org/10.1111/j.1365-2729.2006.00213.x.

Kretzschmar, F., Pleimling, D., Hosemann, J., Füssel, S., Bornkessel-Schlesewsky, I., et al. (2013). Subjective impressions do not mirror online reading effort: Concurrent EEG-eyetracking evidence from the reading of books and digital media. *PLoS ONE 8*(2): e56178. doi: 10.1371/journal.pone.0056178

Kuiper, E., Volman, M., & Terwel, J. (2008). Integrating critical Web skills and content knowledge: Development and evaluation of a 5th grade educational program. *Computers in Human Behavior, 24*(3), 666–692. http://doi.org/10.1016/j.chb.2007.01.022.

Lenhart, A. (2015). *Teens, social media & technology overview 2015.* Washington, DC: Pew Research Center.

Leu, D. J., & Castek, J. (2006). What skills and strategies are characteristic of accomplished adolescent users of the Internet? In *Annual Conference of the American Educational Research Association.* San Francisco.

Macedo-Rouet, M., Braasch, J. L. G., Britt, M. A., & Rouet, J.-F. (2013). Teaching fourth and fifth Graders to evaluate information sources during text comprehension. *Cognition and Instruction, 31*(2), 204–226. http://doi.org/10.1080/07370008.2013.769995.

Margaryan, A., Littlejohn, A., & Vojt, G. (2011). Are digital natives a myth or reality? University students' use of digital technologies. *Computers and Education, 56*(2), 429–440. http://doi.org/10.1016/j.compedu.2010.09.004.

Mason, L., Junyent, A. A., & Tornatora, M. C. (2014). Epistemic evaluation and comprehension of web-source information on controversial science-related topics: Effects of a short-term instructional intervention. *Computers and Education, 76,* 143–157. http://doi.org/10.1016/j.compedu.2014.03.016.

Neuman, S. B. (1988). The displacement effect: Assessing the relation between television viewing and reading performance. *Reading Research Quarterly, 23*(4), 414–440.

Nusername. (2013). AskReddit. Retrieved from User "nusernamed" on the entertainment site Reddit: www.reddit.com/r/AskReddit/comments/15yaap/if_someone_from_the_1950s_suddenly_appeared_today/c7qyp13?context=5#c7qyp13/.

Ouellette, G., & Michaud, M. (2016). Generation text: Relations among undergraduates' use of text messaging, textese, and language and literacy skills. *Canadian Journal of Behavioural Science / Revue Canadienne Des Sciences Du Comportement, 48*(3), 217–221. http://doi.org/10.1037/cbs0000046.

Parish-Morris, J., Mahajan, N., Hirsh-Pasek, K., & Golinkoff, R. M. (2011). Once upon a time: Parent–child dialogue and storybook reading in the electronic era. *Mind, Brain, and Education, 7*(3), 200–211.

Pinker, S. (2010, January). Not at all. Retrieved from http://edge.org/q2010/q10_10.html#pinker/.

Richert, R. A., Robb, M. B., Fender, J. G., & Wartella, E. (2010). Word learning from baby videos. *Archives of Pediatrics & Adolescent Medicine, 164*(5), 432–7. http://doi.org/10.1001/archpediatrics.2010.24.

Richtel, M. (2012, November 1). For better and for worse, technology use alters learning styles, teachers say. *New York Times*, A18.

Rideout, V. J. (2015). *The common sense census: Media use by tweens and teens*. San Francisco: Common Sense Media.

Rideout, V. J., Foehr, U. G., & Roberst, D. F. (2010). *Generation M2: Media in the lives of 8- to 18-year-olds*. Menlo Park, CA: Henry J. Kaiser Foundation.

Roberts, D. F., Foehr, U. G., Rideout, V. J., Brodie, M. (1999). Kids and media at the new millenium. Menlo Park, CA: Kaiser Family Foundation. Available at http://kff.org/hivaids/report/kids-media-the-new-millennium/.

Rosenwald, M. S. (2014, April 6). Serious reading takes a hit from online scanning and skimming, researchers say. *Washington Post*. Retrieved from www.washingtonpost.com/local/serious-reading-takes-a-hit-from-online-scanning-and-skimming-researchers-say/2014/04/06/088028d2-b5d2-11e3-b899-20667de76985_story.html/.

Sanchez, C. A., & Wiley, J. (2009). To scroll or not to scroll: Scrolling, working memory capacity, and comprehending complex texts. *Human Factors: The Journal of the Human Factors and Ergonomics Society, 51*(5), 730–738. http://doi.org/10.1177/0018720809352788.

Schank, R. (2010, January). The thinking process hasn't changed in 50,000 years. Retrieved from www.edge.org/response-detail/11519/.

Segal-Drori, O., Korat, O., Shamir, A., & Klein, P. S. (2009). Reading electronic and printed books with and without adult instruction: effects on emergent reading. *Reading and Writing, 23*(8), 913–930. http://doi.org/10.1007/s11145-009-9182-x.

Szalai, A. (1972). *The use of time: Daily activities of urban and suburban populations in twelve countries*. Den Haag: Moton.

Tamim, R. M., Bernard, R. M., Borokhovski, E., Abrami, P. C., & Schmid, R. F. (2011). What forty years of research says about the impact of technology on learning: A second-order meta-analysis and validation study. *Review of Educational Research, 81*(1), 4–28. http://doi.org/10.3102/0034654310393361.

Troseth, G. L., Saylor, M. M., & Archer, A. H. (2006). Young children's use of video as a source of socially relevant information. *Child Development, 77*(3), 786–99. http://doi.org/10.1111/j.1467-8624.2006.00903.x.

Trushell, J., Burrell, C., & Maitland, A. (2001). Year 5 pupils reading an "interactive storybook" on CD-ROM: Losing the plot? *British Journal of Educational Technology, 32*(4), 389–401.

van Dijk, C. N., van Witteloostuijn, M., Vasić, N., Avrutin, S., & Blom, E. (2016). The influence of texting language on grammar and executive functions in primary school children. *Plos ONE, 11*(3), 1–22. http://doi.org/10.1371/journal.pone.0152409.

Walraven, A., Brand-Gruwel, S., & Boshuizen, H. P. A. (2010). Fostering transfer of websearchers' evaluation skills: A field test of two transfer theories. *Computers in Human Behavior, 26*(4), 716–728. http://doi.org/10.1016/j.chb.2010.01.008.

Wineburg, S., & McGrew, S. (2016, November 1). Why students can't Google their way to the truth. *Education Week.* http://www.edweek.org/ew/articles/2016/11/02/why-students-cant-google-their-way-to.html

Zhang, S., & Duke, N. K. (2011). The impact of instruction in the WWWDOT framework on students' disposition and ability to evaluate Web sites as sources of information. *The Elementary School Journal, 112*(1), 132–154. http://doi.org/10.1086/660687.

CONCLUSION

Beilock, S. (2010). *Choke: What the secrets of the brain reveal about getting it right when you have to.* New York: Free Press.

Brown, P. C., Roediger, H. L. III, & McDaniel, M. A. (2014). *Make it stick.* Cambridge, MA: Harvard University Press.

Bryan, C. J., Yeager, D. S., Hinojosa, C. P., Chabot, A., Bergen, H., Kawamura, M., & Steubing, F. (2016). Harnessing adolescent values to motivate healthier eating. *Proceedings of the National Academy of Sciences, 113*(39), 10830–10835.

Committee on Prospering in the Global Economy of the 21st Century. (2007). *Rising above the gathering storm: Energizing and employing America for a brighter economic future.* Washington, DC: National Academies Press.

Kahneman, D. (2011). *Thinking, fast and slow.* New York: Basic Books.

National Reading Panel (US), National Institute of Child Health, & Human Development (US). (2000). *Report of the National Reading Panel: Teaching children to read: An evidence-based assessment of the scientific research literature on reading and its implications for reading instruction: Reports of the subgroups.* Washington, DC: National Institute of Child Health and Human Development, National Institutes of Health.

National Science Board. (2014). *Science and Engineering Indicators 2014.* Chapter 7, "Science and Technology: Public attitudes and understanding." Arlington, VA: National Science Foundation (NSB 10-01). Retrieved from www.nsf.gov/statistics/seind14/index.cfm/chapter-7/c7h.html/.

Norman, D. (2013). *The design of everyday things.* New York: Basic Books.

Thaler, R. H., and C. R. Sunstein. (2008). *Nudge: Improving decisions about health, wealth and happiness.* New Haven: Yale University Press.

Willingham, D. T. (2012). *When can you trust the experts?* San Francisco: Jossey-Bass.

INDEX

Page references followed by *fig* indicate an illustrated figure and *tab* indicate table

NOTES